Advances in Functional Training

Advanced in Functional Training
Training Techniques for Coaches, Personal Trainers and Athletes

Michael Boyle

Introduction
Mark Verstegen

Foreword
Alwyn Cosgrove

On Target Publications
Santa Cruz, California

Advances in Functional Training
Training Techniques for Coaches, Personal Trainers and Athletes

Michael Boyle

Introduction: Mark Verstegen

Foreword: Alwyn Cosgrove

Cover photo: Scott Cronk
Cover athlete: Ingrid Marcum

Copyright © 2010, Michael John Boyle
ISBN: 978-1-931046-01-5

First Printing November 2009
Second Printing March 2010

On Target Publications
P. O. Box 1335
Aptos, CA 95001 USA
(888) 466-9185
info@ontargetpublications.net
www.ontargetpublications.net

Library of Congress Cataloging-in-Publication Data

Boyle, Michael, 1959-
Advances in functional training : training techniques for coaches, personal trainers and athletes / Michael Boyle ; introduction Mark Verstegen ; foreword Alwyn Cosgrove.
    p. cm.
 Includes bibliographical references and index.
 ISBN 978-1-931046-01-5 (pbk.)
 1. Athletes--Training of. 2. Physical education and training. 3. Exercise. I. Title.
 GV711.5.B68 2010
 613.7'11--dc22
                        2009038240

To Cindy, Michaela and Mark

Because of the three of you my life is better every day

Developing Athleticism

Equipment Choices

Exercises Choices The Basics and Single-Leg Training

In Closing

I was extremely honored when Michael asked me to write the introduction and to lay the foundation for what you are about to read by taking a look back at our first meeting, and where our beloved field was at the time.

In the early '90s, I was a young, idealistic strength and conditioning coach in one of the best positions in college sports. I felt a deep responsibility for my athletes and had a desire to leave no ethical stone unturned, and eventually I left the NCAA setting to create what would become the first independent performance facility in the country, which I called the International Performance Institute.

As glamorous as that sounds, I was alone, in a sea of tennis courts and kids at the Bollettieri Sports Academy, now IMG, in Bradenton, Florida. We had no facilities, staff or resources to do much, and had to earn our way, which is what fuels a naïve, focused coach with undeniable determination.

In hindsight, these limited resources were probably the greatest blessing of all time, as this necessitated a creative, systems-based approach. In time, we built a young, eager team, running an integrated system of mindset, nutrition, movement and recovery. Over the course of four years we made do with what we had, and were honored to support top performers in tennis, football, soccer, baseball, basketball, from juniors to professionals.

In the old days before there was what's now called functional training, a performance industry, and yes, before there was the internet and the associated internet experts providing information overload, there was a time when we heard or read — on paper! — of someone doing something special, usually somewhere between the European Union, Australia, Asia or the Americas.

This is how and when I first met Michael. He had seen a story in *Outside* or *Smithsonian Magazine* on our group, and convinced his family to vacation in Florida, where he could drop in and evaluate firsthand. A month later, we were busy training athletes as Michael sat quietly on the sideline. I had no idea what he was thinking as he observed our controlled chaos through which we rolled thirty pros and a few hundred eight- to eighteen-year-old kids that morning.

Michael was raised by wonderful parents who were educators in hard Boston. His consistent, striving efforts in New England had him coaching the NHL Bruins, Boston University Hockey, and creating Mike Boyle Strength and Conditioning, pumping out athletes in factory-type fashion — including the first true Combine preparation success — and often these all in the same day.

So you can see how Michael would be a hard person to set back, but those were his words of description within the first thirty seconds of our talk that day. What could have set him back? Perhaps being welcomed with open arms during a time when the strength and conditioning industry was high on testosterone, ego and insecurity, and low on respect and open-mindedness.

I had made one simple request: Would he present a talk to our team over our short lunch break? In retrospect, what surprised him was probably our unexpected culture, pulling him in, welcoming him with open arms, our desire to learn from and share with him.

And I also asked him to give us a completely honest evaluation of our sessions. This set the tone of our relationship, and these are some of the values I hope have positively influenced our industry over the last fifteen years.

What does all this have to do with Michael Boyle and his second book on functional training? Everything.

I've spent my life traveling the world seeking the science and people behind successful systems that drive sustainable performance. This book is a great performance that weaves terrific information into proven, effective game plans for you to use personally and with your clients.

If you want to be successful, look deeper at the biggest takeaway from this book: It is the man and the mindset behind this work that should be studied and celebrated. Michael Boyle's lifetime of daily dedication to increasing his knowledge, digesting the information into sustainable systems he passionately implements with his own hands is the true secret to success.

More importantly has been his courage to share his thoughts, often entertaining and unconventional, on difficult subjects that have challenged all of our beliefs, helping to rapidly evolve our field into what we know today. He will be the first person to stand corrected, and often does this himself by sharing not just his successes, but thought-stimulating failures, allowing us to learn in all ways.

In the fifteen years since we first met, we — you included — have created a performance passion, molding a cottage industry into a true global platform that reaches outside athletics and into the game of life. Growth itself is not always positive; growth with integrity is. Our society is plagued, from sedentary adolescents to adults, to short-cutting athletes. The reactive medical model is completely broken, and it has become obvious the true solution lies in proactive options across mindset, nutrition, movement and recovery.

It is up to our performance industry to provide scientific, personalized and efficient systems to lead people to happy, healthy and fulfilled lives. We have a long way to go to in creating a valid, reliable and trusted solution. The only way to do this is together, with open minds, studying, researching, sharing and elevating others as we go.

This is the culture of that early meeting that has acted as the foundation and game plan for growing this industry with benevolent leaders like Michael Boyle, Gray Cook, Greg Rose, researchers and the many others who meet Chris Poirier of Perform Better's high bar to offer our industry educational value with values.

I believe you will find this book to be an insightful, system-based approach to make sense of information overload during this rapidly evolving time in our space. If there is one person to capture this, with his brash yet thoughtful views built through sustainable successes, it is by a man at the absolute top of his game, Michael Boyle.

More so, I hope you walk away with what makes him so successful as a professional. Seek insight into the system to grow professionally, while deepening your passion and responsibility. Michael follows in the contagious state of evolution of the great Al Vermeil, and I hope you'll follow his footsteps for the betterment of our field.

Mark Verstegen
President/Founder Athletes' Performance
Creator of the Core Performance System

In the world of cooking the chef who has been awarded the most Michelin stars is thought to be the best.

In acting a multiple Oscar winner is probably considered number one.

In sports? The most championships or gold medals.

In strength and conditioning we have no such external measure. No checks and balances for our peers to mark off.

It doesn't help that our field is subdivided into strength coaching, powerlifting, personal training, functional training and assessment, all with their own ideas as to who's right and who's wrong.

But out of all of that there is one name that commands respect across our entire field: Michael Boyle.

I first met Michael in the winter of '96 or '97 at a Perform Better seminar in New Jersey. It was one of those moments in a young fitness coach's career when he realizes if he wants to improve, he needs to study this guy's work.

Fast forward ten years and I'm presenting alongside Michael at a similar event. As I listened to his talk, *25 years and 25 mistakes,* it was one of those moments in a ten-years-older fitness coach's career when he realizes yet again if he wants to improve, he needs to study this guy.

And then the final ah-ha moment was when I was on stage that day presenting. Michael sat in the audience taking notes; my first glimpse of him, pen in hand, startled me and I lost my train of thought. I found myself wondering what a guy like me had to offer him in terms of training information... but that's not how he thinks. He is constantly improving and elevating his own standards.

So when you study his work, you are not only getting the results of his more than twenty-five years at a very successful sports training career, you are also getting twenty-five years of Mike's own education, from books, seminars and private conversations with his peers.

It has been said you should seek out and study people who have "been there and done that." I think that's a fallacy. It is better to study those who have been there and done that and are still doing it! Our field is changing so fast these days you need to keep up with people who are still on the cutting edge.

High performance athletic talents seek out Michael Boyle to take them to new heights. Real world people send their kids to him because they know he's just as good at the other end of the spectrum.

And coaches like me go to visit him and we send our staff to learn from him.

This book contains what Michael has learned and practiced since the publication of his first book on functional training, *Functional Training for Sports*. With this book you not only stand on the knowledge contained herein, but also on all the knowledge he has absorbed in the last three decades.

Enjoy.

Alwyn Cosgrove
Results-Fitness.com

We often hear people talk about standing on the shoulders of giants. The true derivation is dwarfs standing on the shoulders of giants. There are numerous historical references to the phrase, but it all comes back to the same thing: Dwarves see farther when they stand on the shoulders of giants. The opportunity is created by the giant and the view is enjoyed by the dwarf. The view of the dwarf surpasses that of the giant only by virtue of the giant.

Often there are times when I feel like Steve Martin in the movie *The Jerk*, ecstatic because I have been validated by seeing my name in the new phone book. I picture Martin running, screaming "The new phonebooks are in!" Or maybe I'm more like Sally Field at the Academy Awards, "You like me, you really like me."

This book is small tribute to those giants who have taught me so much. I am proud to say I call people like Don Chu and Al Vermeil friends, and that somehow I now manage to get mentioned in the same rarefied air they occupied for me as a young strength coach. There are many other giants, too numerous to mention; I will not try for fear of missing more. Just remember we are dwarves, and remember who the giants are.

I am lucky enough to be living a dream. Years ago I sat at conferences and thought how great it must be to hold an audience's attention like Al or Don or Vern Gambetta did. Today I get to present alongside these great coaches on the Perform Better tour, living my dream.

Even better, I get to do it in the company of family and friends. My children often tag along and meet a who's who of fitness and strength and conditioning. They only know Mark or Alwyn as friends who sometimes sleep over. They are blissfully unaware of the magnitude of their meetings.

I am living proof an average guy can make it in this business. I was not a great athlete. I did not have a full time job in the field until I was thirty years old. I don't coach at an athletic superpower. Most of my best published work occurred between the ages of forty and fifty. I fancy myself something of a late bloomer. Hard, consistent work, combined with a lot of caring produces excellent results over time. That I am sure of.

I am humbled by readers, email writers and seminar participants every day. Books continue to sell and websites prosper, all validating the work I love. I am most humbled by the many I taught who continue in our profession. There is no greater reward for your work than to realize you have inspired a young person to enter your field.

Training is simple. A friend said it eloquently: Push something, pull something, and do something for your legs. Add a few rollouts and you have a total body workout. It's not the *what* as much as the *how*. How often, how many? In many cases, just plain how. One leg or two, bars or dumbbells? The truth is, if we keep it simple and hard we will probably be okay.

My life has been a journey in which I wandered from a 110-pound York set to powerlifting to something we called strength coaching. Eventually I passed through strength and conditioning on my way to becoming a performance enhancement specialist.

The beautiful part of the journey is I have some great people with whom I walk.

Along the way I watched others follow the same path. Some lose their way. Some stop in the middle of the path and lie like tired dogs, content they have found a destination when in fact they are only partway through the journey. Those at the beginning of the journey seem to laugh at those of us nearer to the end. It is so easy to feel brilliant when you are young and indestructible, not so easy when entrusted with the training of those other than yourself.

I love Oscar Wilde's quote, "I am not young enough to know everything." I hope young strength coaches continue to read my work and benefit from someone who is farther down the road. I just know I have not stopped too long at any point to lie down and I have no intention of doing that; I love to search and to learn.

The perfect program is to me the Holy Grail. Some day I will be able to look at someone and know exactly what I want to do and why. I can't say that now. These next pages outline the last five years in the journey toward that perfect program.

When you train those who make their living from sport, you assume a responsibility. You must now improve another while not hurting his or her earning potential. When you train someone's children you assume an even greater responsibility. You hope to make better athletes and better people. Both jobs require great thought and great care.

If you are reading this, there is a good chance we are very much alike, and for us, like the perfect wave for a surfer, the perfect program is elusive. In the past ten years I have ridden a roller coaster that probably makes me appear confused to the casual reader.

Information comes at us at a rapid pace, and many of the self-evident truths no longer look so ironclad. Stretch more or stretch less? Squat with one leg or two? What do we really know?

Please read on and explore the continued mystery of strength and conditioning. I hope at the end of the book, you feel as if you have moved another step down the road to that perfect program, the one that produces tremendous gains with no injury.

Michael Boyle
January 2010

Advances in Functional Training

Reconsidering Functional Training

Choosing Functional Exercises
Upper-Body Pulling and Pressing
Vertical Pulling Movements
Horizontal Pulling Movements

Reconsidering Functional Training

We should start with a brief explanation of my path to becoming a believer in functional training. Every time I sent a client with an injury to a physical therapist, the report that came back was short: Most often the injury occurred because a stabilizing muscle was weak and stress was shifted to another muscle. Usually, the weak muscles were stabilizers of the hip, spine or scapulo-thoracic joint.

A trend became obvious: *It always seemed to be the same muscles.*

Therapists frequently pointed at weakness in the deep abdominal muscles (transverse abdominus and internal oblique), hip stabilizers (gluteus medius, adductors and quadratus lumborum and hip external rotators), and scapula retractors (lower traps and rhomboids).

Each weak group seemed to be the cause of a different problem.

- Clients with low back pain were usually weak in the deep abdominals.

- Athletes with knee problems usually had weak hip stabilizers.

- Those with rotator cuff issues universally had issues with scapula retractors and stabilizers.

Since we were repeatedly seeing the same weaknesses, why not address them? We simply made a point of strengthening muscles our trainers and therapists said were consistently weak, even though our athletes had always trained with basic multi-joint exercises.

I didn't do this because it was trendy, I did it because I wanted results. My number one goal is to reduce my athletes' incidence of injury. Even performance enhancement comes in second to injury reduction.

The description of functional training in *Functional Training for Sports* is clear: Functional training is best described as a continuum of exercises that teach athletes to handle their bodyweight in all planes of movement. The coach uses bodyweight as resistance and attempts to employ positions that make sense to the participant.

The concept of functional training seems so intuitive, I used to struggle to find what could be objectionable to others, which it certainly has been. When I read a functional training description of Charles Staley's, I realized why so many people are against the idea. Staley describes functional training in his book *Muscle Logic* as "exercises performed on various devices such as exercise balls, foam rollers and wobble boards, designed to create a more challenging environment for the purpose of involving more of the smaller and more deeply located stabilizer muscles."

He goes on, "Functional training advocates purport that greater stabilizer involvement is the key to enhanced performance and overall training results."

It was obvious I failed in my first attempt to describe functional training, because an intelligent and well-read man like Charles did not see the basic concept of functional training as I saw it.

To me, function is essentially purpose. Functional training can therefore be described as purposeful training.

Functional training and unstable-surface training are not synonymous. Unstable surface training is one aspect of the larger thought process that makes up functional training. Unfortunately, these unstable balance trainers have become so synonymous with functional training, many consider them one and the same.

Functional training is not so much about the gadgets used by physical therapists in rehab, but about the knowledge physical therapists have gained about why injuries occur. This is where people get confused: It's not about the gadgets; it's about the information.

Functional training shifts the focus of exercises to incorporate stabilizer muscles because this is what physical therapists report as the source of injury.

Watching collegiate or professional athletes train like powerlifters, Olympic lifters or bodybuilders began to make less and less sense as my knowledge expanded. It was not that I didn't appreciate the contributions of these sports, it was just that I realized there was so much more as I began to develop a deeper understanding of anatomy and of injury mechanisms.

What functional training really comes down to is the application of functional anatomy to training. It is taking what we know and using that information to select exercises to reduce the incidence of injury and improve performance. Instability is a potential progression, but not the fundamental driver.

Use What Works

When reading this book it is very important to put aside any preconceived notions about the process of strength and conditioning. Think about practicing the art of common sense. Often good ideas seem so basic we discount them based only on their simplicity. As coaches and personal trainers, we continue to jump on and off the latest bandwagons. Try to stay with ideas that work, and be wary of anything that seems too good to be true.

Speed, movement ability, strength and power are all qualities that can and should be improved. Good strength and conditioning coaches are constantly scrutinizing their programs. Every day I learn something that makes me consider a change in the program. These are not knee-jerk reactions, but rather the acceptance that there are many coaches and therapists pushing the envelope and developing better techniques.

As a coach, you can't allow yourself to fall in love with any particular exercises, techniques or philosophies. Your job is to get results, and to choose the methods that give you those results. This means experimenting with everything that makes sense to you, rejecting the things that don't make sense or no longer make sense, and keeping whatever works.

Occasionally you might reject popular exercises. Sometimes you stop using exercises you once liked. And every now and then, you pull something out of the second category and reincorporate it into your programs.

If it works, that's all that matters.

Here no attempts are made to copy the programs of successful teams or athletes. Instead I evaluate each technique or concept for inclusion. Many coaches duplicate the program of the most successful team, but remember, much of that success may be due to recruiting, coaching or genetics. Instead of copying successful teams or individuals, seek the techniques of those who consistently produce great results in less-than-ideal situations.

More is Not Better

Most young athletes and many young coaches think if two sets are good, four sets must be better. In truth, you may be overtaxing the body and disrupting the recuperative process. When you think of a strength program, remind yourself strength training is a game of stimulus and response. The actual workout is a stimulus. The response occurs after the workout. The response is affected by the quality of the workout and by the quality of the recovery. Rest and nutrition have as much to do with success as does the workout program.

The real key to a successful strength program is injury reduction. I used to say injury prevention, but in reality only divine intervention can prevent injury. Injury reduction is a better representation of the goal. Semantics aside, statistics don't lie. If your injuries decrease and your wins increase, you're successful. Wins can obviously be affected by talent and coaching, but in general, injury trends will not be as affected by these factors. Your number one goal is injury reduction, and after that comes performance enhancement.

During my fifteen years of college coaching, I noticed an interesting trend. As we evolved from a traditional power and Olympic lifting program to a more functionally based program, our strength numbers stayed consistent, and our injury incidence decreased drastically. Think about this as you read.

Olympic lifting and powerlifting are excellent systems that teach a strong technical background and emphasize multi-joint lifts. However, much like the invention of modern plumbing and the development of the internet, strength and conditioning is constantly advancing. To be successful we need to advance with it.

Functional Training

Mark Verstegen was one of the first to break out of the track mold coaches were stuck in as he began to teach lateral and multi-directional movement with the same skill the track coaches taught linear movement. This process was a quantum leap for me, and became a quantum leap for my athletes. This was my first step from strength and conditioning coach to performance enhancement specialist. The key to this process was accepting the fact that Mark and his co-workers were far ahead of me in this critical area.

Functional training, core training and the proper use of unstable surfaces are only a few of the examples of advances that should be embraced and incorporated into a sound program. We have far too many ostriches in our profession, content to coach with their heads in the sand.

Technique... technique... technique. Never compromise. Use bodyweight when possible and practical. Do lots of push-ups, feet-elevated push-ups, one-leg squats, chin-ups and dips. Bodyweight exercises are humbling. Use these early and often with beginners. Not only will athletes learn to respect their bodyweight, but they will also see the value of these easy exercises.

Techniques

If you are going to use the squat, teach bodyweight squats first. If athletes can't squat bodyweight with perfect form, they can't squat. Period. They must be able to get through the range of motion. It is normal to be able to squat to a parallel position. Athletes who cannot may need work on hip mobility, ankle mobility or lateral hamstring stretching.

If you choose to have your athletes squat, have them perform parallel squats without fail. Our athletes do nothing but front squats to a femur-parallel position. We even use twelve-inch plyo boxes to ensure depth; we ask athletes to squat to a box that places the femur parallel to the floor. Although we may need different size boxes for different athletes, we arrive at a point for each athlete that defines parallel. These are not Westside Barbell box squats; the athlete merely touches the box to insure depth.

If you use the bench press, no bounce, no arch. Never compromise. As soon as you allow one athlete to cheat or to not adhere to the program, others will follow. Remember why athletes cheat: They cheat to lift more weight. Lifting more weight feeds their egos. Once you allow it to happen, cheating is very difficult to stop.

To make your point, use exercises like pause bench and pause front squats. These exercises can be very humbling. Canadian strength coach Charles Poliquin has a principle called technical failure. Technical failure means you never count a rep after technique breaks down. This principle will encourage your athletes to lift properly. I consistently tell my athletes I don't care how many reps they do; I care how many *good* reps they do.

Strength and conditioning coaching may seem easy in principle, but it's difficult in practice. The key to a successful program is to try to see every set and coach every athlete. This is difficult, time-consuming, and repetitive. In fact, it is impossible.

At the end of a good day in the weightroom, you should be hoarse and tired. A good strength coach will have sore legs and knees from a day spent squatting down to see squat depth.

Choosing Functional Exercises

We'd like to assume coaches are always looking for the best programs and exercises to both reduce the incidence of injury and improve performance. However, when I see the programs many of our elite athletes are given, I am both confused and disappointed.

Coaches continue to prescribe exercises like leg extensions, leg curls and leg presses, even when it appears there is little to support the prescriptions. Functional anatomy is not a theory. What we know about function is factual and is based on science and research.

The idea that we need to isolate a muscle or that we need certain single-joint exercises for injury prevention has not been proven. Coaches need to move forward in their programming and begin to use exercises that make sense and will actually reduce the potential of injury.

The functional continuum was first introduced in *Functional Training for Sports* to illustrate exercise choices on a continuum from least functional to most functional. Exercises are separated into lower-body exercises, upper-body exercises and torso or core strength exercises. The categories are then further broken down into knee-dominant, hip-dominant, upper-body pushing and upper-body pulling exercises. The exercises progress on the continuum from machine-based exercises to exercises done primarily in the standing position. Exercises also progress from a stable system that does not stress stabilizers or neutralizers, to exercises designed specifically to do so. Stabilizers provide stability, while neutralizers prevent unwanted motion.

The first exercise sequence is knee-dominant lower-body exercises. The continuum begins with the lying leg press, as this is the least functional multi-joint lower body exercise I can envision. In a leg press, as with most machine exercises, the athlete simply functions as the engine or force-producer. All of the stability is provided by the machine.

The second exercise on the continuum would be a standing machine squat, progressing up the functional curve to a standing position. The standing position is more sport-specific than lying, and may incorporate additional muscles not stressed in the leg press. However, stability is still provided by the machine.

The third step up the functional continuum is to move to a standing squatting exercise. The athlete is again standing as in the machine squat, but is now self-stabilizing. This will obviously stress the core to a greater degree. Many coaches consider squatting to be a good core exercise even though there is no unilateral or rotational stress. In fact, some coaches think squatting is enough core exercise. The standing two-leg squat is the point where often even good strength coaches stop.

Many coaches use ground-based exercises, but neglect to think a step or two further. The next step in the progression should be to work on one leg.

From a functional anatomical standpoint, it is absolutely critical to be on one leg. How many legs do you run on at a time? Just one. Have you ever had an athlete pull his hamstrings bilaterally? Not a chance. The muscles that support the lower leg in single-leg stance — the quadratus, glute medius and adductors — are not nearly as active in double-leg exercises.

The final step in the continuum is a one-leg squat while standing on an unstable surface. Now the athlete must engage the prime movers, stabilizers and neutralizers while dealing with the additional proprioceptive input provided by instability.

We'll cover each of the advances rungs of the continuum in the pages that follow.

Using Functional Exercises

Functional exercise makes some old-school coaches nervous. Opponents of the concept of functional training are consistently trotting out poorly done studies to call functional training a fad. Recently I was told functional exercise is fine for rehab and will help restore proprioception, but it doesn't work with healthy athletes. My experience does not bear this out: In six years of professional or Olympic-level soccer, our athletes had no ACL tears. This is obviously anecdotal, but powerful nonetheless.

The concepts described in the functional continuum can be applied to any region of the body. To use an overused cliché, think outside the box. Don't do what you've always done. Don't do what everyone else does. Don't copy powerlifters or weightlifters; they are training for their sports, not yours. Many of the concepts of powerlifting or Olympic-style lifting can be applied to a sound strength program, but remember, those sports are different because in our other activities we infrequently have two feet in contact with the ground. You don't have to take exercises like squats or deadlifts out of your program, but instead complement them with assistance exercises higher on the functional continuum.

This book will provide exercises and programs examples, but to give you the basic idea:

• *Instead of leg extensions,* use split squats or another single-leg squat variation. Split squats incorporate balance, flexibility and single-leg strength.

• *Instead of leg curls,* use a single-leg straight-leg deadlift. The hamstring is more of a hip extensor than a knee flexor. In fact, the hamstring is actually a resistor of leg extension in sprinting. Leg curls do not provide useful, real-world strength.

• *Instead of dumbbell bench press*, try an alternating dumbbell bench press where you have the client stabilize the dumbbell at the top. This will develop core strength, shoulder stability and single-arm strength.

When choosing exercises, ask yourself why each is in the program. If the reason is because everyone else does them or because that's the way you have always done it, think again.

The functionality of an exercise should be a key factor in choosing exercises for athletic development. Functional exercises will, by definition, be specific to a sport or activity. Progression from double-leg to single-leg exercises is important to most ground-based sports.

Upper-Body Pulling and Pressing

In most strength training programs, pulling movements such as chin-ups and rows are still given little emphasis. Instead, most coaches and trainers have their athletes and clients perform lat pull-downs for the muscles of the upper back under the mistaken assumption this is all that is necessary. In addition, many programs completely ignore rowing movements. This type of program design leads to overdevelopment of the pressing muscles, to postural problems, and eventually to shoulder injury.

A well-designed upper-body program should include a proportional ratio of sets of horizontal pulling and vertical pulling to overhead and supine pressing exercises. There should be at least one set of a pulling exercise for every set of pushing.

A poor ratio of pulling to pressing leads to overdevelopment of the pectorals and underdevelopment of the scapulae retractors, and predisposes athletes to overuse shoulder injuries, especially rotator cuff tendinosis.

The incidence of rotator cuff tendinosis among athletes who perform a great deal of bench press and bench press variations is extremely high. Many powerlifters accept shoulder pain as a part of their sport in much the same way swimmers or tennis players do. The reality is with a balanced program very few athletes should experience anterior shoulder pain. Anterior shoulder pain is not due to the bench press itself, but more likely to the lack of an appropriate ratio of pulling movements.

The real key is for the athlete to possess a good ratio of pulling to pushing strength. This is best estimated by comparing an athlete's maximum number of pull-ups to his maximum bench press weight. Consideration must be given to bodyweight, but an athlete capable of bench pressing well over bodyweight should also be capable of pulling his bodyweight, regardless of size.

For example, a 200-pound male athlete who can bench press 300 pounds should be able to perform twelve to fifteen chin-ups, and a 300-pound male athlete who can bench press 400 pounds should be able to do five to eight.

Females may actually perform better in the ratio of chin-up to bench press. We have found female athletes capable of bench pressing their bodyweight can perform anywhere from five to ten chin-ups.

Vertical Pulling Movements

A well-designed strength program should include at least three sets each of two chin-up variations weekly, as well as a minimum of three sets of two rowing movements per week. Either the specific type of vertical and horizontal pull, or the number of repetitions should change every three weeks; in some cases, both should change.

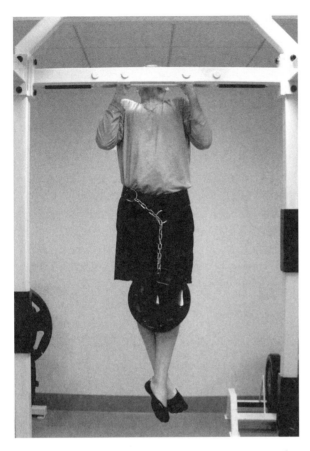

An important point is not to get caught in the trap of adding chin-ups to your program, but not training them as a strength exercise. Vertical pulling movements should be cycled in conjunction with horizontal pressing movements like the bench press.

If you are performing sets of three in the bench press, perform sets of three in your vertical pulling movements. If you are performing pyramids, do the same with vertical pulls.

Our male athletes very rapidly gain upper-back strength with this type of program. It is not unusual for men to perform five chin-ups with a forty-five-pound plate attached to a dip belt, and female athletes sets of three chin-ups with anywhere from five to twenty-five pounds.

Treat vertical pulling as a strength exercise and you will see large increases in strength, and, most importantly, decreases in shoulder pain.

Horizontal Pulling Movements

Horizontal pulling movements are critical for two reasons.

• The addition of rowing motions to the program will help prevent injury.

• Rowing exercises are a true antagonistic movement to the bench press. Although chin-ups and their variations are important, rowing movements specifically target both the muscles and movement patterns that directly oppose those trained on the bench press.

Despite their importance, rows are even more frequently omitted from strength programs. Rowing motions are an area of functional training undergoing great change. Recent advances in athletic training and physical therapy have shown the body is linked both anteriorly and posteriorly in a diagonal pattern. Force is transmitted from the ground through the leg to the hip via the biceps femoris and the glute max. The force is then transferred across the sacro-iliac joint into the opposite latissimus dorsi.

The key in this system of cross-linkage lies not only in stabilizing the hip, but in engaging the muscles used in the proper motor pattern.

For this reason, all rowing motions except the inverted row and rotational row are performed with only one foot in contact with the ground. With one foot on the ground and the load in the hand opposite that foot, the athlete must now engage the biceps femoris and glute to transfer force from the ground via the pelvic stabilizers and the hip rotators.

The hip rotator group and pelvic stabilizers are of particular importance because all force transferred from the ground must move through a stable hip to properly transfer to the upper body.

Until very recently, the hip rotator group has been effectively ignored. The hip rotators are the "rotator cuff" of the lower body, but don't get the attention the shoulder rotator cuff muscles of the upper body get. All force originating from the ground, whether a golf swing or a home run, must transfer through a strong, flexible and stable hip rotator group. The hip rotators must be given particular attention in program design.

We'll get into specifics later in the book, but first we need to cover what I consider the biggest change in training philosophy in recent years, joint stability and joint mobility as a focus in our training.

Mobility and Flexibility

The Joint-by-Joint Approach

Movement Screening

The Functional Movement Screen

Assessing Strength, Flexibility and Mobility
The Bodyweight Squat

Mobility Drills

Foam Rolling

Rolling versus Massage

Static Stretching
Shortened Muscles
Active-Isolated Stretching

The Joint-by-Joint Approach

Joint	Primary Needs
Ankle	*Mobility (sagittal)*
Knee	*Stability*
Hip	*Mobility (multi-planar)*
Lumbar Spine	*Stability*
Thoracic Spine	*Mobility*
Scapula	*Stability*
Gleno-humeral	*Mobility*

If you are not yet familiar with the joint-by-joint theory, be prepared to take a quantum leap in thought process. My good friend, physical therapist Gray Cook, has a gift for simplifying complex topics. In a conversation about the effect of training on the body, Gray produced one of the most lucid ideas I have ever heard.

We were discussing the findings of his Functional Movement Screen (FMS), the needs of the different joints of the body, and how the function of the joints relate to training. One beauty of the FMS is it allows us to distinguish between issues of stability and those of mobility; Gray's thoughts led me to realize the future of training may be a joint-by-joint approach, rather than a movement-based approach.

His analysis of the body is a straightforward one. In his mind, the body is a just a stack of joints. Each joint or series of joints has a specific function and is prone to predictable levels of dysfunction. As a result, each joint has particular training needs.

This joint-by-joint idea has really taken on a life of its own, one I certainly didn't envision. It seems like everybody's familiar with it; it's become so common knowledge people fail to reference Gray Cook or me as the developers of the idea.

The table in the next column looks at the body on a joint-by-joint basis from the bottom up.

The first thing you should notice is the joints alternate between mobility and stability. The ankle needs increased mobility, and the knee needs increased stability. As we move up the body, it becomes apparent the hip needs mobility. And so the process goes up the chain — a basic, alternating series of joints.

Over the past twenty years, we have progressed from the approach of training by body part to a more intelligent approach of training by movement pattern. In fact, the phrase "movements, not muscles" has almost become an overused one, and frankly, that's progress. Most good coaches and trainers have given up on the old chest-shoulder-triceps method and moved to push-pull, hip-extend, knee-extend programs.

Still, the movement-not-muscles philosophy probably should have gone a step further. Injuries relate closely to proper joint function, or more appropriately, to joint *dysfunction*. Problems at one joint usually show up as pain in the joint above or below.

The primary illustration is in the lower back. It's clear we need core stability, and it's also obvious many people suffer from back pain. The intriguing part lies in the theory behind low back pain. The new theory of the cause: loss of hip mobility.

Loss of function in the joint below — in the case of the lumbar spine, it's the hips — seems to affect the joint or joints above. In other words, if the hips can't move, the lumbar spine will. The problem is the hips are designed for mobility, and the lumbar spine for stability. When the intended mobile joint becomes immobile, the stable joint is forced to move as compensation, becoming less stable and subsequently painful.

The Process is Simple

- Lose ankle mobility, get knee pain

- Lose hip mobility, get low back pain

- Lose thoracic mobility, get neck and shoulder pain, or low back pain

Looking at the body on a joint-by-joint basis beginning with the ankle, this makes sense.

The ankle is a joint that should be mobile and when it becomes immobile, the knee, a joint that should be stable, becomes unstable; the hip is a joint that should be mobile and it becomes immobile, and this works its way up the body. The lumbar spine should be stable; it becomes mobile, and so on, right on up through the chain.

Now take this idea a step further: What's the primary loss with an injury or with lack of use? Ankles lose mobility; knees lose stability; hips lose mobility. You have to teach your clients these joints have a specific mobility or stability need, and when they're not using them much or are using them improperly, that immobility is more than likely going to cause a problem elsewhere in the body.

If somebody comes to you with a hip mobility issue — if he or she has lost hip mobility – the complaint will generally be one of low back pain. He (my editor suggests I can get away with the generic pronoun "he" instead of writing he or she and him or her throughout the entire book; I hope she's right) won't come to you complaining of a hip problem. This is why we suggest looking at the joints above and looking at the joints below, and the fix is usually increasing the mobility of the nearby joint.

These are the results of joint dysfunction: Poor ankle mobility equals knee pain; poor hip mobility equals low back pain; poor t-spine mobility, cervical pain.

An immobile ankle causes the stress of landing to be transferred to the joint above, the knee. In fact, there is a direct connection between the stiffness of the basketball shoe and the amount of taping and bracing that correlates with the high incidence of patella-femoral syndrome in basketball players. Our desire to protect the unstable ankle came with a high cost. We have found many of our athletes with knee pain have corresponding ankle mobility issues. Many times this follows an ankle sprain and subsequent bracing and taping.

The exception to the rule seems to be at the hip. The hip can be both immobile and unstable, resulting in knee pain from the instability — a weak hip will allow internal rotation and adduction of the femur — or back pain from the immobility.

How a joint can be both immobile and unstable is an interesting question.

Weakness of the hip in either flexion or extension causes compensatory action at the lumbar spine, while weakness in abduction, or, more accurately, prevention of adduction, causes stress at the knee.

Poor psoas and iliacus strength or activation will cause patterns of lumbar flexion as a substitute for hip flexion. Poor strength or low activation of the glutes will cause a compensatory extension pattern of the lumbar spine to replace the motion of hip extension.

This fuels a vicious cycle. As the spine moves to compensate for the lack of strength and mobility of the hip, the hip loses more mobility. Lack of strength at the hip leads to immobility, and immobility in turn leads to compensatory motion at the spine. The end result is a kind of conundrum, a joint that needs both strength and mobility in multiple planes.

Your athletes and clients must learn to move from the hips, not from the lumbar spine. Most athletes with lower back pain or hamstring strains have poor hip or lumbo-pelvic mechanics and as a result must extend or flex the lumbar spine to make up for movement unavailable through the hip.

The lumbar spine is even more interesting. This is clearly a series of joints in need of stability, as evidenced by all the research in the area of core stability. The biggest mistake we have made in training over the last ten years is an active attempt to increase the static and active range of motion of an area that requires stability.

Most, if not all, of the many rotary exercises done for the lumbar spine were misdirected. Physical therapist Shirley Sahrmann in *Diagnosis and Treatment of Movement Impairment Syndromes* and James Porterfield and Carl DeRosa in *Mechanical Low Back Pain: Perspectives in Functional Anatomy* all indicate attempting to increase lumbar spine range of motion is not recommended and is potentially dangerous. Our lack of understanding of thoracic mobility caused us to try to gain lumbar rotary ROM, and this was a huge mistake.

The thoracic spine is the area about which we know the least. Many physical therapists recommend increasing thoracic mobility, though few have exercises designed specifically for it. The approach seems to be "We know you need it, but we're not sure how to get it." Over the next few years we will see an increase in exercises designed to increase thoracic mobility. A leader in the field, Sahrmann was early to advocate the development of thoracic mobility and the limitation of lumbar mobility.

The gleno-humeral joint is similar to the hip. The gleno-humeral joint is designed for mobility and therefore needs to be trained for stability. The need for stability in the gleno-humeral joint presents a great case for exercises like stability ball and BOSU push-ups, as well as unilateral dumbbell work.

In the book *Ultra-Prevention,* a nutrition book, authors Mark Hyman and Mark Liponis describe our current method of reaction to injury perfectly. Their analogy is simple: Our response to injury is like hearing the smoke detector go off and running to pull out the battery. The pain, like the sound, is a warning of some other problem. Icing a sore knee without examining the ankle or hip is like pulling the battery out of the smoke detector. The relief is short-lived.

Every day, I learn more and more about the body. What I learn allows me to be a better coach and a better educator. Often, what I learn contradicts what I formerly believed, and you may find a few of those reversals between this book and its predecessor.

My recommendation to all coaches and personal trainers is to learn Gray Cook and Lee Burton's Functional Movement Screen (FMS) and take a group of athletes through the screen. I guarantee you'll find things you would miss looking at movement. The reason for this is the reason we need to be careful with the whole functional training thing. In my experience, the better the athlete, the better the compensation. Elite athletes always find a way to perform a skill and make it look easy. The red flags don't disappear, they just go into hiding.

The only way to analyze the motion of an elite athlete is to slow him down and look at static postures, active ranges of motion and stability. The red flags hide until they become a full-blown injury. Then we are forced to back up and attempt to fix what is now broken. The approach of many of the experts in strength and conditioning is if it's not broken, don't fix it. In other words, wait until it breaks and then ask a physical therapist to fix it. With a tool like the FMS, we get to close a few barn doors before the horses get out.

A coach or personal trainer who works with a wide range of athletes and clients, as most do, can use this one simple screening system. The key to understanding and using the screen lies in realizing it is just what the name implies. It is a screen. It is a basic tool to look at patterns of movement and bilateral imbalances. It is not meant to be a program design system.

The FMS is a great way to begin a program. The FMS and its results create an immediate bond between the client and trainer or the athlete and coach. Even if the program is not individualized in any way, the athlete or client feels his unique concerns are now being addressed.

The Functional Movement Screen (FMS) was developed by Cook and Burton as a simple system for screening both athletes and non-athletes for potential injury. The most common question I get in regard to the FMS is if I use the FMS with our teams. The answer is yes, but probably not the way you might think.

To understand why we use the Screen we need to begin with why I like Gray Cook: He helps me to achieve my goals. I want to get my athletes better. Gray's ideas help me do that.

I have no financial interest in the FMS or any of Gray's business ventures. In spite of that, I may be one of his biggest supporters and his best salesman.

What this process really is about are results and best practices. How can I get the best results for my athletes? If my athletes achieve, if my teams wins, if my clients are free of pain, everything is right with my training world.

Gray's advice for an individual is clear: Attack the worst pattern. The process is simple. Run the screen, look at the results, work on the problem patterns.

In teams settings we do the same thing. My staff and I have used the FMS with enough athletes to see trends across a wide variety of sports. In hockey the hip flexion pattern tested in the hurdle step assessment tends to be the most significant problem. As a result we designed a lot of our warm-up and pre-hab work to go after the hip flexion pattern.

Another weak pattern in testing our hockey players was rotary stability. This meant we needed to upgrade our core work.

In addition, we perform the FMS on any injured athlete who comes to our facility, and on all our personal training clients.

Losing Control of the Program

One area many strength and conditioning coaches get concerned with is losing control of their programs. That will never happen unless you let it. It's your program. I don't run Gray Cook's program and you don't have to either. I don't agree with Gray on everything. In fact, we use very few of Gray's corrective strategies as we have not found them group-friendly. However, that does not mean I can't use the screen or the information obtained from the screen to help me improve my program. The truth is as I understand more, I integrate more.

The real question is do Gray Cook and the screen have the ability to make us better at our jobs and help us improve our athletes? For me I absolutely know they do. The things I have learned from Gray have been invaluable in my evolution as a coach.

NFL strength and conditioning coaches like Jon Torine and Jeff Fish have developed group corrective strategies they like. I have also, but still use my favorite corrective exercises as a general team warm-up. There's no harm in an athlete doing additional corrective exercises even if they do not apply to his needs.

One solution that Gray has advocated is the use of the Turkish get-up or parts of the get-up as a group's corrective strategy. If you analyze the get-up, you see scapular stability, core stability and hip mobility, as well as single-leg patterns.

Gray realized athletic teams, the military and other groups who wanted to use the FMS would feel limited by some of the corrective suggestions. His solution was the *Kettlebells from the Ground Up* project called *The Kalos Sthenos* — Greek words that make up our word callisthenics. The project consists of two DVDs and a manual that reviews the movements behind the kettlebell get-up or the Turkish get-up.

One get-up involves fourteen movements from top to bottom. It has a high neural demand and challenges both mobility and stability. In the manual, each step has corrective suggestions. The get-up has a left-right component, which lends itself to the exposure of asymmetry, a fundamental component of the FMS. In addition, each part of the get-up uses one or two patterns of the FMS.

The strength coach familiar with the FMS will see many options for warm-up and corrective exercises within the program. Three to five get-ups per side can be an excellent warm-up and corrective combination. If a complete get-up is not possible for an athlete, have the athlete do three circuits of the corrective exercise suggested at the problem segment of the get-up. Cook states, "If you did nothing the FMS suggested, but let the get-up catch the problem and worked on the difficult parts of the get-up, you would witness a huge improvement in the FMS."

Screening or Selling

Influence of the Functional Movement Screen

Stop thinking of the FMS as an assessment and start thinking of it as the best tool you can have to sell your athletes on your program. The FMS may not change what you do, but it will change how your players perceive what you do. The FMS results reinforce good program-design concepts, because a well-designed program yields good FMS scores.

Mike Boyle Strength and Conditioning was one of the first groups to use the Functional Movement Screen after Gray came to Boston and taught the screen to us in 2002. At the time, we noticed one significant thing: Our coaches all scored very high. The coaches at the time were all former MBSC athletes who had spent years on our program, and the results were clear... what we did worked. A program of functional exercises with lots of single-leg work and intense core work produced excellent scores.

We then began to screen groups of normal athletes, athletes who did conventional bilateral training and machine training. The results were the opposite. Dysfunction was everywhere. The net result? The scores of our coaches reinforced to them that the program they believed in produced superior results when tested independently. And the scores and obvious inabilities demonstrated by others reinforced what was lacking in other training.

It's easy to sell core training to an athlete after he bombs the rotary core stability test. I once had a professional athlete tell me the test was impossible. I had to do it successfully three times to get him to believe it could be done. This guy could not even balance in the two-point position, much less move, yet he was playing in the NFL as a receiver. After implementing a corrective strategy, his improvement was rapid and his injury risk decreased substantially.

The concepts obtained from the Functional Movement Screen reinforced everything we believed, and added an entire level of thought process to what we did. The knowledge gained from Gray and from the screens drove us to new levels.

When I first encountered him, he preached the idea of stability before mobility. From the standpoint of developing exercise progressions, that was one of the smartest things I'd ever heard. We began to design all our strength progressions to develop stability first before progressing to mobility.

We also began to plan all our warm-up progressions to develop mobility, but only at the right joints. In a sense our approach to functional training became in a way anti-functional, using our joint-by-joint approach to simultaneously pursue stability in some areas like knees and lumbar spine, and mobility in others, such as ankles, hips and t-spine.

At the same time Gray continued to develop ways to distinguish between mobility and stability issues. In simple terms a consistent problem is a mobility issue.

The best example is the squat; if an athlete is unable to perform the overhead squat, or any squat for that matter, but in a supine position can flex the hips above ninety degrees and keep a flat back, the athlete has a stability issue. The presence of mobility in an unloaded motion coupled with a loss of mobility against gravity clearly indicates a stability problem.

The reverse would be the true mobility problem. This is best illustrated by an athlete who cannot get into the overhead squat position in standing or when lying on the back.

In the first example the athlete is capable of the range of motion, but is incapable of controlling it. In the second situation, a true mobility problem, the athlete does not have the mobility necessary to do the movement. The lack of control ability leads to an apparent loss of mobility.

This is the essence of how stability affects mobility. The body does not allow motion it cannot control. That control is achieved by decreasing range of motion.

An inconsistent problem — adequate passive ROM, inadequate active ROM — is a stability problem. A consistent lack of ROM is a pure mobility issue. The key point is stability issues will not be solved by mobility work. In contrast mobility work will probably enhance stability.

Developing Progressions

When using the Functional Movement Screen, we take the information gained and use it to develop exercise progressions. In order to do that, we need to think about movement patterns and use the concept of stable to mobile.

Movement Progressions or Exercise Progressions

The main differentiation lies in understanding the concepts of mobility and stability and how these ideas apply differently to movement progressions and exercise progressions. For movement, think about active range of motion exercises without external loads. In movement, proper mobility must precede the development of stability.

For exercises of strength, think about movements to which we intend to add loads beyond bodyweight. In strength training exercise progressions, the athlete must be stable prior to adding movement such as multi-planar actions.

As he continued learning, Gray's philosophy evolved, and he now uses the following continuum:

Mobility before stability before movement.

Athletes must develop proper mobility. When mobile they can move into the positions to develop stability. Mobility and stability can then be added to movements.

The actual continuum is as follows.

• Mobility: Freedom of movement at movable segments. The term broadly includes and covers both joint range of motion and muscle and tissue flexibility.

• Stability: The ability to control motion at a particular segment in the presence of force, tension, load, and movement.

Stability is made up of two progressive levels of control:

• *Static:* Isometric control of all directions while under load or tension, such as the shoulders in a deadlift or the hips in a tall-kneeling chop or lift.

• *Dynamic:* Control of joint alignment and integrity in a particular direction or plane of movement, while movement or force is generated in another direction or plane of movement. Examples: the hips in a deadlift or squat, extension drive without losing hip alignment; shoulder girdle in the chop and lift, although the humerus moves across all three planes, the scapula is maintained in the middle third of its movement.

Movement is the combined act of posture and control in the presence of active and reactive patterns of manipulation, moving stuff, and locomotion — moving self. This is the point where controlled mobility and dynamic stability come together with the other attributes of fitness like power, strength, speed, endurance. Movement equals function.

Gray writes, "In this continuum, mobility comes first because you cannot have control — stability — if freedom of movement is not present. Stiffness could be confused for stability if there's no freedom of motion. is not present. Static stability precedes dynamic stability. Dynamic stability precedes movement."

The key is to learn to follow patterns. If we want to control excessive motion in an exercise, we must initially eliminate potential sources of that motion. Cook's idea is to use transitional postures. In other words, many exercise progressions for strength exercises begin in a kneeling, half-kneeling, or lunge position.

If you want an athlete or client to develop control or stability at a particular joint, such as the lumbar spine, it will be easier if we eliminate the knee and ankle joints and begin in a kneeling stance.

Each stance has benefits. Tall-kneeling on the knees with the hips extended will create great glute emphasis, as the muscle is no longer needed to control the knee, only the hip. Half-kneeling, one knee down, one knee up, flexes the hip and as a result restricts motion at the lumbar spine.

In our exercise progressions, we tend to favor tall-kneeling for our athletes as a starting point. In contrast, standing creates the greatest number of issues, as there is the maximum number of joints to control. We always progress to standing as our end goal, but generally begin a tall-kneel, half-kneel or high split-stance.

Let's look at the diagonal lifting pattern to illustrate. The exercise progression initially emphasizes stability and the progression is one of increasing mobility.

Half-Kneeling Stable Lift

This is a pull-push pattern done with a long bar attachment like the Cook bar or Core bar. Motion occurs primarily in the shoulders and elbows, while the core remains stable.

Half-Kneeling Sequential

In the half-kneeling sequential lift, a shoulder turn is added and a triceps rope replaces the long bar. The pattern is still clearly a push-pull, but with a shoulder turn. The shoulder turn is advocated by physical therapist and educator Shirley Sahrmann to encourage motion at the thoracic spine rather than at the lumbar spine.

We call this a sequential lift because it is initially taught as a three-part action. Step one is a pulling action similar to a diagonal upright row. Step two is a slight turn of the shoulders. Step three is a diagonal press. This is taught sequentially to ingrain the pull-turn-press action. It is important to note some mobility has been added at the thoracic spine via the shoulder turn.

Standing Lift

The third exercise in the progression is the standing lift. The standing lift now takes on a diagonal squat-to-press action. The exercise moves from the somewhat mechanical action of the sequential lift to a very fluid movement more like an Olympic lift. The thinking is the pattern of pull-push has been properly ingrained and core control established. The key again is added mobility as the hips and knees become a part of the action.

Step-Up Lift

The last stage of the progression is to add a single-leg dimension. The single-leg action adds an additional pelvic stability component.

The progression moves from a core stability exercise to a dynamic single-leg total-body power exercise. This is the beauty of using the information obtained from Gray Cook and the Functional Movement Screen to develop exercise progressions. The idea is no longer about fixing individual issues with the screen, but rather working more globally to develop better integrated progressions for rotary stability.

Cook has advocated chops and lifts as excellent exercises to correct asymmetries and to enhance stability. Our job as coaches is to develop progressions from these ideas.

Adding Strength to Dysfunction

Another area where Cook's thoughts provide insight is in exercise selection. Gray frequently says, "Don't add strength to dysfunction." What he's saying in the simplest sense is if you can't squat, don't squat. An athlete or client who cannot perform the overhead squat to a least score a two in the screen should not be squatting. In essence if we allow him to do squats, we are simply adding strength on top of dysfunction.

The client still has a poor movement pattern, but the poor pattern can now be demonstrated with external load. This is a common high school and college football mistake and may be at the root of many athletes' back pain. An athlete who squats poorly is encouraged by a well-meaning coach to get strong. Instead, the initial emphasis should be to get mobile or to perfect the squat pattern. However, very few coaches do this. Instead, they add strength to dysfunction.

Our current approach is initially to work on mobility to obtain or develop the squat pattern. The only modification will be to elevate the heels to improve the athlete's position. Our feeling is if you can't squat low, don't squat heavy. Instead, we work on mobility and simultaneously work on single-leg strength.

This is a matter of risk-to-benefit ratio. Loading dysfunctional patterns can only lead to injury as the body tries to manage the additional stress applied to a fragile and flawed system.

Gray illustrates this with the idea of *difficult versus beneficial*. An exercise can be difficult and not be beneficial. In addition, difficult can often be unsafe.

The In-Line Lunge

There is one small area in which I disagree with Gray: We add a one-leg squat to our version of the Functional Movement Screen. Gray cautions against this, however we added the one-leg squat because I think the patterns of a supported single-leg movement — the split squat or Cook's in-line lunge — is distinctively different than the one-leg squat. A one-leg squat is what we would classify as a static unsupported exercise. The pelvic implications of what we see in a split squat versus a one-leg squat can be quite different, so we do both.

I think the in-line lunge should be renamed the split-stance squat. The in-line lunge is not a lunge at all, it's a split squat by definition. The split squat is what we refer to as a static exercise. In other words, the feet don't move. A lunge has motion and would be classified as a dynamic exercise. The lunge has a transitional component.

I believe what Gray intended to look at is a single-leg pattern and the in-line lunge —our split-stance squat — accomplishes that.

FMS Examples in Team Settings

Below are a few simple examples of the team problems encountered in the screens and how we solved them.

Hockey Example

Problem: Eighteen athletes out of twenty screened received a score of two on the hurdle step. This obviously indicated a dysfunctional pattern of hip flexion, and it led us to look at psoas and iliacus function. Our players operate in constant hip flexion and are inhibited or inefficient in standing.

Solution: Work on hip flexion from the top down and from the bottom up or as Gray would say, clean up the pattern. In this case we added hip-flexion activation exercises to our warm-up and hip-flexion strength exercises to the end of our workouts.

Football Example

Problem: Abundance of overhead squat scores of two out of a possible three. Our problem seemed to revolve around ankle mobility.

Solution: Add ankle mobility and hip mobility exercises to the warm-up.

These are two examples of simple problems with easy solutions. The beauty of the FMS system is we don't overanalyze, we just attack the problem pattern.

Case Studies

Below are three distinct examples of how the results of the Functional Movement Screen lead to career-changing solutions for professional athletes. In all three cases below, the athletes had experienced injuries other sports medicine professionals had a difficult time explaining.

Oblique Strain
in an NBA All-Star Guard

FMS Finding — a zero in the in-line lunge on the right leg

A zero score is given if the athlete cannot do the movement without pain, and is obviously a major red flag. In this case the athlete was unable to adequately flex the rear foot, his left, well enough to perform a right leg in-line lunge. When questioned about the problem, the athlete revealed a severe case of turf toe, a sprain of the big toe, he had not mentioned previously as he felt it unrelated to his abdominal issue.

The history of turf toe was significant as the athlete had also altered his gait pattern as a result of the painful toe. The alteration was to walk on the outside of the foot with the hip externally rotated.

The net result was a significant loss in hip mobility over a period of time. The lack of hip mobility placed greater stress on the core musculature and resulted in the oblique strain. Externally rotated hips take away hip mobility for spin moves. Spin moves that should have occurred at the hip were now placing excessive strain on the core, eventually resulting in an oblique strain. Without performing the screen, we may never have discovered the turf toe or the change in gait pattern. The screen led us right to the problem.

Chronic Hamstring Strains
in an NFL Wide Receiver

FMS Finding — a one score in rotary stability and a three in rotary mobility

This athlete was in a potential career-ending situation after sustaining hamstring strains each of the previous two seasons, resulting in significant lost game time.

The new FMS does not contain the older rotary mobility test, however I often do the test when I have an individual who complains of back pain. The combination of poor rotary stability and excessive rotary mobility is the perfect storm of back pain. Athletes who possess great mobility with no control are the most at risk.

In further conversation with this athlete, the plot thickened. Once in the NFL, the athlete stopped most strength training due to numerous back strains sustained in a conventional college strength program. An athlete like this should have never been spinal-loaded in training. However, discontinuing strength training was not the answer, and had put the athlete in a difficult situation.

Our solution was a unilateral strength program with minimal spinal loading to develop the glutes. Previous rehab attempts had centered on the hamstrings. However, the hamstring issues were a symptom of poor glutes, not the cause of the strains.

In the absence of glute strength, hamstrings, no matter how strong, will fail every time. Hamstrings are a secondary extensor. This was a classic case of the Shirley Sahrmann axiom *any time a muscle is injured, look for a weak synergist.* A program developed around single-leg squats, bridging and slideboard leg curls kept this athlete at the top of the NFL receiving lists once we discovered and fixed the problem.

FMS and the Strength Coach

Using the FMS in team settings is as simple as doing the screen and looking at the trends. Look for trends and design a team program that corrects your trends.

What you need to do is combine your favorite tools with the FMS findings. Look at your problem patterns. Work to improve your problem patterns in the warm-up or in the workout, or ideally in both. The results of the FMS in a team setting may not allow you to help each individual, but they will clearly help your team.

Gray Cook sums it up by saying:

"Some coaches shy away from the FMS because they feel they will lose some degree of autonomy, thinking they must submit to the FMS suggestions and corrections. They may also be aware the FMS will expose deficiencies in their programming and suggest changes in program design. We all hate to take a shot to our confidence, but our confidence rarely correlates to our level of effectiveness. The book *Blunder, Why Smart People Make Bad Decisions* by Zachary Shore demonstrates how we neglect to expose ourselves to objective feedback either consciously or unconsciously. This book is a must if you are responsible for programming, teaching and analyzing data. Protect your brain from your ego!

"The role of a strength coach is to manage risk, refine functional movement and enhance performance. The FMS will assist with the first two and influence the third indirectly. Movement pattern deficiency correlates with injury risk, and the screen offers a view of movement against an objective, reproducible baseline. A strength coach avoiding a tool like the FMS is like a speed coach avoiding a stopwatch. If a speed coach is not scared of a stopwatch, a good strength coach should not be scared of the FMS.

"Mike is a great example. The FMS did not change much in his program, but it reinforced his good ideas. Mike yielded good conditioning with respectable movement patterns. This, along with great coaches and sound programming, is probably the secret behind the low injury record Mike managed to stack up year after year.

"We can't be scared of objective tools that measure a variable we are ultimately responsible for controlling! You will learn either way. It will reinforce your program or offer the best possible improvement you could make."

Gray was kind enough to provide some closing recommendations.

- Don't push movement when mobility and stability are compromised.

- Don't continue programming that does not yield clean movement patterns.

- Don't risk injury when you can screen for it in less than ten minutes.

- Don't be scared of objective appraisal of your work.

- Don't let others find your mistakes; always check your work.

- Don't lump movement tests together with performance tests. You will miss the weakest link.

Bottom line: Not using the FMS is a major mistake. Get to a workshop and learn the screen. You will not be the same coach or personal trainer after the workshop, and I can promise that is a good thing.

Assessing Strength, Flexibility and Mobility

Flexibility is range of motion around a joint. Mobility is how well the joint moves. Range of motion can be limited by both inflexibility and by poor mobility.

This especially becomes an issue at the ankle. The easiest way to assess ankle mobility versus ankle flexibility is to look at the range of the athlete's active and passive dorsiflexion.

In order to fully understand how this works, we need to enter the world of assessment. Even if you don't use the movement screen, as a bare minimum assessment, an athlete should perform an overhead squat. If the athlete can overhead squat to a parallel position with the toes pointed forward, you can safely proceed to any squat variation. Athletes who cannot overhead squat to a position with the thighs parallel to the floor are deficient in either ankle, hip or hamstring flexibility.

Most athletes can overhead squat to the proper depth by raising the heels on a one-by-four board or a wedge. If elevating the heels solves the problem, you can safely assume the issue is in an ankle or both ankles.

• Elevating the heels will not harm the knees in any way. The idea that elevating the heels increases the stress on the knees is not supported by any scientific research.

• Athletes in the sports of powerlifting and Olympic lifting have been wearing shoes with a built-up heel for decades. Lifting shoes were specifically designed to slightly elevate the heel.

At this point there are two possibilities, ankle flexibility or ankle mobility. I mention both because we see more and more athletes whose problem is not flexibility but is instead mobility.

Determining the difference is easy. Place the athlete in a long sitting position on a table. Passively dorsiflex the athlete's ankle. If the ankle range of motion is limited but the athlete does not report a stretching in the gastroc, the issue is mobility, not flexibility. This athlete will respond to ankle self-mobilization, rather than stretching.

Ankle Self-Mobilization

Have the athlete stand with the toes a few inches away from the wall and dorsiflex the ankle so the heel stays in contact with the floor and the knee touches the wall.

Have him repeat this ten times on each side, gradually moving the toes further from the wall. Pay attention to symmetry; if one knee does not reach the wall from a distance the other reaches easily, continue working to bring that ankle up to par. Don't allow the athlete to work the more mobile ankle at a greater distance than the less mobile one.

Omi Iwasaki, director of physical therapy at Athletes' Performance Los Angeles, was nice enough to supply this technique. We use it as part of our daily mobility drills, described on page 45.

The Bodyweight Squat

Coaches should always begin lower-body strength training by teaching an athlete to perform bodyweight squats. Athletes must be able to bodyweight squat before being allowed to use any type of external load. This is the strength and conditioning equivalent of walking before we run. Watching an athlete squat bodyweight reveals important information about strength, flexibility and injury potential.

Athletes who have difficulty keeping the knees from moving past the toes are deficient in either flexibility or strength. An understanding of the importance of knee-dominant squatting versus ankle-dominant squatting is vital.

When most athletes hear the directive to squat, their minds tell their bodies to lower their hips the easiest way possible. For weaker athletes, the easiest way is often one that does not stress the weak muscles, usually the quadriceps. Weaker athletes or athletes returning from injury often attempt to lower the center of gravity by initially driving the knees forward over the toes until the limit of ankle range of motion is reached. Then and only then does the movement begin to center on the knee joint.

This type of ankle-dominant squatting leads to excessive knee flexion in order to reach a position where the thighs are parallel to the ground.

Rehab patients are often directed to squat to a ninety-degree knee angle. A knee angle of ninety degrees can be reached far before a parallel squat is achieved. Strength coaches do not define squat depth by knee angle, but rather by a parallel relationship of the *femur to the floor,* which often results in a knee angle greater than 135 degrees if the athlete is an ankle-dominant squatter.

This type of ankle-dominant squatting is frequently seen in athletes with knee pain.

Teach your athletes to bodyweight squat in a manner that minimizes range of motion at the ankle and maximizes range of motion at the knee. Once the athlete has mastered the technique of bodyweight squatting, the athlete can progress to the hands-free front squat.

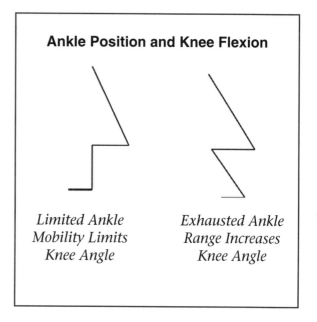

Ankle Position and Knee Flexion

Limited Ankle Mobility Limits Knee Angle   *Exhausted Ankle Range Increases Knee Angle*

Full front squats are always used in our program. The full squat is defined as one in which the top of the thigh is parallel to the floor. Half-squats or quarter-squats should never be used. No one does half- or quarter-curls to save the elbows; the knees should be no different. Partial squats cannot fully develop the glutes, hamstrings and lower back. In addition, half-squats and quarter-squats present a greater risk of back injury due to the heavier weights used in partial movements.

Athletes with normal flexibility can squat to a position with the thighs parallel to the floor with no heel elevation. Less flexible or less mobile athletes can use heel elevation as discussed earlier.

Increased strength in squatting movements is the first step in developing speed and increasing the vertical jump, and achieving a full range of motion bodyweight squat is the first step in the process for our athletes.

These are eight essential mobility drills to weave into your warm-ups. The nice thing about these exercises is anyone can do them. Everyone may not be able to do them well, but they can do them. And think about this: The people who can't do these well need them the most.

Number One
Thoracic Spine Mobility

The thoracic spine is one of the least understood areas of the body and was previously the realm of physical therapists. Sue Falsone, director of performance therapy at Athletes' Performance, may be single-handedly responsible for introducing the athletic world to the need for thoracic mobility, and for showing a simple way to develop it.

The important thing about t-spine mobility is almost no one has enough and it's hard to get too much. We encourage our athletes to do thoracic mobility work every day.

To perform our primary thoracic mobility drill, all you need is two tennis balls and some tape; just tape the two balls together and go to work doing a series of crunches beginning with the balls at the thoracolumbar junction. The ball peanut sits under the erectors and effectively provides an anterior-posterior mobilization of the vertebrae with every little mini-crunch.

The head should return to the floor after every crunch and the hands come forward at a forty-five-degree angle. We do five reps at each level and then slide down about a half-roll of the ball, working from the thoracolumbar junction up to the beginning of the cervical spine. Stay out of the cervical and lumbar areas; these are not areas that need mobility work.

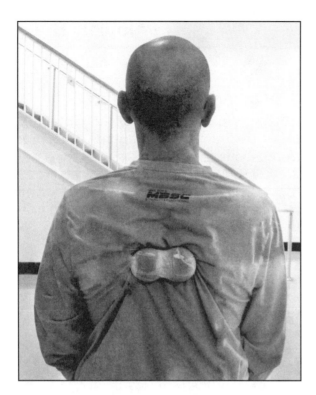

This drill is done first, just after we foam roll, which will be described on page 51, because the athlete is already on the floor. The rest of the mobility work is done standing.

Number Two
Ankle Mobility

Just as with thoracic mobility, it is rare to find a person who doesn't need ankle mobility work. Whether for an athlete who experienced a previous ankle sprain or a woman who wears heels every day, ankle mobility is step two in our warm-up. The first key to ankle work is to understand it is a mobility drill, not a flexibility or a stretching drill.

Have the client rock the ankle back and forth, not holding the stretch, using Omi Iwasaki's ankle self-mobilization drill discussed in the previous section.

The second key is to watch the heel. It is essential for the heel to stay in contact with the floor. Most people who have ankle mobility restrictions immediately lift the heel. I often hold the heel down for beginners so they get the feel of what I'm looking for in the movement.

The third key is to make it multi-planar. I like fifteen reps, doing five to the outside toward the small toe, five straight, and five driving the knee in past the big toe.

Self-mobilizing the ankle involves a gentle rocking motion. Teach the client how to send that rocking action into the joint. That's the simplest way to look at it is we're feeding motion into the joint.

Our mobility work, which we build into our warm-ups, starts at the ankle and works up. We do our sagittal-plane ankle-rocking drill against the wall, then we move to our leg swing drill at the wall to get frontal-plane ankle mobility.

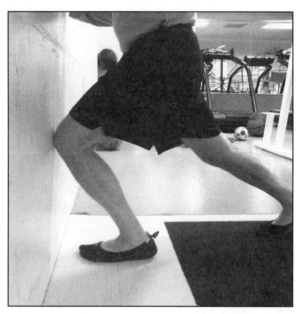

Number Three
Leg Swings

Leg swings are an interesting exercise. I used to think of leg swings as a hip mobility exercise and a dynamic adductor stretch. This is another day for the PTs to take a bow. Physical therapist Gary Gray describes leg swings as a great transverse plane mobility exercise for the ankle. Yes... the ankle. Watch an athlete with poor ankle mobility do leg swings and you will see the foot move into external rotation with each swing.

The key to leg swings is to keep the foot in contact with the floor and to drive rotary motion into the foot and ankle. The action of the leg swinging creates mobility at the ankle in the transverse plane.

Numbers Four, Five, Six
Split Squats, Lateral Squats and Rotational Squats

This is a precursor to what many call a lunge matrix. The lunge matrix is another Gary Gray concept, but one with a small flaw. Athletes must have proper mobility to perform a lunge matrix, and must gradually familiarize themselves with the movements to avoid extreme soreness.

To avoid soreness and develop mobility, we perform an in-place matrix for three weeks prior to moving to a lunge matrix. Another great thing about an in-place lunge matrix is an idea of strength coach Dan John. Dan is fond of saying, "If something is important, do it every day." We can do single-leg work every day, some for mobility development, some for strength, and the in-place lunges fit into this mold.

Split squats are an in-place precursor to a lunge, and develop sagittal plane mobility.

Lateral squats are an in-place precursor to a lateral lunge and develop frontal plane mobility. This is an area where many people are restricted. The key here is to watch the feet. In the lateral squat, the feet must remain straight forward. External rotation is a compensation.

Lateral squats are a bit counter-intuitive. A wider stance makes them easier, not harder, but most people will begin narrow. Try to get the client's feet three-and-a-half to four feet apart. I use the lines on the flooring, usually four-foot rolls, or the width of the wood on the platform as a gauge.

Rotational squats may be misnamed; these are not really rotational, but instead are the proper precursor to rotational lunges. Here again, watch the foot position. The feet are at right angles to each other as opposed to being parallel as in the lateral squat.

Most often we see a lunge matrix that is actually a series of forward lunges done in different directions. Many who think they are doing multi-planar lunges are actually doing panoramic lunges; they do the same lunge facing in several directions.

The rotational squat prepares the trainee for rotational lunges and continues to open up the frontal and transverse motion of the hips. Many may recognize lateral and rotational squats as groin stretches, and in fact, they are nothing more than a dynamic version of the popular groin stretches.

The big limiting factor in hip mobility is often flexibility in the muscles versus the motion of the joints. Hip capsular mobility is best left to trained therapists.

Number Seven
Wall Slides

I have to tell you, I love wall slides. Talk about bang for the buck, these…

- Activate the low trap, rhomboid and external rotators

- Stretch the pecs and internal rotators

- Decrease the contributions of the upper traps

The gleno-humeral joint needs to be mobile and the scapular-thoracic joint needs stability. To accomplish both, we use wall slides, another Sahrman exercise. In a wall slide, we get rid of elevation, pull everything down, and then need to be able to move the gleno-humeral joint in the

presence of a stable scapula. This is really the essence of shoulder health.

Use wall slides; you will be amazed. Many of your clients won't even be able to get into the position. This is not unusual. Another thing that may surprise you is an asymmetry of the shoulders. A third surprise might occur when they try to slide overhead. Many people will immediately shrug, indicating a dominance of the upper trap.

The keys to the wall slide:

• Scapulae are retracted and depressed.

• Hands and wrists are flat against the wall; the back of both hands must touch the wall.

• During the slide up, have the client press gently into the wall with the forearms.

Stop your client at the point of discomfort. The anterior shoulder will release and ROM will increase over time. Don't allow force.

Regression: Forward wall slide — Clients who can't get full external rotation should use the same exercise facing the wall.

Progression: Have your clients who master the back version do wall slides sitting Indian-style with their backs against the wall.

Start your older or deconditioned client with a forward wall slide, and finish the slide with retraction. The shoulders slide up the wall at a forty-five-degree angle, and then retract the shoulder girdle away from the wall, squeezing posteriorly.

The regular wall slide has the shoulder girdle working at about ninety degrees. When shifting to the forward position, this is decreased to between thirty and forty-five. As the client gets better, he'll almost be doing the wall slide with his nose against the wall, sliding the forearms directly up the wall. Somebody who's not quite as good will be at a forty-five-degree angle,

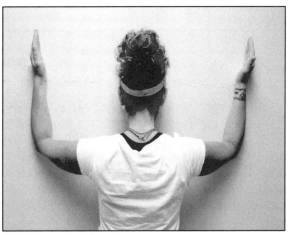

with the nose maybe six to eight inches off the wall.

If your client is completely unable to stabilize the scapulae during wall slides, the regression tool is a Velcro belt around the chest.

Number Eight
Big X Band

The Big X Band is an improvement of the original mini-band walk, wherein we added an upper-body component. The only problem was many people did not retract the scapulae; instead they shrugged, activating the wrong muscles. Physical therapist Alex McKechnie, who has become a sports hernia rehab expert, uses Theraband to create the fascial slinging effect of the body. I borrowed and simplified that by cutting a three-quarter-inch Superband to create a big X for a great total-body activation exercise.

Have your client step on the band, then grab the band by the hands, crossing over to create the X. The client then side-steps in the mini-band walk fashion.

The Big X-Band activates the glute medius, as well as the entire posterior chain. It does it in an anatomically correct manner by using the diagonal relationship of opposite hip to shoulder.

Give these drills a try in your program warm-ups. It will take your athletes five or ten minutes, and in a short time they'll feel better. When people feel better, they also perform better.

Soft Tissue Therapy

Soft tissue work goes by many names. Physical therapists use the term soft tissue mobilization. Chiropractors usually use the acronym ART for Active Release Technique. Massage therapists just call it deep tissue work. The magic is in the hands: It's all pressure applied to tissue to deform it and cause a chemical reaction.

Soft tissue therapy, whether for chronic muscle strains or for tendon issues, is like weight training. Treatment is actually a stimulus. In effect, what the therapist is doing is irritating the tissue to produce a chemical response. The chemicals produced are what begin the healing process. This is why soft tissue work is often painful and can ache the following day, similar to DOMS.

According to physical therapist Dr. Donnie Strack, soft tissue mobilization stimulates the formation of fibroblasts, which help take immature and randomly aligned Type 3 collagen seen in tendinosis, and changes it back to a stronger, more parallel mature Type 1 collagen.

In other words, massage changes the quality of the muscle fibers.

A major change in the attitude toward injury prevention and treatment has been evidenced by the awareness of hands-on techniques like massage, Muscle Activation Technique (MAT), and ART, which can work wonders on injured athletes.

We appear to be moving away from the injury care of isokinetics and electronics to a more European-inspired process that focuses on hands-on soft tissue care.

Massage fell out of favor during the physical therapy boom of the 1980s not because it was ineffective, but because it was not cost-effective. With the increase in use of modalities like ultrasound and electrical stimulation, athletic trainers and therapists could treat more athletes, more rapidly.

In Europe and in elite athlete situations such as high-level track and field and swimming, a disdain for a modality-based approach and an affinity for European-inspired massage held fast. Eventually, the performance world caught on to the idea that manipulation of the soft tissue helps athletes to either stay healthier or to get healthy faster.

The success of physical therapists with soft tissue mobilization and MAT manipulation, and the number of chiropractors using ART has clearly put the focus back on the muscle. MAT is a soft tissue technique developed by Greg Rospkof using manual muscle testing, isometric contractions and tissue work primarily to the origin and insertion of the muscle. It theoretically turns on the muscle by stimulating the areas of highest proprioception. I have had it done and it works.

The message at the elite level is to get better and healthier, get a good manual therapist in your corner.

One thing that's fundamentally different now from when the original *Functional Training for Sports* book was written is there was no emphasis on tissue quality... tissue work... rolling, stretching. I can't believe there was no reference to static flexibility and no reference to foam rolling just a few years ago. We had no concept of changing tissue density.

Foam Rolling

Foam rollers are the poor man's massage therapist, soft tissue work for the masses. As strength and conditioning coaches and personal trainers watched elite level athletes tout their success with various soft tissue techniques, the obvious question arose. How can we mass-produce soft tissue work for large groups of athletes at a reasonable cost?

A decade ago strength and conditioning coaches, athletic trainers and physical therapists would have looked quizzically at a thirty-six-inch-long round piece of foam. Today nearly every athletic training room and most strength and conditioning facilities contain an array of foam rollers in different lengths and densities.

Physical therapist Mike Clark is credited with the initial exposure of the athletic and physical therapy communities to the foam roller and to what he called self-myofascial release, another term for self-massage. In one of Clark's early manuals published as a pre-cursor to his book *Integrated Training for the New Millenium*, he included a few photos of self-myofascial release techniques using a foam roller.

The technique illustrated was nearly self-explanatory: Get a foam roller and use bodyweight to apply pressure to sore spots... kind of a self-accupresssure technique. These photos began a trend that is now probably a multi-million dollar business in the manufacture and sale of these foam tools.

A foam roller is a cylindrical piece of extruded hard-celled foam. Think pool noodles, only a little more dense and larger in diameter. These are available in a number of densities from relatively soft foam, slightly harder than a pool noodle, to newer high-density rollers with a much more solid feel. The feel of the roller and the intensity of the self-massage work must be properly geared to the age and fitness level of the client.

Clark's initial recommendation was not as a self-massage technique, but more of an accupressure concept. Athletes or patients are instructed to use the roller to apply pressure to sensitive areas in the muscles. Depending on the orientation of the therapist, these points are alternately described as trigger points, knots, or areas of increased muscle density. Regardless of the name, those in the fields of athletics and rehab are familiar with the concepts of sore muscles and the need for massage.

The use of foam rollers has progressed in many circles from an acupressure-type approach to self-massage. The roller is now used to apply sweeping strokes to the long muscle groups like the calves, adductors and quadriceps, and small, directed force to areas like the TFL, hip rotators and glute medius.

When you picture a muscle as a band with a knot in it, the foam roller is what unties the knots. This is what allows us to create tissue length, and what allows us to stretch.

Athletes should be instructed to use the roller to search for tender areas or trigger points, and to roll these areas to decrease density and over-activity. As a general rule of thumb, ten slow rolls are done in each position, although there are no hard and fast rules for foam rolling. Often athletes or clients are encouraged to simply roll until the pain disappears.

Gluteal Group and Hip Rotators

Here are the subtle hip areas that respond well to the foam roller and the techniques we use to address them.

The client sits on the roller at a slight tilt and moves from the iliac crest to the hip joint to hit the glute max. To address the hip rotators, the affected leg is crossed to place the hip rotator group on stretch.

TFL and Gluteus Medius

The tensor fascia latae and gluteus medius, although small muscles, are significant factors in anterior knee pain. To address the TFL, the athlete begins with the body prone and the edge of the roller placed under the TFL, just below the iliac crest.

After working the TFL, the athlete turns ninety degrees to a side position and works from the hip joint to the iliac crest to address the gluteus medius.

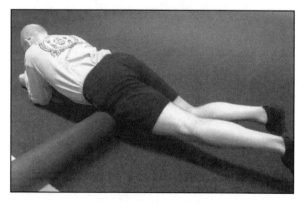

Adductors

From a tissue density standpoint, glutes and adductors are where you're going to get your big changes. Adductors are a somewhat forgotten bodypart. We're in a situation with adductors where people are thinking anterior chain, posterior chain, knee-dominant, hip-dominant, and the adductors don't really get much thought. A great deal of time and energy is mistakenly focused on the quadriceps and hamstring groups, and very little attention paid to the adductors. There's a huge area of opportunity for the roller to decrease density in that adductor triangle.

There are two methods to roll the adductors. The first is a floor-based technique that will work well for beginners. In the floor technique, the user abducts the leg over the roller and places the roller at about a sixty-degree angle to the leg.

The rolling action should be done in three portions beginning just above the knee in the area of the vastus medialis and pes anserine. Ten short rolls should be done covering about one third of the length of the femur. Next, the roller should be moved to the mid-point of the adductor group and again rolled ten times in the middle third of the muscle. Finally, the roller should be moved high into the groin almost to the pubic symphysis for another ten rolls.

The secondary technique for the adductors should be used after the athlete has acclimated to the previous technique. This method requires the use of a training room table or the top of a plyometric box. Sitting with the leg over the roller allows the athlete to shift significantly more weight onto the roller and to work deeper into the large adductor triangle.

Foot Rolling

Rolling the plantar fascia daily over a ball for a minute or two will provide relief to many of your clients who suffer from foot pain.

Regular use of a ball, beginning with a softer ball like a handball or tennis ball and working toward the size and density of a golf ball, contributes to a healthier state of the back fascial line, which begins at the foot.

We'll briefly discuss the fascial lines later, which I expect to be an area of attention in our field in the coming years.

When to Roll

Coaches and therapists are not in universal agreement over when to roll, how often to roll or how long, so only general guidelines can be provided.

Rolling offers great benefit both before and after a workout. Foam rolling prior to a workout can help to decrease muscle density and allow for better warm-up. Rolling after a workout may help aid in recovery from strenuous exercise.

It appears rolling can be done on a daily basis. In fact, Clair and Amber Davies, authors of *The Trigger Point Therapy Workbook*, actually recommend trigger point work up to twelve times a day in situations of acute pain.

How long an athlete or client rolls is also individual. In a personal training setting, we allow five or ten minutes for soft tissue work at the beginning of the session prior to the warm-up, and with our athletic team members in a group setting we do the same.

Rolling versus Massage

Static Stretching

Massage therapy is the best choice whenever possible because hands work better than foam. Hands are directly connected to the brain and can feel changes in tissue density. If cost was not an issue, we'd have a team of massage therapists on call for the athletes at all times.

However, this is not realistic. Most athletes struggle to afford the services of a qualified coach or the cost of a facility membership. Prevention is generally not a covered cost for healthy athletes; with no ability to get reimbursed, the cost of massage therapy alone could approach or surpass the cost of training. The foam roller can provide unlimited self-massage for under twenty dollars. You do the math.

Good massage work and good self-massage work may be uncomfortable, much like stretching. It is important athletes or clients learn to distinguish between a moderate level of discomfort related to a trigger point and a potentially injurious situation.

Foam rolling can be hard work, particularly for weaker or overweight clients because the arms are heavily involved in moving the body. In addition, it can border on painful and should be used with discretion in those clients with less muscle density. Foam rolling should never cause bruising. The athlete or client should feel better after a brief session with a foam roller.

The use of foam rollers and other rolling implements has exploded over the past ten years and will continue to increase. Foam rollers are a small investment to see a potentially significant decrease in the number of soft tissue, non-contact injuries, and offer a remarkable relief from low-grade body aches for your adult personal training clients.

In the field of strength and conditioning the pendulum always swings. A classic example is the use of and subsequent disdain for static stretching. Static stretching has gone from the best way to warm up to something no one should ever do.

Research in the '80s demonstrated static stretching prior to exercise could decrease power outputs. This led to a huge overreaction, the elimination of static stretching and the birth of the dynamic warm-up. This was both a plus and a minus. Dynamic flexibility work has been a huge benefit to the performance world as a warm-up technique.

The reality is static stretching was a poor way to warm up for exercise, and dynamic flexibility and active warm up is superior. However, the net effect was a total disdain for static stretching at any time, for any purpose. The truth lies somewhere in the middle.

An active warm-up prior to high intensity exercise is the best way to prevent acute injury. In other words, if you want to decrease hamstring and groin pulls, you need to perform dynamic flexibility exercises prior to practice, games or lifting sessions.

However, there is also truth on the other side of the coin. A lack of flexibility is a causative factor in many of the gradual onset injury conditions that plague today's athletes and aging adults. Overuse problems like patella-femoral syndrome, low back and shoulder pain relate strongly to long-term tissue changes that don't respond to dynamic stretching.

The fact is athletes need a combination of both active warm-up exercises and static stretching. For many coaches, the solution is active warm-up before exercise and static stretching after.

Although this seems reasonable, the process is somewhat flawed. Post-workout stretching does not seem to produce gains in flexibility. The key may lie in performing static stretching near the beginning of the workout, followed by a dynamic warm-up. Static stretching would be done to increase flexibility while the muscle is most prone to increase in length. Dynamic warm-up should follow to prepare the muscles for exercise.

Coaches need to think about length changes for long-term injury prevention, and dynamic warm-up for short-term injury prevention. Both are critical.

Tissue can change in two ways, length and density. We foam roll to decrease density, and we stretch to change length.

I have consulted the best physical therapist in the world and he firmly believes to change tissue length, we have to stretch when the muscles are cold. The theory is warm muscle elongates and then returns to its normal length. Cold muscle may actually undergo some plastic deformation and increase in length.

In Our Program

We foam roll for five minutes to decrease the density of the muscle. Muscles respond to injury and overuse by increasing in density. Think of foam rolling as ironing for the muscles, a necessary precursor to stretching.

Then we static stretch. Yes, static stretch, and yes, before the workout. Once the tissue density has been dealt with, we work on changing the length. Many top soft-tissue experts recommend muscles be stretched cold, without the benefit of a warm-up. Simply roll, and then stretch.

Next we use a dynamic warm-up. This is done after rolling and stretching. Any potential power decreases should be negated by the dynamic warm-up that follows a static stretch.

The process for our athletes every day is the same:.

- Foam roll to decrease knots and trigger points

- Static stretch to work on increasing flexibility

- Follow with a dynamic warm-up

Positioning is everything. Be specific about how you want someone to stretch. Most people don't stretch well; they just try to look like they're stretching.

Good stretching is uncomfortable, but not painful. Know the difference. A little discomfort means your athlete is well positioned.

- Activate the antagonist

- Do long statics

- Use active stretches

Use the athlete's bodyweight to assist. The athlete should be both comfortable and uncomfortable at the same time. Stretch all areas.

Carolina Hurricanes trainer and strength coach Peter Freisen has a theory: He thinks it is more dangerous to be overly flexible in one muscle group than to be tight in all of them. Eliminate or abbreviate the stretches your clients are good at and work harder on the ones they don't like.

Roll First, then Stretch

To consider the idea of stretching without rolling first, picture a band with a knot in it, and as you stretch, you're pulling on both ends of that band and the knot is getting tight. The roller unknots the knot before the stretching begins.

When we have injured athletes, invariably, every single time, without fail, we are told by the physical therapists there are muscle length issues. Almost all those muscle length issues also involve a density component.

If you take one thing from this book, it's this: Start rolling. Start stretching. If all of your athletes are not rolling and stretching, you're five steps behind.

If you don't have the Thomas Myers book, *Anatomy Trains*, get it. Myers is a Rolfer, an original student of Ida Rolf. In his book, he draws on the physical laws that govern the body and describes the concept of lengthened muscles being locked long and shortened muscles being locked short. In some ways this challenges the Janda-based NASM idea of simply stretching the short side and strengthening the weak or long side.

It also explains why this doesn't seem to work well in older clients. Older clients have undergone structural change in both the bones and the muscles that will not be reversed with a foam roller, some stretching and a few strength exercises. Muscles in a chronically stretched position — think scapulae retractors — become locked long. In effect they develop more collagen and less elastin in response to the constant tension.

On the flip side, the pecs in the front become locked short. This is really important if you're a personal trainer. It's foolish to think you can undo years of soft tissue change with stretching. It is also tough to counter eight to ten hours of sitting with one hour of standing. Don't stop trying; just realize what took years to do will take years to undo.

Bottom line, stretching is highly underrated. To keep athletes healthy long-term, add good old-fashioned stretching to the workout.

We do active-isolated stretches during the rest period between sets. In fact, all stretches done during the workout are active-isolated stretches, not static stretches. In active-isolated stretching, the stretch is held for one to two seconds, and there is a conscious effort to contract the antagonist muscle.

This type of stretching can be done during the workout without compromising the neurological efficiency of the muscle. Aaron Mattes is a leader in the area of active-isolated stretching; you can read more at stretchingusa.com.

Using active-isolated stretching has two significant benefits.

• The rest period is used for something other than conversation. This allows us to increase the total training effect of the sessions, as flexibility has now been addressed during the strength or power session. It also keeps the focus on training with fewer distractions that come with down time.

• Stretching the muscles in use correlates to a decrease in soreness from the workout. This is not a research-based concept, but empirically our athletes have drawn this conclusion on their own.

Injury Reduction

Pain during Rehab

Tendinitis or Tendinosis

Injury Prevention Suggestions

Upper-Body Injuries

Rotator Cuff Support

Anterior Knee Pain
> *Glute Medius and Adductors in Knee Pain*
> *Single-Leg Training and Knee Pain*

ACL Injury Prevention

Adductors Sports Hernia
> *Hip Flexion and Adduction*
> *Soft Tissue Therapy*
> *Sports Hernia Prevention*
> *Rehabilitation Concepts*

Every good strength and conditioning coach should be paranoid about injuries.

The key to injury prevention and rehab is a sound understanding of functional anatomy. We need to stop repeating the mistakes of the past and begin to realize we still have a lot to learn from an anatomical and biomechanical perspective. Memorize Shirley Sahrmann's statement, "When a muscle is strained, the first thing to do is look for a weak or underactive synergistic."

When we consider injuries, we know they happen for a reason governed by the laws of physics and controlled by functional anatomy.

If you only understand one thing about injuries, understand this: Injuries do not occur because of the muscle that's injured. That's very, very rare. Pulled hamstrings, pulled quads... anytime you see a muscle that hurts, you have to consider why. And that is going to lead you to look at the synergistic muscles and ask why this injured muscle has to do too much work. What's not doing its job to cause this other muscle to overwork?

I use the analogy to look for leaks in the roof, not in the wall. When you see a water stream running down the wall, your automatic assumption is the roof is leaking. You know you need to get outside and look on the roof.

Our model of the body is clearly not that way. Our current therapy is more like we see a water stain on the wall, and we paint over the stain. That's our sports training medical system in a nutshell: Cover over the problem.

We really have to look deeper to find the source of the problem as opposed to looking at the pain site.

The reality is athletes will get hurt from time to time. The key is to minimize exposure to potentially injurious situations and exercises. Strength is one of the best injury prevention tools in sport, but getting injured while training not to get injured is as stupid as it sounds.

Although some might argue I'm getting caught up in semantics, we should use the term *reduction* instead of prevention when talking about injury. No matter what we do as athletic trainers, sport coaches or as strength and conditioning coaches, we can't prevent injury, we can only reduce the incidence. Using the word prevention is giving ourselves too much credit.

Professional sport uses the avoidance of injury as the measuring stick of success in strength and conditioning. Pro teams don't test squats or deadlifts. I don't know one professional sports team that does one-rep-max strength testing.

One of my early influences was former NY Giants, NE Patriots and San Francisco 49ers strength and conditioning coach, Johnny Parker. I remember Johnny saying, "Who needs testing? We have sixteen tests a year!" The NFL uses a statistic called Starters' Games Missed. The NHL uses a similar stat called Man Games Lost to Injury. Success as a strength and conditioning coach at the professional level is measured by keeping the best players playing.

What people don't understand is all training is about assumption of risk. How much risk should I assume with this particular athlete or client? The way I train my college team is slightly different than the way I train my younger NHL guys, and it varies significantly from how I train my veterans. Many of my older clients no longer do conventional squats or Olympic lifts. Their bodies no longer tolerate it.

We do jump squats, kettlebell swings, and lots of single-leg stuff with these trainees because the objective is to keep them playing.

My college athletes do hang cleans, hang snatches, front squats and bench presses, a much more conventional approach. The key is finding the right tool for the job.

Every day we make decisions that affect both the short-term and long-term health of our athletes and clients. Take that job seriously, and read and study extensively.

There are a lot of hurt people reading this book who got that way the same way I did, by laying it on the line. There was a time I believed everyone should have a sore back for a week after a deadlift workout, and that everyone iced their shoulders and took Advil after every pressing workout. I now know that isn't true. I want my athletes to have all the benefits science and experience can provide.

Technical Failure

Charles Poliquin uses the term technical failure to define the point where a set ends when the athlete can no longer do another correct rep. I'm a big believer in the technical failure concept. The set ends at technical failure, not when you can't cheat through another rep. I'd always rather undertrain than overtrain. Tomorrow is another day. The healthy trainee returns to train another day, while the hurt guy goes to physical therapy.

I want my athletes to lay it on the line every set with perfect technique and stop when their technique fails. I also want them to go all out during our conditioning sessions. Plenty of people enjoy the weightroom, but are remarkably unfit. I'm a strength and conditioning coach, and I put a premium on conditioning as well as strength.

Painful Exercise

People who know my background often ask for training advice. Most of the time they ignore it because the advice does not contain the answer they want. They say, "It only hurts when I run," and I answer, "Don't run."

If you have an injured athlete and are wondering whether a certain exercise is appropriate, ask the basic question, "Does it hurt?" The key here is the question can only be answered yes or no. If the answer is yes, the client is not ready for that exercise, no matter how much you want to use it.

Any equivocation in the pain question is a yes. "After I warm up it goes away" is still a yes answer.

If your athlete is injured, use your common sense. Exercise should not cause pain. This seems basic, but athletes ignore pain all the time; they rationalize. Discomfort is common at the end of a set in a strength exercise or at the end of an intense cardiovascular workout. The additional discomfort of delayed onset muscle soreness (DOMS) often occurs the days following an intense session. This is normal. This discomfort should only last two days and should be limited to the muscles, not felt in the joints or tendons.

Pain at the onset of an exercise is neither normal nor healthy, and is indicative of a problem. Progression in any strength exercise should be based on a full, pain-free range of motion that produces muscle soreness without joint soreness. If you need to change or reduce range of motion, there's a problem that needs attention.

Progression in cardiovascular exercise should also be pain-free and should follow the ten-percent rule: Do not increase time or distance more than ten percent from one session to the next. I have used these rules in all of my strength and conditioning programs and have been able to keep literally thousands of athletes healthy.

Tendinitis or Tendinosis

Most people who think they have tendinitis actually have tendinosis. The difference is not just one of semantics; it's an issue of understanding. We can't have chronic tendinitis. If it's chronic, it's probably tendinosis.

In tendinosis the tendon undergoes a structural change in response to the chronic stress placed on it, and possibly from the poor initial injury treatment.

The condition is different, and the treatment is different. Ice and anti-inflammatories do little for tendinosis, as the condition is no longer an inflammatory one. My good friend Dr. Donnie Strack, makes a great point: Continued use of anti-inflammatories actually weakens a tendon and delays healing.

In reconditioning an athlete with a tendinosis condition, it may be necessary to endure some tendon pain to produce the proper remodeling effect. In fact, Dr. Strack points out it may not just be necessary, but according to some studies it's a must.

If there's no soreness in a tendon rehab program, research shows reps or external weight should increase. This is an isolated exception to the no-pain rule. The painful stress to the tendon acts much like soft tissue work to initiate a healing response.

Acceptable pain is localized to the target tissue, and the tissue is painful to touch. There should be no swelling and no motion restrictions. The pain should follow a DOMS-like pattern and be gone in two or three days.

Injury Prevention Suggestions

There are two basic categories of injuries we commonly see. Lower-body training tends to cause back trauma. Most back injuries are acute and are a result of a technical failure. Upper-body injuries are generally overuse in nature and related more to what the trainee may *not* be doing.

Here are my basic recommendations to make training both safe and effective.

Switch to Front Squats

Back pain has three root causes as it relates to lifting. Torque (forward lean), compression (high spinal loads), and flexion are what cause most back injuries. Front squats lessen torque, compression and flexion, and are therefore inherently safer than back squats.

Your clients can probably front squat badly, but it's a lot easier to back squat badly. In general, if a person front squats poorly, he'll dump the bar, sidestepping a back injury.

However, there are three major reasons people still do back squats instead of front squats.

- They always have — a bad reason, but people really hate change.

- They can lift more weight. Ego is always a big problem.

- They perceive front squats as difficult due to poor wrist flexibility.

Front squats decrease spinal load and improve back position — two positives in my book. My athletes and clients haven't done a back squat in years and we have very little back pain. We still front squat relatively heavy; our college players front squat between 300 and 350 pounds to a powerlifting depth, at bodyweights of 180-200 with no wraps.

Forget the Leg Press

If your clients can't squat, please don't put them on a leg press. I'd like all of my athletes and clients to front squat, but once an athlete has a history of back pain, we use alternatives.

One choice we *don't* use is the leg press; we never leg press. I haven't had a leg press in one of my facilities for over ten years. The leg press is good for only one thing: inflating the ego. There are far better ways to work the lower body if a client is unable to squat; they just don't allow him to use huge weights.

Avoid Knee Wraps

Knee wraps are not an injury-prevention tool. They're an elastic launching pad to allow more weight to be lifted. Knee wraps don't protect the knee. If you have a knee issue and like the feel of something on your knee, use Neoprene sleeves.

I'm a raw guy all the way. No belt, no wraps. For those who compete in powerlifting, it's a different story. Throw on the gear in the last few weeks to get ready, but don't train with it.

Try Belt Squats

This is an old Westside favorite and is a great way to work the lower body when injured. I generally prefer to work the lower body with single-leg exercises if an athlete can't squat, but we've had athletes in the past do nothing but belt squats for an entire season to rest sore backs and later had the same athletes squat PRs.

Belt squats are particularly good if the athlete is a low-bar, forward-lean squatter.

Use Single-Leg Squats

There are many variations of the single-leg squat, which are covered in detail later in the book. Most lifters don't like one-legged squats because they're hard, and they take coordination. However, if you want to minimize back stress and maximize leg work, make your clients get used to them.

We don't need a lot of weight to get a great leg workout because bodyweight immediately becomes a part of the load. Our athletes one-leg squat to a soft touch on a twelve- or fourteen-inch box and have used a hundred pounds of external load — a twenty-five-pound dumbbell in each hand and a fifty-pound weight vest.

The additional benefit of the one-leg squat is great stabilizer loads on the abs and adductors.

Dump Conventional Deadlifts

I know this will anger the powerlifters, but I'm a former powerlifter and I don't like deadlifts. Go to a powerlifting meet and watch the entire meet. You'll see great squat technique, but you won't see many flat-back deadlifts. It isn't easy to deadlift well. It's much easier to deadlift heavy than to deadlift well, and nothing is worse for a back than flexion under load.

I do, however, love single-leg versions of the modified straight-leg deadlift. With single-leg deadlifts, the hamstring gets all the load while the back gets half.

Now this is a general thought about deadlifting, and it's especially applicable in situations where you can't be on hand to supervise every rep. We'll discuss deadlifts in detail in the section on specific exercises.

Clean from the Hang Position

Hang cleans are safer than cleans from the floor. Cleans from the floor are easier for short people; hang cleans are the great equalizer because everyone starts from the same position. It's often difficult for taller athletes to get into a proper start position for a clean from the floor. This again puts the low back at risk as athletes attempt to position themselves for the clean.

Teach Dumbbell or Close-Grip Snatches

The snatch is actually a better and safer lift than the clean. Cleans can be limited by flexibility, and the catch position of the clean can be difficult to master.

One reason many coaches don't like the snatch is they've never tried it.

- Don't teach snatches with a snatch grip.

When I realized snatches would be a great lift for our athletes, I began to implement them into our programs. Within a week athletes complained of shoulder pain. In two weeks so many complained, I took snatches back out of the program.

It was not until I revisited the snatch with a clean grip that I truly began to see the benefits. The only reason Olympic lifters use a snatch grip is to reduce the distance the bar travels, and as a result lift more weight. Close-grip snatches markedly decrease the external rotation component and also increase the distance traveled. The result is a better lift, only using less weight.

The best way to learn to snatch is to snatch a dumbbell first. The dumbbell snatch is the first explosive lift we teach and if using only one Olympic-type lift, we choose the dumbbell snatch. Dumbbell snatches work on core strength and unilateral shoulder strength, as well as hip and leg power.

Upper-Body Injuries

Upper-body injuries relate more to the exercises we're not using than to the ones we are. Lack of pulling strength is probably the reason so many lifters have rotator cuff problems. Most people are out of balance and have rotator cuff issues because of it.

This boils down to two things: not enough rowing — horizontal pulling — and not enough vertical pulling, the chin variations.

Our athletes have zero incidence of rotator cuff tendinosis, and most can also do a one-rep-max chin-up with more than they can bench press.

The pull-to-push ratio should be a minimum of one to one. In other words, a 180-pound athlete who can bench 280 should be able to perform a supinated-grip chin-up with a hundred pounds.

The chin-up weight is calculated by adding external load on the dip belt to bodyweight. Coach a supinated grip to spare the shoulders, and start from the bottom. Those who can do this rarely have shoulder issues.

Treat your vertical pulls just like the bench. Cycle them. Do heavy triples. Whatever you do for horizontal presses, do the same for vertical pulls.

I don't have a ratio for rows, but an athlete with proper pulling strength should be able to dumbbell row about eighty percent of what he can dumbbell bench. In other words, an athlete performing dumbbell bench presses with one-hundred-pound dumbbells for five reps should be able to dumbbell row with eighty-pound dumbbells for five.

In addition, all athletes should eventually be able to perform ten to fifteen inverted rows with the bar at bench press height and the feet elevated eighteen inches. In the inverted row, the athlete should be able to touch his chest to the bar without cheating.

I've never seen an NFL lineman who couldn't do one chin-up, but have seen many who couldn't do one quality inverted row. Many strong bench pressers will not be able to do a single one initially, and will immediately cop-out with stuff like, "I'm not flexible enough to do that."

You need to remind your athletes if they can lower a bar to the chest, they should be able to pull the chest to the bar. I've seen many 400-pound bench pressers who couldn't do five good bodyweight reps. What these athletes lack is true scapulae retraction strength, and you can help your athletes regain it by horizontal pulling.

Rotator Cuff Support

Physical therapist John Pallof, currently practicing at our facility, has taught us excellent rotator cuff exercises using the Keiser functional trainer to develop posterior cuff strength and scapulae stability. Many of these are the same exercises that can be done with tubing or potentially with dumbbells. However, the sequences are best done on a smooth machine that allows for small increases in resistance. Remember, the rotator cuff is made up of small, often weak muscles, and smaller increases are required.

I prefer the Keiser equipment to tubing due to the issue of length and tension. Tubing resistance increases as the tubing is stretched. In other words, as the tubing is lengthened, the resistance is increasing. This means we get maximum resistance at end range. This can be a benefit or a drawback depending on what we are training.

Dumbbells often present the reverse problem. As the client moves through the range of motion with dumbbells, the load stays constant. As the leverage advantage increases, dumbbells get too easy. The Keiser machine provides even, smooth resistance in one-pound increments throughout the range of motion, and this is critical in rotator cuff training.

Good descriptions of the rotator cuff muscles use the term dynamic ligaments when describing the rotator cuff. Due to the flimsy nature of the anterior capsule, the rotator cuff is the strongest support structure for the shoulder, in essence a series of dynamic ligaments. The key with the cuff, as with all muscles, is to do both strength training and specific speed training.

John's exercises are standard cuff exercises done at 90/90, but with great attention to detail, such as allowing no shrug. Some are for scapular stability, some for strength.

In addition we do lots of overhead throws for what I consider specific deceleration work. Multiple functions require multiple training environments.

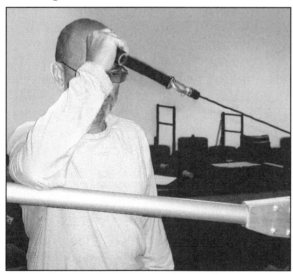

The YTWL shoulder series you probably already do is our phase one program. These exercises are done in a non-functional manner to teach clients how to use the middle and lower trap in place of the upper

trap, and to help strengthen the often weak lower trapezius and rhomboids.

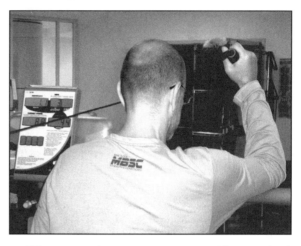

The second series was inspired by Michol Dalcourt, a writer, trainer and coach: Move the YTWL exercises to standing. We first go to a half-kneeling position, then move to standing YTWLs.

The third series are the 90/90 exercises John Pallof recommended for our overhead athletes. The first 90/90 is simply a horizontal adduction done supine. The emphasis is maintaining scapula stability and horizontally adducting the humerus. The second two are 90/90 external rotation. The next series is the reverse of the first, a resisted scapula adduction and retraction.

Anterior Knee Pain

Anterior knee pain goes by a number of names, but unfortunately has few effective treatments. Names like chondromalacia patella, patella tendinosis and patella-femoral syndrome are all used to describe various types of often-debilitating anterior knee pain. Treatment is often focused on the knee joint, the primary pain site, and that's a large part of the problem in treating knee pain.

In reality, the knee may be the repository of pain that emanates from issues at the hip or the foot. A knee-centered approach to treatment of knee pain becomes a symptom-based approach versus a cause-based approach; treatment often focuses on eliminating a key symptom versus trying to address the cause.

Current research is leading to the conclusion many of the overuse conditions of the knee are not conditions of the knee at all. All of the conditions mentioned in the opening paragraph may be related to poor stability at the hip, but present as knee pain. The analogy frequently used to describe why this occurs is the rope analogy. If I put a noose loosely around your neck, stood in front of you and pulled on it, you would tell me the back of your neck hurt. If I stopped pulling on the rope, your neck pain would disappear. Nothing was ever really wrong with your neck — the neck was simply the endpoint at which you felt the pull.

This is similar to the effect of the glutes pulling on the IT band, resulting in pain at the knee. The IT band transmits forces from the glutes to the patella tendon. Pain is felt in the patella tendon much like the back of the neck feels the pull from the rope.

Another potential cause of anterior knee pain may be a loss of ankle mobility. The zeal of athletic trainers to stabilize the ankle with shoes, tape and braces has led to athletes playing with ankle joints that function as if fused.

In the sport of basketball, a leading sport for anterior knee pain, serious ankle sprains are less frequent, yet patella-femoral pain has reached near epidemic levels. The desire to over-stabilize the ankle joint has led to a phenomenon we now call the high ankle sprain, and to a spate of patella tendon issues. The high ankle sprain was virtually unknown twenty years ago, and may be a by-product of over-stabilizing ankles.

Interestingly, soccer has few ankle or patella-femoral problems, yet soccer players use a low-cut, lightweight shoe on grass. Training with less artificial stability at the ankle joint probably protects the ankle and the knee.

Over the past decade, anterior knee pain has been blamed on poor VMO development, poor patella tracking and numerous other causes. Most treatments have centered on trying to reduce the pain at the pain site with various treatments like ice, taping and ultrasound.

Instead, an aggressive strengthening program aimed from the hip down, particularly the eccentric control of knee flexion, adduction and internal rotation may be more effective.

According to a 2003 study done by researchers Ireland, Willson, Ballantyne and Davis and published in the *Journal of Orthopaedic and Sports Physical Therapy,* "Females presenting with patella-femoral pain demonstrate significant hip abduction and external rotation weakness when compared to non-symptomatic age-matched controls."

Our lower extremity strengthening done with emphasis on hip control, in combination with a program of progressive single-leg plyometric training to address the eccentric and neural stability components may allow many trainees to experience long-term relief.

Glute Medius and Adductors in Knee Pain

Recent research has validated what up until now was an empirical feeling. All athletes training in our facility are evaluated for hip pain via palpation of the glute medius if they complain of anterior knee pain. We found nearly a one-hundred-percent correlation between knee pain and glute medius tenderness. All of our athletes with anterior knee pain had direct point tenderness in the glute medius on the affected side.

Soft tissue work on the glute medius caused a significant reduction in the pain at the patella in almost every case. Most also had marked weakness in manual muscle testing for the glute med. The conclusion is obvious: Weak hip stabilizers cause a lack of control of knee and hip flexion with an additional component of adduction and internal rotation. These control issues result in a painful sensation in the patella-femoral joint or the patella tendon.

Further study caused us to look at the adductors, another hip stabilizer in the lateral subsystem. In addition to looking at lateral hip structures as a potential causative factor in knee pain, we also began to look at the strength and over-activity of the adductors. We found weakness in the adductor muscle group, with a preference to substitute hip flexors, as well as obvious tender trigger points in the adductors.

Single-Leg Training and Knee Pain

The key from both a cause and a solution standpoint lies in the modern sagittal-plane dominant, double-leg-oriented strength training so prevalent in the American training system. It's clear the key to solving anterior knee pain lies in control of hip, knee and foot movement in the frontal plane, and single-leg exercises must be employed in both strength training and power training to address these issues.

The single-leg strength training must center around single-leg *unsupported* exercises like one-leg squats and one-leg deadlift variations. Knee-dominant single-leg exercises like split squats and rear-foot-elevated split squats may provide adequate stress in the sagittal plane, but do not provide enough work for the hip structures in the frontal or transverse planes.

The athlete must be standing on one foot with the opposite foot having no contact with either the floor or any other object, in other words a true unsupported one-leg squat. In essence, the act of standing on one foot and performing a single-leg squat becomes a tri-planar exercise even though the athlete is moving in only the sagittal plane.

Having only one foot in contact with the ground forces the hip structures, the abductors and external rotators, to stabilize against movement in both the frontal and transverse planes.

In these single-leg unsupported exercises we will allow less than full range of motion to develop hip control. This is a major exception in our system of training, as we otherwise always use full ROM exercises. This is true progressive range of motion exercise.

The objective is always to get to a full pain-free range with bodyweight before the addition of any external resistance. The exception will be the addition of five-pound dumbbells to allow weight shift toward the heel. The progression is in range versus load to cause the progressive control of hip motion.

The following treatment program is suggested for patella-femoral pain syndromes.

Step One

Soft tissue work on the glute medius with a tennis ball and foam roller, or by a qualified therapist or trainer if available is our first step.

Step Two

Use reactive neuromuscular training (RNT) for the hip abductors in conjunction with a strengthening program for the knee and hip extensors, focusing on single-leg unsupported exercises and progressive range of motion if necessary.

The term reactive neuromuscular training can be confusing as the same term has been used by two well-respected physical therapists to describe entirely different ideas. Mike Clark of the National Academy of Sports Medicine uses the term reactive neuromuscular training in place of the word plyometrics.

Physical therapist Gray Cook, on the other hand, uses the term reactive neuromuscular training to apply to an entirely different concept: Cook's idea of RNT involves applying a stress to a joint in opposition to the action of the muscles.

To effectively target the hip abductors, a band is placed around the knee and the leg is pulled with an adduction force. The addition of the adduction force will in effect turn on the abductors.

In a therapy or personal training situation, the adduction force can be provided by the therapist or trainer with Theraband. In a group situation, the adduction force can be provided by a piece of Theratube or a mini-band.

The glute medius fires to counter the adduction force of the tubing; this idea comes courtesy of Shad Forsythe, performance specialist at Athletes' Performance, Los Angeles, and will be covered further on page 225.

Step Three

In step three, we strengthen the hip extensors, to include three distinctly different patterns.

Pattern one is a straight-leg pattern as in the one-leg straight-leg deadlift, actually a misnomer as the knee is intentionally bent to twenty degrees.

Pattern two is a bent-leg pattern that incorporates the mechanics learned in the bridging exercises covered in the core training section later in the book.

Pattern three is a leg-curl move incorporating the hip-extensor function of the glutes.

Pattern One

- Reaching single-leg SLDL

- Single-leg SLDL

- Low-pulley or horizontal pulley anterior reach (twenty-degree knee flexion, flat back)

Pattern Two

- Single-leg bridge variations

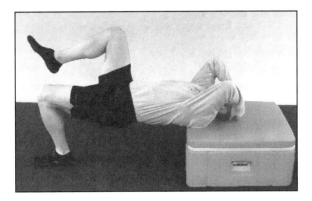

Beginning floor-based and work to a hip lift or hip raise from a bench or a twelve-inch plyo box. These are the best glute exercises no one ever does and the subject of a great body of work from Coach Bret Contreras.

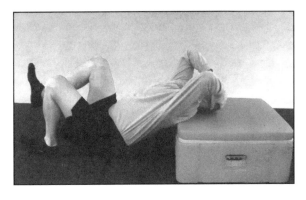

These exercises target the glutes and the hip rotator group with the addition of instability.

Pattern Three

- Slideboard leg curl variations

The key with the slideboard leg curl is the glutes function isometrically to maintain hip extension, while the hamstrings act to flex and extend the knees. Any flexion of the hip negates the effectiveness of this class of exercises. Even one degree of motion at the hip negates the glute function.

The best teaching progression is to begin in a bridge with the glutes and abs contracted, and eccentrically lower into an extended position.

Step Four

- Concentric training of hip abductors

Although many would argue isolated single-joint training is not functional, it is still necessary to train the concentric action of the hip abductors. This can be done with side leg lifts or with standing abduction on a Pilates reformer or Shuttle MVP.

Additional Points

Core

Core training should always be included in any sound program, but with patella-femoral pain, both quadruped and bridge variations should be used for emphasis on glute max and glute med function.

Conditioning and Muscle Endurance

Retro walking is another excellent exercise for the client with patella-femoral pain. Backward walking provides less stress to the knee joint and is actually just a series of closed-chain terminal knee extensions. Backward walking can begin with a treadmill program of intervals at progressively higher inclines and progress to walking backward with a weighted sled.

Eccentric Strength

Eccentric strength work should focus on single-leg plyometrics with emphasis on landing skills; jumps should be forward, with hops done forward, medially and laterally. The Shuttle MVP can be used to develop landing skills for athletes returning from injury or athletes with poor strength-to-bodyweight ratios.

The key to battling patella-femoral pain is to adopt a well-rounded approach that works on the source of the pain versus the site of the pain, and takes into account all of the functions of the lower extremity.

ACL Injury Prevention

The key to understanding functional anatomy is to realize everything changes when you stand on one leg. From an anatomical standpoint, this is undeniable, and for knee injury prevention, it's a vital consideration.

ACL injury prevention programs often consist more of packaging than new concepts. Calling a program an ACL prevention program may be nothing more than a way into the head of the athletic trainer, physical therapist or coach.

ACL injury prevention is just good training; the program we use for ACL injury reduction is actually the same program we use with everyone. As coaches we have to realize we should be practicing great injury prevention concepts with all our athletes and weekend warriors.

Because female athletes are much more likely to experience ACL injuries, those who coach women tend to be more interested in the protocol. Estimates run to over 100,000 ACL tears per year, about a third of these being high school female athletes. ACL injury prevention may be the thought that gets the women's basketball coach to buy into your strength program.

When training the female athlete, we need to stop lamenting the plight of women and start doing something about it. Complaining about the number of injuries that occur in women will do nothing to change the situation.

Neither will studying things like menstrual cycles. We cannot change gender, however we can change lower-body strength and stability. Certain contributing factors — Q angle, intercondylar notch, menstrual status — are all in the "things we cannot change" category.

One area of study is the effect of menstrual cycle on probability of ACL tear. My question is what do we do when we know? Will we see parents holding their daughters out of the big game because it is a risky time period? Not likely.

ACL Injury Reduction Strategies

ACL reduction is simple, but systematic. We need to work on all of the items listed below. This is not a menu to pick from; it's more like a recipe. Don't leave out a key ingredient.

- Active warm-up

- Power and stability — eccentric strength equals landing skills

- Strength development —emphasis on one leg

- Change of direction concepts — learning how to stop

- Change of direction conditioning — developing conditioning

Strategy One
Active Warm-Up

A good warm-up is the first step in an ACL prevention program. Guess what? A good warm-up is the first step in any program. A proper warm-up develops single-leg strength, dynamic flexibility and increases proprioception. And the best active warm-up exercises activate one muscle while elongating another.

- High-knee walk

- Leg cradle

- Walking heel to butt

- Back lunge

Strategy Two
Develop Stability
and Eccentric Strength

If active warm-up is the first step, the development of stability and eccentric strength is the most important step. In many of the popular ACL prevention programs, this is the major failing. Most programs concentrate too much on jumping and not enough on hopping.

Understand this: *A jump and a hop are not the same.* Everything changes when we stand on one leg, and everything changes when we *land* on one leg. The key to injury reduction is developing the ability to land on one leg. Eccentric strength is the ability to land properly.

Understand the terminology:

- Jump: two legs to two legs — This is the basis for many programs, but is not the mechanism for ACL injury prevention.

- Hop: right leg to right leg or vice versa — Hops are neglected in most programs, but are actually the key to ACL prevention. Hopping must be done forward, medially and laterally.

- Bound: right leg to left leg

- Skip: two foot contacts per foot

Progressing Plyometrics

Plyometric phases should last a minimum of three weeks, and jumps and hops can be done twice per week. In our system we do our plyometric exercises every training day, but we don't repeat the same exercise twice in one week.

Phase one

Jump or hop up to a box: This decreases the effect of gravity and lowers eccentric forces. Jumps are done forward. Hops should be done forward, medially and laterally.

Phase Two

Jump or hop over an object: In phase one we decrease the effect of gravity and the subsequent eccentric force. In phase two we reintroduce the acceleration due to gravity by jumping or hopping over an object. The same idea applies as above, but instead of jumping or hopping onto a box, the jumps and hops are done over a hurdle. Hurdles of varying sizes from six inches to thirty inches can be used.

If the quality decreases with the addition of gravity, strength is an issue. Do not proceed to the next phase. In fact, return to the previous phase.

Strength and conditioning legend Al Vermeil makes the statement, "The bigger or weaker the athlete, the smaller the obstacle."

Phase Three

Introduction of elasticity: In phase three, the same exercises are used as in phase two. The difference is in phase three a bounce is added.

Phase Four

True plyos: This is the reactive work we commonly recognize as plyometrics.

Strategy Three
Strength Development

Strength development is the second big key. In ACL prevention the strength program must be geared toward a functional single-leg approach.

Keys

• Handle bodyweight — single-leg progressions

• Develop functional strength — no machines

• Develop single-leg strength — difference in hip mechanics

• Perform both knee-dominant and hip-dominant single-leg exercise

Ideally all athletes should progress to a true single-leg squat and a loaded one-leg straight-leg deadlift.

Strategy Four
Change of Direction Concepts

The idea of teaching change of direction is a foreign one to most coaches. We like to distinguish between teaching movement versus timing movement. In many agility programs, athletes run from cone to cone. In our change of direction program, the consideration of effective movement is taught.

Simple drills are used to teach athletes to stop and to crossover. Many of the concepts build on ideas and landing skills taught in the plyometric exercises.

Strategy Five
Change of Direction Conditioning

The notion of change of direction conditioning is not new. However, the heavy influence of track coaches and technology have had a negative effect over the past couple of decades. Many conditioning programs shifted to a track-style interval program based around linear distances like 110-, 220- and 440-yard runs. Even worse, many athletes began to condition on cardiovascular equipment like the stationary bike, elliptical trainer or stairclimber.

What is often missing in modern conditioning programs is the planned incorporation of stops and starts. Injuries occur in acceleration and deceleration. We need to incorporate stopping and starting into the conditioning program to minimize injuries on the field of play. On the days we don't do change of direction running, we incorporate the slideboard for lateral conditioning.

As a strength and conditioning coach, understand and appreciate your athletic trainer. Develop a cooperative relationship, not an adversarial one. If you are an athletic trainer or physical therapist, cultivate your strength coach, make him part of the team.

A good cooperative relationship makes the job easier. Strength coaches need to become a part of the rehab team and athletic trainers need to realize a quality strength and conditioning program will decrease workloads in the training room.

The bottom line is a good strength and conditioning program is also the best ACL prevention program.

No ingredient is non-essential; all of them must be included.

Understanding Sports Hernia

One area of increasing interest to many in the fields of performance enhancement and physical therapy is the sports hernia. In order to understand the concept of sports hernia, the first thing we need to do is describe it. In the technical sense, the sports hernia is a tear in the lower abdominal wall in the inguinal area. Unlike a classic inguinal hernia, there is rarely a significant tear that results in a bulge. Instead, there is a gradual onset of pain in the lower abdominal area, usually beginning as groin pain.

A number of different conditions fall under the umbrella of sports hernia. However, the most interesting thing about the sports hernia is it almost always begins as groin pain, not as abdominal pain. Most sports hernia sufferers will describe a groin injury that gradually progressed into a painful lower abdomen. This often-overlooked fact may be the real key to solving or understanding the problem.

Sports hernias are not traumatic. There is no singular incident, but rather a gradual progression. What begins as groin pain progresses into abdominal pain; the sports hernia may be a secondary injury. Sports hernias may be the reaction of the abdominal muscles to a groin injury, or more specifically, the reaction of the abdominal muscles to a change in the mechanics of the hip joint.

To backtrack a bit, let's first examine the word groin and the idea of a groin pull. The groin area as commonly described in sports and sports medicine includes the muscles that flex the hip, the muscles that adduct the hip and, surprisingly, some of the hip extensors. Groin is really a garbage term, a catch-all used to describe all of the adductors and flexors of the hip.

This is where things begin to get interesting. The adductor group is comprised of five muscles: adductor magnus, gracilis, pectineus, adductor longus and adductor brevis. Because we are taught origin-insertion anatomy, we visualize these muscles in their singular, uni-planar role as adductors. We tend to adopt a simplified view of adduction as a motion done purely in the frontal plane. However, like all things, nothing is as simple as it appears.

I have worked with athletes with sports hernias in both high-level soccer (MLS) and high-level ice hockey (NCAA and NHL). In the summer of 2006, I participated in and coordinated the successful rehabilitation of two athletes who had sports hernia surgeries. One was an NHL player, the other was an NCAA Division 1 hockey player.

I enlisted the assistance of an outstanding manual therapist, Dr. Donnie Strack, DPT. Donnie evaluated both players and found each had significant soft tissue restrictions in the pectineus. They had both at some point experienced a groin pull or adductor strain that was treated conventionally with ice and rest.

Both players were allowed to return to play after the symptoms subsided, but neither player received appropriate soft tissue work to this critical area.

Dr. Strack's mentor, physical therapist Dr. Dan Dyrek, uses the term benign neglect to describe such treatment of injuries. The assumption is an absence or decrease in symptoms is the same as healing, which of course is not always true.

All of our adductor muscles have a secondary, multi-planar role. Two of the adductors are also weak hip flexors. The pectineus and the adductor brevis act to assist in hip flexion. In other words, they flex and adduct.

Hip Flexion and Adduction

Sports hernias are near epidemic in two sports, hockey and soccer. What do hockey and soccer have in common? One very critical point. The recovery of the skating stride in hockey is a combination of hip flexion and adduction. What muscles do we envision being overworked and injured? Obviously those that both flex and adduct. Striking a soccer ball? You guessed it, the flexion and adduction combination.

What do these adductors and flexors also have in common? They insert just below the abdominals right in the area of the sports hernia.

The remaining three adductors are extensors *and* adductors. Adductor magnus, adductor longus and gracilis aid in adduction, but by virtue of their position of insertion on the pelvis, also aid in extension of the hip.

Two muscles get overworked, the pectineus and adductor brevis, and a strain occurs. Rehab is often inadequate. The location of the strain makes soft tissue work difficult. In fact, many athletic trainers, particularly if gender lines are involved, are reluctant to perform soft tissue work in the high adductors. Soft tissue work can also be neglected due to time or skill constraints.

If rehabilitative exercise is performed, the focus is on frontal plane adduction, which does not directly address the unique function of the injured muscles. In frontal plane adduction, the long adductors can substitute and mask the issue with the flexor and adductors.

Wraps and elastic devices are often used to mask symptoms or to decrease pain. The result of this process of benign neglect is an eventual tear of the abdominal wall secondary to a groin strain in the pectineus or adductor brevis.

Soft Tissue Therapy

Here's where the athletic trainer and physical therapist crowd gets mad at me. Currently, the only therapists I use for my athletes or clients are manual therapists. I am lucky enough to have a long time relationship with Dr. Dan Dyrek. Dan is a genius and a master of soft tissue. His entire business revolves around soft tissue mobilization.

If you are an athletic trainer or a physical therapist, develop your soft tissue evaluation and treatment skills. Most athletic trainers and physical therapists don't do massage in this country because it's too hard and it's not cost effective. This has to change to stem the tide of sports hernias.

If you have an athlete with a lower abdominal issue, find a good manual therapist. This is not easy; they are few and far between. Surgery may help, but it will not be the entire answer. Resolution of scar tissue is the final piece of the puzzle. You need to get to the original source of the injury and deal with it. This can only be done by a soft tissue professional.

Many in the medical world will disagree with my thoughts. I have discussed the sports hernia phenomenon with numerous well-respected colleagues and have gleaned a few theories. One of my conversations with Gray Cook yielded this gem: Cook theorizes most athletes would do as well without surgery as with surgery if they would actually take time to rehab. The surgery is almost a method of forced rest to allow healing.

Stretching

Another thought comes from Pete Freisen, athletic trainer for the Carolina Hurricanes of the NHL. Pete thinks a large predisposing factor in ice hockey athletes is many players stretch the adductors, but not the hip flexors. The adductors are easy to self-stretch, while the hip flexors require either great concentration or the assistance of a partner. The result is often athletes who have great frontal plane mobility at the hip with limitations in the sagittal plane, basically one large degree of freedom and one limited one.

Consider the forces on the hip capsule and lower abdominal wall when there's excessive abduction with a big block in extension. If you think of this mechanically, it makes sense. The discrepancy of hip ROM probably sets these athletes up for an abdominal tear and potentially for labral damage.

Freisen said he would rather have tight or loose athletes than athletes who are tight in one plane and loose in another. Cook would define this as an asymmetry. In Cook's Functional Movement Screen research, asymmetry was a greater predictor of injury than a symmetrical restriction. Asymmetrical range of motion at the hip may be another precursor to sports hernia.

Hip Internal Rotation

An additional area of concern in sports hernia is hip internal rotation. Most of the athletes who experience a sports hernia lack hip internal rotation, a transverse plane deficit. Just as we misunderstood the role of the adductors, our athletes may be over-lengthening the wrong muscles, the adductors in the frontal plane, and leaving other muscles, the hip flexors and hip external rotators, critically short. The result is a hip that lacks extension and internal rotation, but has great ROM in conventional frontal plane adduction. This forces the pelvis to move in compensation, and stress to be shifted to the lower abdominal wall.

The potential result is a sports hernia.

Sports Hernia Prevention

Prevention of any injury begins with appropriate screening techniques. As already discussed, for screening athletes we use Gray Cook's seven-part Functional Movement Screen to predict risk of injury. It should be done in its entirety on every athlete at least once. Of particular interest in the sports hernia area is the FMS hurdle step, a test of the hip flexion pattern.

An impaired hip flexion pattern usually demonstrates a lateral shift of the pelvis when attempting to flex the hip. In the impaired hip flexion pattern, usually the deep flexors, psoas and iliacus, are weak or inhibited. This forces the athlete to use the quadratus lumborum to hip hike to create the illusion of hip flexion. In essence, lateral flexion of the pelvis from the spine raises the hip.

Cook advocates not focusing on individual muscles, but rather on fixing the pattern. To fix the pattern, we have adopted a top-down approach to recruit the deep hip flexors. For more on this, see the hip flexion section, page 113.

In addition to improving the hip flexion pattern, prevention of sports hernias must also center on developing proper hip range of motion and core stability. Hip motion and core stability are linked. Impaired hip motion leads to excessive pelvic motion, and excessive pelvic motion may be why a groin pull progresses into a sports hernia.

From a flexibility standpoint, the hip must be stretched into extension and internal rotation, as well as into abduction. In many cases abduction stretching should be limited while the rest of the hip in effect catches up.

After static stretching, a program of multi-planar active mobility and strength must be established. Strength emphasis should be on unilateral strength. Unsupported single-leg squats, one-leg straight-leg deadlifts, lateral squats progressing to lateral lunges, and rotational squats progressing to rotational or transverse plane lunges should form the core of the lower-body program.

Plyometric training should address multi-directional hops and bounds, and lateral conditioning on a slideboard should be performed at least twice a week. The slideboard is unique in that it supplies eccentric stress to the adductors and concentric stress to the abductors.

Sequence

Organization is key. For overall injury prevention, we always follow a sequence of

- Foam roll

- Static stretch

- Dynamic warm-up

- Strength

In a program designed for injury prevention, none of the factors are optional. You cannot elect to foam roll and omit static stretching or elect to static stretch without rolling prior. Each piece of the puzzle has a specific purpose, and the prevention program suffers when parts are omitted.

Athletes must be given time to roll and be told the key areas in need of attention, like the hips, adductors and t-spine. Athletes must be given specific stretches to perform and, more importantly, be both told and shown how to do each stretch.

Most athletes perform fake stretching. In fake stretching athletes get improperly positioned and make an attempt to look like everyone else. This is generally done to compensate for a large deficit. Those who like to stretch are generally flexible and probably don't need to stretch; those who dislike it are those most in need.

Try to find stretches that allow athletes to use their bodyweight to help or that use props like boxes, tables or rollers.

After the basic foam roll, static stretch and dynamic warm-up, the next step in prevention is to perform specific strength exercises for the hip flexors and psoas training above ninety degrees. I like a three-step progression.

- Step one — Supine hip flexion

- Step two — Standing hip flexion

- Step three — Standing hip flexion, adduction and prone hip flexion

Prevention Keys

Look for an excessive abduction and limited extension pattern. Generally an athlete with a seated V-type stretch of greater than 110 and a neutral Thomas position has an imbalance.

Train hip flexion above ninety degrees to improve psoas function. This can be done as a warm up or activation. Think ten-second holds, not reps.

Train hip-flexion patterns progressing to a flexion and adduction pattern. Pay attention here: Make sure your athletes use a flexion and adduction pattern. Those with issues will instinctively internally rotate the hip and in essence recreate a hip flexion pattern.

Things to Avoid

Avoid the surgeon. Surgeons do surgery. That's their business. Doctors work on what I call the 1-2-3 model, the three Is.

- Ingest anti-inflammatories

- Inject more anti-inflammatories

- Incise…that is, to cut

We want to avoid the 1-2-3 model. If your client returns to the doctor without improving, surgery will be schedule, but surgery should be the last resort. And if the client has not really committed to a full rehab program, that's even more reason to avoid surgery.

If athletes were willing to take time off and listen to the trainers and therapists, innumerable surgeries could be avoided. I have seen at least three professional athletes scheduled for surgery who were able to avoid them by committing to a proper rehab program of exercises and soft tissue work.

We should never let a surgeon go in to take a look around. This means the doctor is unsure, but wants to do surgery anyway. Usually this means he will go in, repair any small tear he sees and often "release" the adductors. This only makes more scar tissue.

My feeling, and the feeling of many therapist colleagues, is sports hernia surgery will be like the lateral release in the patella femoral joint, a surgery that had limited success and thankfully eventually went out of style.

Rehabilitation Concepts

One of the most successful methods in dealing with sports hernias focuses on decreasing motion. Many current rehab protocols focus on training the deep abdominal muscles to stabilize the pelvis. Although this may be an initial part of the solution, an approach that simply emphasizes core stability may be doomed to long-term failure.

Eventually the tissues must be re-exposed to high velocity loads and contractions. If this is not done, re-injury is a predictable result. Every failed sports hernia rehab fails when velocity is introduced.

Developing core stability in the presence of poor tissue quality only puts off the inevitable re-injury. Don't short-change soft tissue attention.

Another area of concern lies in the open-chain versus closed-chain debate. Many therapists and coaches have been misdirected and believe all lower body work must be closed-chain. The recovery stride in both sprinting and skating is a pure open-chain movement. The athlete must convert from an explosive abduction and extension action done in a closed-chain fashion, to an explosive flexion and adduction pattern done in an open-chain position.

It is possible we have become too closed-chain oriented without actually looking at function. Many therapists are attempting to use closed-chain concepts to solve an open-chain problem. This is one reason I like the slideboard for all athletes and one reason we don't see a significant number of sports hernias in our athletes. All of our athletes, regardless of sport, use the slideboard.

The beauty of the slideboard is the adductor and hip flexor muscles are exposed to eccentric, closed-chain loads as the athletes slide across the board. However, in the transition the same muscles are used to recover the leg in an open-chain flexion and adduction action. The slideboard provides two levels of essential stress to the tissues critical in rehab.

The major problem with the slideboard is in mediating or controlling the stress. This can initially be done by controlling velocity and by providing adduction assistance to the adductors.

Velocity is controlled by asking the athlete to move slowly across the board. Our description of the initial exposure to the board is public skating, a pace used when holding hands with a member of the opposite sex on an iced-over pond.

Assistance is provided by placing a Lifeline lateral resistor on the athlete's ankles. The lateral resistor, which you can get at Perform Better, functions as an additional adductor and acts to pull the free leg and decrease stress on the target tissues.

Sports Hernia Rehab

The real key to sports hernia rehab is a program of gradually increased velocity. Many athletes feel fine initially because the tissue is not lengthening at a rapid rate, but deteriorate at the end when the velocity of tissue lengthening increases. In addition, rehab rarely includes appropriate soft tissue treatment and as a result is doomed to failure.

The first two to three weeks of rehab should focus on wound care and pain management. The strength and conditioning coach should have little involvement until the athletic trainer or physician has determined the athlete can begin rehab. Somewhere around week two or three post-surgery, the athletic trainer, team doctor and physical therapist will begin to allow a controlled exercise program.

Our first three-week phase of rehab begins approximately two weeks post-surgery and focuses on healing. We get the athlete working out again without forcing stress onto the groin and abdominal area. This involves removing exercises that indirectly apply load to the abdominals. The most notable things we avoid are pull-up variations and single-leg knee-dominant exercises like split squats and one-leg squats.

Phase One
Weeks Two through Four

Core

Core work focuses on the hips and glutes with almost no direct ab or groin work. In rehab, we strengthen around but not over the acute area. We strengthen the abs and adductors indirectly initially when possible, incorporating one basic exercise for each area.

All exercises except the adductor squeezes and rollouts are done for three sets of ten-second isometric holds, increasing by ten seconds per week. Rollouts and adductor squeezes begin at two sets of ten, adding two reps per week.

Always ask if an exercise hurts. *This is a yes or no question.*

- Cook hip lift — single-leg bridge holds

- Quadruped hip extension — McGill birddogs

- Side bridge — short lever

- Supine psoas holds

- Supine or side-lying adduction — squeeze an Airex or Pilates ring if pain-free

- Stability-ball rollouts — the only direct ab work and done only if pain-free. Larger diameter balls offer less stress.

Lower-Body Strength

Focus again is on low-stress exercises. Begin at three sets of ten, adding two reps per week or two reps per day.

- Bodyweight squats — add a weight vest, work up to bars

- Reaching single-leg straight-leg deadlift

In addition, mini-band work can be done for the abductors as part of a general warm-up.

Phase Two
Weeks Five through Seven

In phase two we continue to progress all of the above exercises and add a short-stance split squat if it can be done pain-free.

A short-stance split squat is done in more of a 90/90 position to apply less stress to the anterior hip and anterior core. We want to begin to move to lunge-type stances, but not aggressively. The stance can be lengthened if the exercise is pain-free on both sides.

Again, we follow a progression of bodyweight to a weight vest, and eventually to a bar. It is important to note up to this point we were working in the sagittal plane.

Physical therapist John Pallof had an excellent progression concept: John proposed a progression from sagittal plane via squats, to frontal plane by adding lateral squats and eventually to transverse plane. We further modified this to work mobility first and strength second.

In phase two, week two we add a bodyweight lateral squat. This is a low-velocity frontal plane exercise. Some might view this as stretching or mobility work, which it is, but like many of our warm-up exercises, it will be loaded later. It is critical for the lateral squat to precede the lateral lunge. This maintains the integrity of our model of gradually increasing velocity and tissue stress.

In phase two, week three, we add a rotational squat. This is the last step in preparation for the bodyweight lunge circuit or lunge matrix we add in phase three.

Hip-dominant work progresses by adding load to the single-leg straight-leg deadlifts, and by adding slideboard or stability-ball leg curls. The slideboard leg curl is an excellent progression from the core work, as it combines the actions of bridging into a concentric and eccentric hamstring exercise.

In phase two of our velocity-based model, we introduce low-intensity agility ladder work and begin to add low-intensity linear box jumps of twelve to eighteen inches, again always with the warning the exercises should not produce pain.

Core work and strength work continue to progress with a goal of returning to normal strength levels.

Lower-Body Strength

Here we add single-leg knee-dominant exercises.

Core work continues to progress in the number of reps, six sets of ten seconds in this phase. Mini-band work continues as part of a general warm-up.

Week One

- Short-stance split squat, 3x10 each leg

- Front squats, 3x10, done after split squats. This is a departure from normal because it's rehab.

- Single-leg straight-leg deadlift using one dumbbell or kettlebell

- Slideboard leg curl

Week Two

- Add lateral squats, 2x10 each side

Week Three

- Add rotational squats, 2x10 each side

Begin at three sets of ten, adding two reps per week or two reps per day.

Phase Three
Weeks Eight, Nine and Ten

In phase three, we add increased velocity by switching from eccentric to concentric contractions in a more dynamic manner.

In phase one and two, we classify the knee-dominant exercises as static, supported exercises. This means the pelvis is supported by the opposite limb in contact with the ground or a bench, and the body is not moving forward or back; it's static. This is in comparison to a lunge, which is a dynamic exercise. In dynamic exercises gravity and bodyweight begin to add additional decelerative stress.

In phase three we also introduce static, unsupported exercises. These are true one-leg squats where the pelvis does not have the benefit of an additional support foot.

Plyometrics are progressed adding all normal phase one stability-based plyos. This is a mix of box jumps (single- and double-leg), lateral and medial hops (right to right or left to left), and lateral bounds (right to left).

Ladder work will also progress in intensity. At this stage, we begin slideboard work with lateral resistors, and add sled pushes and crossovers.

We also move to phase one of our normal straight-ahead speed progression, adding a drill called Lean-Fall-Run. Lean-Fall-Run is exactly as it sounds. The athlete stands tall and literally falls into a five- or ten-yard sprint.

With a rehab client, the instruction is three quick steps and coast. One set of five sprints is done with a walk-back recovery.

Lower-Body Strength

- At this point, we add lunges and one-leg squats.

- Core work stays at six sets of ten seconds in this phase.

Split squat, lateral squat and rotational squat are now done for one set of ten on each side as part of the warm-up.

Day One

- Single-leg squats, 3x10 each side, beginning with five-pound dumbbells

- Front squats, 3x10. These are done after the single-leg squats, still a departure from normal during rehab.

- Single-leg straight-leg deadlift — one dumbbell or kettlebell, continuing to progress loads five or ten pounds per week.

- Slideboard leg curl —add weight

Day Two

- Forward lunge replaces the single-leg squat.

Phase Four
Weeks Eleven, Plus

Here our in-place squat circuit — split, lateral, rotational — is replaced by a lunge matrix circuit. This is still a bodyweight multi-planar warm-up. The athlete should now be able to train normally with teammates, but will be carefully monitored.

Plyos and speed continue to progress. Because the athlete begins to add phase one sprint and plyos in phase three, he is two phases behind the plyometrics.

There is still much to learn in the area of sports hernia rehab. This section should give you food for thought and a base to build upon in regard to prevention and rehabilitation.

The Approaches in Core Training
Core Stability
The Science of the Core
Terminology

Anterior Core Training

Glute Activation and the core

Rotational Training

Core Advances

Awareness in Rotational Training

The Core Exercises

Core Stability Exercises

Supine Progression

The Superficial Core

My previous books, *Functional Training for Sports* and *Designing Strength Training Programs and Facilities,* go into great detail about what we knew about core training when they were written, and I make no apologies for learning and changing based on new knowledge.

Our core programming has changed every year for the past seven or eight years. All the changes were and are based on the latest research. We've used the knowledge of Paul Hodges, Stuart McGill, Shirley Sahrmann, Mark Comerford and others to improve the health and performance of our athletes.

We now know we can't just squat for core training, which for core work activate primarily back extensors like longissimus and multifidus. The bottom line is squats are great for developing the posterior aspects of the core, but do little for the anterior muscles according to Jeffrey McBride's research in the Neuromuscular Lab at Appalachian State University. In fact, push-ups and side bridges are superior to squats for the external obliques

Most of the better exercises for the anterior core — sometimes called the deep sleeping abdominal muscles — are more in what some consider the "sissy" category. .

Will bilateral exercise of any type truly work the core muscles as they're intended to work in a unilateral activity? Let's look at the research and try to use the information for the betterment of our athletes and clients.

Simply defined, core stability is the ability to create movement in the legs and arms without compensatory movement of the spine or pelvis, and in the broadest sense allowing force to move from the ground through the hips, spine or scapulo-thoracic joints without energy leaks.

Energy leaks are defined as points at which energy is lost during the transfer of force from the ground, and are a result of the body's inability to stabilize a particular joint. Torso strength encompasses core stability, hip stability and shoulder stability, and most importantly, the ability to move force from the ground to the extremities while maintaining stability in the aforementioned areas.

As the study of the interrelationship of low back pain and the training of the abdominal muscles continues, it's clear the paradigms will continue to shift. One such shift is occurring currently.

Previously I have written and spoken extensively about the Australian methods of training the deep abdominal muscles. The work of Richardson, Hodges and Jull, through their landmark book, *Therapeutic Exercise for Spinal Segmental Stabilization in Low Back Pain,* has significantly advanced our knowledge of core anatomy and muscle function. In actuality, that book and the research that preceded it have forever changed the way training is performed.

Some practitioners in the field rejected the Australian concepts for a broad range of reasons. The most notable and credible among these critics is the Canadian researcher, Dr. Stuart McGill. McGill provides a sound biomechanical rationale for why hollowing, as he refers to the Australian draw-in maneuver, will actually decrease stability. McGill advocates a technique he refers to as bracing in place of the hollowing or drawing in we'd been doing previously.

Paul Hodges
Australian Core Philosophy

This approach was initially based on the Richardson, Hudges and Jull book. This was a landmark work in 1999, and the research formed the basis for the original core revolution.

This is where the draw-in idea began, and is also the stuff that aggravates the weightlifter crowd. It's important to remember the writers are therapists who study low back pain. The fact that we can't figure out how to correctly apply what they do doesn't make them wrong.

Paul Chek was the first in the US to embrace these concepts and brought the stability ball into our realm. Like so many other theories, the uninformed ran away with the idea. My guess is the authors feel differently about some of their ideas now, but the old concepts were firmly entrenched by people like Chek and by Mike Clark at NASM.

I have an orthopedic surgeon friend who says, "Don't be the first guy to use a new technique, but don't be the last guy either." Many coaches got carried away with using a blood pressure cuff under the back and a lot of the draw-in techniques, but that doesn't mean it's all bad.

The McGill Research

Stuart McGill is a Canadian researcher who took the next step. McGill's books, *Low Back Disorders* and *Ultimate Back Fitness and Performance,* are the current state of the art in low back health.

McGill is in agreement with much more of the Australian core philosophy than he disagrees with, the major difference being McGill favors a technique he refers to as "bracing" over the Australian technique of drawing in. This has become a huge disagreement, but is in my mind a tempest in a teapot.

The exercises used and concepts applied are very similar. The difference is in how you elect to stabilize the core. I use a little bit of both concepts, and I like Gray Cook's idea best: Just tell the client to get tall and skinny.

Gary Gray
and the Functional Approach

The functional approach has no real connection to the first two. In the functional approach, most of the conventional wisdom of core training is rejected. True proponents of the functional approach believe it's non-functional to lie on the ground and attempt to use individual muscles or groups of muscles. All their core training is done standing.

I thought Paul Hodges and the Australians were right about the draw-in, sucking in the gut when you lift. Now I think Stuart McGill is closer to right with bracing. And Shirley Sahrmann has always been pretty much right.

None of this matters if you find a way to keep the core stable. For that, program more front and side planks. When these get easy for your clients, progress them. Elevate the feet, unload a foot, get the extremities unstable. Forget about squats and deadlifts being enough core work. Jeffrey McBride's research invalidates that thought.

The point is a number of really smart people have been effectively skinning the same cat in very different ways.

Terminology

Drawing in

The action of bringing the rectus abdominus toward the spinal column. Ideally this is done by contracting the transverse abdominus and internal oblique muscles.

Hollowing

Another description of a drawing-in action that assumes the action results in a decrease of waist diameter.

Bracing

The technique taught and favored by McGill involves a simultaneous co-activation of the transverse abdominus, internal obliques, external obliques and rectus abdominus. In bracing there is no attempt to decrease the diameter of the waist, only to activate the muscles.

Although I am clearly not qualified to dispute Dr. McGill's research, I have a point of theoretical disagreement. McGill's research shows drawing in or hollowing can decrease the base of support and stability of the spine. However, we teach drawing in as a neuromuscular awareness exercise, not as the primary vehicle for stability, and McGill agrees hollowing may act as a motor re-education exercise.

In addition, most of our athletes fit the classic Janda lower-crossed-body model, with an almost protruding abdominal wall and a significant lumbar lordosis. In these athletes, teaching drawing in simply brings the rectus into normal alignment from a position of concavity. The athlete is not hollowing, but bringing the abdominal wall back to its intended position of stability.

In other words, the goal is to bring the abdomen back to its normal anatomical alignment. Drawing in for a lordotic athlete would not decrease the base of support as McGill suggests.

Performing draw-in exercises literally sets the table for all other stability exercises. We are teaching athletes to contract a muscle they may not be capable of contracting voluntarily. Clients unable to draw in will not be able to properly stabilize in any other movement pattern; an athlete who cannot draw in would not be able to brace as effectively. The purpose of the draw-in exercises is not really to be exercises in themselves, but to teach clients to properly set the core musculature in all activities.

Initially the draw-in concept is applied in quadruped or bridging exercises. The draw-in is the foundation on which all other stability exercise is built. Whether you choose to draw-in or brace, the execution of quadruped or bridging exercises remain the same.

Anterior Core Training

Based on the work of Stuart McGill and Shirley Sahrmann, we now know core function may be more about what you *shouldn't* be doing than what you *are* doing. Two terms becoming more and more popular in core training are anti-rotation and anti-extension, and in fact, the focus of our core training now is these main actions.

The strength guys say to forget doing abs, just do heavy squats and deadlifts. Don't even say the word core around them. The functional guys say lying down is not functional, and seem to be against any core training not done standing. If we proceeded logically we would see both groups at least agree all good core training is done standing. As is sometimes the case, I disagree with both parties.

The function of the anterior core is absolutely not flexion. That is where I fully agree with the functional guys. When does anyone ever do anything in real life that looks like a crunch?

I agree with the functional folks: Lying on your back doing abs is not only a waste of time but probably dangerous. Look at McGill's method for causing disk damage in a lab setting — repeat flexion. Ideally we need an anterior core exercise that doesn't involve flexion.

Function of the anterior core is the prevention of extension. Core training may just be more about the *prevention* of motion than about the *creation* of motion.

Everyone needs a strong core, and exercises like ab wheel rollouts, which strengthen your anterior core by resisting extension, are the gold standard.

The problem with the rollout was never that it was a bad exercise. It just wasn't the right place to start. Our athletes who struggled with the wheel simply weren't strong enough for it, which is why I took it out of our programs.

It's best to start with stability balls. The weaker the athlete, the bigger the ball we start with. As you look at the ab wheel and a stability ball, look at the difference in terms of where the body angle is when using the ab wheel and using the ball. There's really no difference. Think of the stability ball as an oversized ab wheel; your goal is to work down until your athlete can use the regular-size wheel safely and productively.

Our rollout progression goes from stability balls to ab wheels to TRX rollouts or fallouts, which don't change the difficulty of the eccentric action, but add a whole new dimension to the concentric.

From the great strength coach, Dan John: *I love those damn five-dollar ab wheels. I loved them when they came out in the '60s; I loved them when they returned with the advent of the internet, and I love them as my favorite anterior-chain exercise now.*

I agree with Dan. However, we have a small problem: We need a progression. Ab-wheel rollouts are tough. Too tough. That's the reason I abandoned them years ago. Athletes got exceptionally sore or were unable to hold a stable lumbar spine.

The key in my mind was to find a progression to get my athletes to safely do ab-wheel rollouts, which took us to the ball rollouts. The stability ball is a big wheel; the bigger the ball, the easier the exercise. Beginners will use a seventy-five-centimeter ball; with older, deconditioned clients, put the ball against the wall and use it almost as a straight-up roller.

Phase One
Front Planks

If your athletes or clients can't hold a perfect plank for forty seconds, start there. Remember a perfect plank looks like the person horizontally standing. It's not a prone crunch.

Phase Two
Stability-Ball Rollouts

The stability ball is like a big wheel. The weaker the athlete, the bigger the ball. It is essential everyone starts with stability-ball rollouts. I don't care how strong you think your athletes' abs are, do yourself a favor and program stability-ball rollouts twice a week for the first three weeks. If you start them with a wheel, there is a good chance you will strain a few abdominal muscles.

Phase Three
The Ab Dolly

Ab dollies are a bit pricey, but they make a nice transition to the wheel. I am all about progressions that keep our athletes healthy, and the ab dolly makes the transition from the stability ball to the wheel much easier. It's a physics thing; the ab dolly allows the user to be on the elbows first to get a short-lever rollout.

Phase Four
The Wheel

If you have an ab dolly, you don't really need a wheel. Your athletes will grasp the sides of the ab dolly with their hands to lengthen the lever. I like the wheel better because we get better diagonals as we get more advanced, but for phase four it really doesn't matter. The key is the moving piece is now a full arm's length away.

Phase Five
Valslide or Slideboard Rollouts

The Valslide or slideboard now adds a frictional component. Instead of the wheel rolling, bodyweight creates a drag. This again makes the exercise harder, particularly the concentric return portion. The athlete has to pull the body back in.

Phase Six
TRX Rollout

The TRX rollout or fallout is a great progression as the lever arm is now the entire body. You can play with the length of the TRX or the foot position to vary the difficulty.

Bodysaw

The bodysaw can be done on a TRX with the feet in, or on a slideboard. This is an excellent progression from a rollout as the full length of the body now comprises the lever arm.

I love this exercise because it also works off the plank concept. The bodysaw actually combines the concept of planks and rollouts.

To perform the bodysaw, the athlete will begin in a front plank with the feet either in the TRX foot cradles or on a slideboard. The athlete should then slide back so the shoulders move toward the rear and are no longer over the elbows. The greater the core strength, the greater the ROM.

Glute Activation and the Core

To really understand core training we need to look at the key compensation patterns that occur when someone attempts to train the core. Substituting lumbar extension for hip extension is the major culprit in many of the problems we see. This is one of the primary problems in lower back pain and will be one of the key areas we work to improve our knowledge and training experience over the next few years.

In discussing this, McGill uses the term gluteal amnesia. Mike Clark might call it a problem of reciprocal inhibition or synergistic dominance. Both are Jandaists, if I may be so bold as to make up a word. Dr. Vladimir Janda was one of the pioneers of manual medicine in Europe. He introduced many of the concepts of muscle imbalance on which some of the concepts of core training and functional training are now based.

Both McGill and Clark identify the same problem: Are the glutes weak because the psoas is tight, or is the psoas tight because the glutes are weak? It may be a classic interdependent, chicken-and-egg scenario. Either way, proper strengthening of the glutes will be the best cure.

We may not even be strengthening, but instead reeducating the neuromuscular system. In point of fact, most early strength gains are more neural than contractile.

In order to remedy poor glute function, the athlete needs to be able to set the core and fire the glutes. Initially this is best done in quadruped position to eliminate hamstring contribution.

Sahrmann presents another series of thoughts in her game-changing book; she believes anterior hip pain can be the result of poor glute function and the resultant synergistic dominance of the hamstrings.

Sahrmann describes the biomechanical explanation by citing the lower insertion point of the hamstrings on the femur. If the hamstrings are consistently called upon to be the primary hip extensor, the result will be anterior hip pain in addition to hamstring strains. The anterior hip pain is a result of the poor angle of pull of the hamstrings when used as a hip extensor.

If I can make one clear statement of what I believe now about training as it applies to the core, it's this: Glute activation, or, more importantly, lack of glute activation, may be the root of all our core training failures and the primary source of low back pain.

As we look at more and more athletes, both injured and healthy, the inability to activate the gluteus maximus and glute medius stands out as the root cause of at least four major injury syndromes.

- Low back pain relates strongly to poor glute max activation, with poor glute function causing excessive lumbar compensation.

- Hamstring strains relate strongly to poor glute max activation. Think about synergistic dominance.

- Anterior hip pain relates strongly to poor glute max activation. This relates to the poor biomechanics of hamstrings as hip extensors.

- Anterior knee pain relates strongly to poor glute medius strength or activation.

Sahrmann makes another of her many lucid points: When assessing the factors that contribute to an overuse syndrome, one of the rules is to determine whether one or more of the synergists of the strained muscle are also weak. When the synergist is weak, the muscle strain is probably the result of excessive demands.

This means don't focus on the pain site, focus on the pain source, a recurrent them in my philosophy and in this book. In the bigger picture, coaches should look at every non-traumatic, non-contact injury as having a root cause in either poor program design or weakness of synergists.

In this case, the source keeps coming back to the glutes. We perform glute activation at the beginning of every workout to attempt to develop better conscious awareness of the function of the glutes and to hopefully wake the glutes up so they will be greater contributors to the workout.

The idea of glute activation can become a problem because you will be asking your athletes or clients to continually touch their rear ends. In addition, you will be continually touching people's rear ends. A word to the wise: In our litigious society, perceived sexual harassment is a problem. Be careful as you tread in dangerous but necessary water.

Glute Activation Keys

• Perform glute activation as the first thing in your warm-up

• Straight-leg mini-band or Superband X-walks are great for glute medius

• For glute max use either quadruped hip extension or the Cook hip lift

One small problem to contemplate: When does glute activation become resistance training versus core training? I must confess to being unsure at this point. There is a thin line between hip-dominant exercise and core training.

The solution may be to do your core work — stability, quadruped and bridging — on the days you are doing your hip-dominant lower body exercises, or perhaps to perform some type of hip-dominant exercise every day.

Let me be clear: Perform glute activation prior to *every* workout.

Global Muscles

The future of torso or core training will be in combining all of the movements necessary without overemphasizing or underemphasizing a particular muscle or movement.

If I look at my failings over the last few years, it would be in not training the larger global muscles. So much emphasis was placed on draw-in exercises and on stability, many of our athletes could not perform sit-up exercises.

To limit flexion we are currently using straight-leg sit-up and Turkish getup progressions in our core work instead of the conventional curl-up and crunches. In fact we are encouraging our athletes and clients to flex their hips more and their spines less.

My philosophy now is fast rep speed for movers — the global muscles — and slow for stabilizers.

With global muscles we're using primarily multi-joint exercises and need to work to accelerate the load. Therefore, we move fast.

With local stabilizer muscles, a rapid contraction will quickly override the small muscles and kick on the big global muscles. Slow is key for working stabilizers.

Rotational Training

Rotational training is really the blending of core training and strength training and is in fact an essential part of both core training and proper strength development.

We can probably trace the roots of rotary training probably to Maggie Knott and Dorothy Voss, physical therapists who expanded on neurophysiologist Dr. Herman Kabat's diagonal patterns of proprioceptive neuromuscular facilitation (PNF) from the 1950s. Although we now recognize PNF more as a neuromuscular stretching technique, the idea was originally far more extensive. Knott and Voss advocated diagonal patterns of exercise to involve both sagittal plane prime movers and the muscles responsible for transverse and frontal plane motion.

Physical therapists began to realize these diagonal patterns of extension and rotation were a vital part of movement and started to use them to provide a more real-world aspect to rehab. Specialists in rehab began to understand movement is multi-planar, and the highest form of rehab involved diagonal patterns of flexion and extension combined with rotation.

Thomas Myers in *Anatomy Trains* discusses what he calls the spiral and functional lines of the body, while Janda made us aware of the integrated workings of the musculature across the critical junction from the glutes to the opposite-side lat. This area, known as the thoracolumbar fascia, along with the hip joints, allows us to move force from the ground to the extremities.

The most frequent diagonal patterns we use to address these lines are called chopping and lifting patterns. Chopping is a pattern of flexion and rotation, probably best illustrated by the actions of chopping wood, or, from an athletic standpoint, throwing a baseball. Lifting is the pattern of extension and rotation, a multi-plane pushing action. Mark Verstegen describes lifting patterns as a rotational push-press.

The chop and the lift as exercises were introduced to the athletic world by Gray Cook. Gray advocated diagonal patterns of trunk flexion with rotation — the chop — and trunk extension with rotation — the lift. His 1997 article *Functional Training for the Torso* was a quantum leap in training, combining the concepts of conventional strength training with the concepts of rehab to produce a new category of strength exercise: Rotational Training.

Cook originally described sequences of chopping and lifting, moving from a regular kneeling or a half-kneeling position with one knee down, up to standing.

Cook has since modified his original versions so the chop-and-lift exercises are initially exercises in which the arms transfer force in a diagonal pattern through a stable torso.

In Gray's view the initial concept of rotary training involves stabilizing against a rotational force rather than simply rotating.

Shirley Sahrmann's thoughts support Cook. She wrote, "During most daily activities, the primary role of the abdominal muscles is to provide isometric support and limit the degree of rotation of the trunk... A large percentage of low back problems occur because the abdominal muscles are not maintaining tight control over the rotation between the pelvis and the spine at the L5- S1 level."

The initial chopping and lifting patterns involve movements primarily in the frontal plane that force the athlete to isometrically resist rotation with the muscles of the core.

Athletes must be able to prevent rotation before we allow them to produce it. The action of moving through a chopping or lifting pattern prior to introducing the rotary component is a necessary precursor to the actual motions of chopping and lifting. It is important to be able to isometrically resist the forces of rotation before those forces can be used in a propulsive manner.

Performance enhancement expert Mark Verstegen probably deserves the credit for taking Cook's concepts into the field through his work at Athletes' Performance. In the Athletes' Performance philosophy, rotary training is viewed as a program component much like squatting or pressing.

The chop-and-lift exercises presented here have been modified from Cook's original ideas. The initial exercises challenge trunk stability through the use of a cable column. To properly perform these exercises, a special handle — the Cook bar, a twenty-inch-long bar fitted with an eyehook — is needed for the cable column. These handles can be obtained from Perform Better.

In *Functional Training for Sports* these exercises were done standing. The influence of my work at Athletes' Performance led me to alter my view and we now begin with a half-kneel position.

Level One

Half-Kneeling Stability Chop

In the half-kneeling chop, have the athlete kneel at the cable column on the inside knee with the outside knee up. Grasping the handle with hands approximately fourteen inches apart, the athlete will pull to the waist with the outside hand, and press down with the inside hand.

This should be a distinct push and pull action, and should be performed without altering the position of the torso. Watch for hips shifting right or left, or for the inability to stabilize the scapula.

A big key in the half-kneeling exercises is to get the athlete to concentrate on firing the glute on the inside leg. Firing the glute and drawing in the abs will create a stable tall-kneel.

As this is a cable-column exercise, three sets of ten can be done and the weight increased in week two, or you can use a set weight and an 8-10-12 progression, increases reps each week from eight to ten to twelve. This is our basic progressive resistance concept.

Half-Kneeling Stability Lift

The lift is the opposite of the chop. To do the lift, the cable column is placed in its lowest position. The half-kneel is again inside knee down, grasping the handle with the hands fourteen inches apart.

The action is pull and push, pulling one hand to the shoulder and pressing the opposite hand overhead while keeping the pulling hand at shoulder height. Have the athlete press to a position directly overhead. Watch for a shifting of the hips.

Again, three sets of ten can be done and the weight increased in week two, or you can use a set weight and an 8-10-12 progression. Both of these lifts should be done with no more than twenty to thirty pounds at first.

Level Two

Half-Kneeling Sequential Chop

The next exercise in the rotary progression is a half-kneeling sequential chop. In the sequential chop, trunk rotation is now introduced in a pull-turn-push sequence.

This is a logical progression from the stable chop. Posture is still maintained through drawing in the abdominals and firing the glute, but now rotation is introduced. The handle is replaced by a triceps rope to allow for rotation.

• The athlete grasps the handles and rotates the shoulders to face the cable column.

• A two-handed pulling action is used to bring the hands to the chest.

• After pulling to the chest, the head and shoulders turn away from the cable column and the athlete executes what looks like a diagonal triceps press-down. This is the pull-turn-push action alluded to above.

A three-part sequence allows the coach or trainer to teach the motion without fear of compensation. Rotation is introduced, but in a very controlled manner.

Half-Kneeling Sequential Lift

In this lift, the action is now a pull-turn-press action. This is the beginning of Mark Verstegen's rotational push-press concept. The rope handle is again substituted for the long handle. The ropes are gripped with the thumbs up, and the initial action takes on the appearance of a close-grip upright row.

As above, the athlete grasps the rope with the head and shoulders turned toward the cable column. Abdominals are drawn in and the glute is fired.

The athlete pulls with both hands to the chest, rotates the trunk, and presses diagonally past the opposite shoulder. The level three progression is a lunge-position chop-and-lift.

Dynamic Chop-and-Lift

To create a level four exercise, both the dynamic chop and the lift now move to a standing position and truly become multi-joint extension-rotation or flexion-rotation exercises. The emphasis is now on teaching the athlete to transfer force from the ground, through the trunk and into the hands in the diagonal chopping and lifting patterns. The dynamic standing lift is one of the most sport-specific actions that can be performed in the weightroom.

Coaching the Dynamic Standing Lift

Have the client continue to grasp the handles with the thumbs up.

Position the client perpendicular to the cable column with feet slightly wider than shoulder-width apart.

The lifter begins in a squat position with the hands outside of the leg closest to the cable.

The action is now squat-rotate-press down in a rapid, fluid motion.

We'll continue to make advances in this area through research and writings of people like Stuart McGill, Paul Hodges, Shirley Sahrmann and Gray Cook. The new concept of the core is simple: *Core is anti-rotation. Core is the prevention of motion.*

What's really new is when we now talk about core strength, we really mean core stability. We're going to train rectus abdominus, internal oblique, external oblique to prevent motion of the lumbar spine with our rollout progressions.

Core training is at the center of the functional versus non-functional and isolation versus integration arguments. I have been on both sides of this argument; my work in the weightroom over the past few years has totally changed my opinion. Many athletes cannot properly use the glutes or the abdominals. These inabilities are at the heart of many dysfunctions, causing problems from low back pain to hamstring injuries.

Isolative core work may be important to rewire neural patterns and correct these dysfunctions. I am clearly not advocating a return to single-joint exercise, but isolated work in the core is a necessity for those athletes dealing with low back pain or returning from injury.

The definition of the core continues to move outward, and truly does encompass the hips and the scapulo-thoracic joints.

From core stability, to core strength, to hip stability and into rotary training, it is clear our approach to training is changing rapidly. The days of uni-planar, rectus-dominant abdominal work are gone, and are being replaced by an ever-evolving series of exercises that emanate primarily from the world of physical therapy.

The type of attention we put on the core has changed a great deal the past few years. We had all been very Australian-influenced, highly influenced by Paul Chek, and the idea of draw-ins were really, really big.

There is very little in either of my earlier books we still use for core training. Those books were loaded with crunch-type exercises we just don't do anymore.

For us, draw-ins are pretty much out. It's rare for our athletes to do draw-ins, but we do use them with our rehab people. Spinal rehab clients have to do draw-ins; you have to teach them how to draw in, how to use that musculature because they can't do it when coming out of back pain situations. At our facility healthy athletes no longer do the little isolated draw-ins we'd used in the past, but when someone comes to me with a bad back, I still use some of the draw-in exercises.

Even now we might be under-reacting a little bit as we do no crunching and no rotation. What's really big now is anti-extension and anti-rotation training, which might be an over-reaction and we may find two or three years from now we'll be doing a little bit of crunching and a little bit of rotation. I don't think so, but I do think we're in the over-reaction stage right now.

Awareness in Rotational Training

Part of the process of moving from a sagittal plane orientation to an emphasis on unilateral training and multi-planar training has been a huge push toward developing flexibility in rotation. Athletes competing in a sport that requires rotation, like baseball, hockey or golf, were urged to develop more rotation in the lumbar area.

Like many performance coaches, I fell victim to this flawed concept. I was one of the lemmings, blindly following the recommendations of others and using exercises I now consider questionable or even dangerous. As a back pain sufferer, I wrote off my own discomfort as age-related and continued to perform rotary stretches and dynamic rotational warm-up exercises.

It took time, but eventually we eliminated a whole group of stretches and dynamic warm-up exercises that were once staples of our programs.

In *Diagnosis and Treatment of Movement Impairment Syndromes,* Sahrmann states, "During most daily activities, the primary role of the abdominal muscles is to provide isometric support and limit the degree of rotation of the trunk ... A large percentage of low back problems occur because the abdominal muscles are not maintaining tight control over the rotation between the pelvis and the spine at the L5- S1 level."

Here's the key: The lumbar range of motion we were trying to create is potentially injurious.

The ability to resist or to prevent rotation is more important than the ability to create it. Clients must be able to prevent rotation before we should allow them to produce it. James Porterfield and Carl DeRosa in their book *Mechanical Low Back Pain* came to the same conclusion as Sahrmann.

Porterfield and DeRosa wrote, "Rather than considering the abdominals as flexors and rotators of the trunk, for which they certainly have the capacity, their function might be better viewed as anti-rotators and anti-lateral flexors of the trunk."

Sahrmann goes on to note a key fact overlooked in the performance field:

"The overall range of lumbar rotation is calculated to be approximately thirteen degrees. The rotation between each segment from T10 to L5 is two degrees. The greatest rotational range is between L5 and S1, which is five degrees.

"The thoracic spine, not the lumbar spine, should be the site of greatest amount of rotation of the trunk.

"When an individual practices rotational exercises, he or she should be instructed to think about the motion occurring in the area of the chest."

Sahrmann places the final icing on the cake with this: *Rotation of the lumbar spine is more dangerous than beneficial, and rotation of the pelvis and lower extremities to one side while the trunk remains stable or is rotated to the other side is particularly dangerous.*

Most people now do rotational exercises for thoracic mobility. Why would we want to drive thoracic mobility through the stable core? Why use the hips and legs as a driver to get at the t-spine when we have to go through the lumbar region? If this area is weak and unstable, we're going to get stress on the passive structures of the lumbar spine and not nearly enough rotational stress on the thoracic spine.

It's very important to notice the differences in rotation movements. For example, lateral med ball tosses against a wall involve hip internal and external rotation, not lumbar rotation. Stop and consider your rotational exercises, and make sure your choices involve rotation in the hip or thoracic joints, and not through the lumbar region.

With this in mind, I have eliminated the following types of stretches we were using to increase lumbar range of motion. This includes seated and lying trunk rotational stretches, such as windshield wipers.

We also eliminated dynamic exercises designed to increase trunk range of motion, such as the dynamic bent-leg trunk twists, the dynamic straight-leg trunk twist, and the scorpion.

Most people don't need additional trunk range of motion. The evidence from the experts is clear what we really need is the ability to control the range we have.

Although dropping these exercises may seem extreme to some, I have seen a significant decrease in the complaints of low back pain since removing them from our training programs.

In fact, a great deal of our emphasis is now placed on developing hip range of motion in both internal and external rotation. The future will see coaches working on core stability and hip mobility, instead of working against themselves by simultaneously trying to develop core range of motion and core stability.

It drives people crazy when I say this because these trunk rotation exercises are on every athletic performance DVD, but that's where we are now: We no longer seek to increase lumbar range of motion.

The Core Exercises

In addition to the anterior core and chop and lifts previously discussed, my favorite exercises work the core as anti-rotators or as stabilizers. It's key we rethink our ideas about core training and begin to look at anti-rotation as the main goal.

There are a lot of great core exercises. Just remember the core is a cylinder. It has a back, sides and a front. Work all sides into your programming.

Core Strengthening Exercises

Feet-Elevated
BOSU Ball Push-Ups

This might be my favorite core exercise. I can only say this: Don't knock it 'til you've tried it with your feet eighteen inches off the ground and with a twenty-pound weight vest strapped around your torso. It's great for the core and for the overall shoulder girdle.

TRX, Jungle Gym or
Blast Strap Inverted Rows

All three of these strap set-ups function in a similar manner, offering an improved version of the inverted row to incorporate the rotator cuff and the core.

These begin supinated, palms up, and end pronated, palms down. This incorporates an element of external rotation not present in a regular inverted row, adding rotator cuff strengthening and stability.

Besides being a great addition for the rotator cuff, it's also a shoulder-saver. Being able to rotate freely is great for shoulder health. Keeping the body straight as if shot from a cannon is great for the core, particularly for the glutes.

Landmine Twists
Extreme Core Trainer

I have to give strength and conditioning coach Loren Goldenburg credit for turning me on to the landmine, what we now call the extreme core trainer, but the credit for how to use it goes to Stuart McGill. The extreme core trainer has become a core training essential at our facility. It allows us to work the anti-rotator function of the core in a standing posture. This is a device that really satisfies all of the core training proponents. It doesn't get much better than that.

In the landmine, we want to produce the largest arc with no movement of the core — anti-rotator training. This is what McGill has been talking about. Train these muscles to do exactly what they do: prevent movement.

McGill often speaks about sparing the spine, while Porterfield and DeRosa talk about training the core as anti-rotators. This anti-rotator concept is a milestone for me in core training. The core muscles are stabilizers first. This is the reason we see such great core activity in isometric bridges.

Front support and side support positions provide the greatest stimulus to the rectus abdominus and the external obliques. Both are isometric exercises.

The extreme core trainer is a great anti-rotation piece that allows us to apply a big rotary load to the core, the essence of what low back experts describe as anti-rotation exercises.

One-Arm Dumbbell Snatch

I love the one-arm dumbbell snatch. It's great for core stability and for shoulder stability. I love the fact the overhead load goes to one shoulder and to one side of the trunk. The core effect is the reason I like the lift so much.

Very often in sports we need unilateral shoulder stability while in a bilateral lower body stance. Imagine the pushing or pulling done in so many sports: Unilateral upper body, combined with bilateral lower body — it just screams one-arm dumbbell snatch.

Convertaball Twists

The Convertaball twist is another exercise into which Stuart McGill breathed new life. I remember seeing Paul Chek perform this exercise and saying to myself, "I could never ask a client to do that." The exercise seemed too dangerous. The idea of combining explosive trunk rotation with a abrupt violent ending was appalling to me.

After listening to Stuart and reading Porterfield and DeRosa's book, I realized it wasn't the exercise that bothered me, it was the way it was performed. I went from thinking never, to thinking advanced progression.

The key in McGill's version is the ball is moving and the athlete is doing everything in his power to *not* rotate. Just as in the landmine, here we're training the anti-rotator function of the core versus the rotator function.

The core musculature is forced to stabilize against an aggressive rotary force and collision — an advanced exercise, but definitely a beneficial one. As we reconceptualize this exercise, this exercise becomes a stability exercise. We're applying high velocity loads to stabilize against instead of going with them. This changes the nature of the exercise.

The problem is we've had the balls come apart, breaking loose from the rope, so until the manufacturer fixes this issue, we're no longer doing this exercise. When a 300-pound lineman is going real fast, a break is not a real pretty sight.

As much as I like the exercise, until the balls are redesigned, I caution against these.

Keiser Push/Pulls

This sagittal driver is another of the best core exercises you can program. It's also one of the more difficult to teach. It can be done on any functional trainer apparatus; I'm partial to Keiser.

The big key is the core is used to stabilize against sagittal plane motions that are attempting to produce rotary force. If the torso or shoulders turn even slightly, the core effect dissipates. The exercise forces the trainee to use the core again in its primary function — the prevention of rotation.

It's almost like a sawing action, like those rock-em, sock-em robot toys. Have the client fire the glutes and contract the abs and don't allow the motion to shift.

Get the client to think *Don't rotate, don't let the shoulders move, don't rotate the shoulders.*

Kettlebell Slideboard Lunges

A sneaky exercise, I love slideboard lunges. Valslides make this an excellent option for trainers or groups without access o slideboards.

By loading the hand opposite the working leg, a rotary force is applied to the working hip.

The glute is an external rotator, as well as an extensor. The kettlebell provides an internal rotation force that stimulates the external rotator capability of the glute. A uni-planar exercise becomes multi-planar, and is great for the core.

One-Leg Squats and Straight-Leg Deadlifts

Single-leg squats and single-leg straight-leg deadlifts both stimulate the pelvic stabilizers. These are covered in detail later in the book.

Floor-Based Core Stability Exercises

Quadruped Progression

Floor-based core stability exercises may have been part of the core over-reaction. It does not appear healthy, symptom-free athletes and clients need to spend extended periods performing some of these core stability exercises.

However, core isolation exercises can be incorporated in the active warm-up part of a session. We now use these exercises with our healthy clients as activation or warm up, and focus on anti-extension or anti-rotation exercises as our core exercises.

The exercises illustrated will form the basis of rehab for low back pain, as well hip issues. Once the bridging and quadruped patterns are taught, transfer that function into the single-leg strength exercises.

Bridging and quadruped exercises are designed to promote glute function and stability. Gray Cook classifies these exercises as core stability because there is no movement of the spine.

Cook states the concept simply: In order to be doing a core stability exercise, there must be no movement of the core.

Exercises that cause the spine to move are considered core strength exercises.

Stu McGill's research has validated my thoughts relative to quadruped exercise, and I believe it is essential for all athletes to work through this progression.

The quadruped exercises are frequently viewed as rehabilitation exercises, and have largely been ignored by strength and conditioning coaches and athletic trainers. Many coaches view quadruped exercise as boring and a waste of time. The quadruped exercises may not make sense at first glance, but that's only because these exercises are often performed incorrectly. In many cases the results of these exercises done poorly become the opposite of what was intended.

Quadruped exercises should teach athletes *how to recruit the glutes while maintaining a stable torso.* Instead, athletes often learn they can mimic hip extension by extending or hyper-extending the lumbar spine.

The purpose of this quadruped progression is to teach the athlete to stabilize the torso with the deep abdominals and multifidus muscles and to simultaneously use the hip extensors to extend the hip.

Quadruped refers to the starting position; most of the exercises are actually done in a three-point stance.

The multifidus component is not present until the hip or arm is extended. The multifidi are incorporated when the athlete has to stabilize against the rotational component produced by lifting an extremity.

The pelvic floor is a sensitive issue because coaches are dealing with discussions of body areas and body functions with athletes who may not be mature enough to understand the essential nature of engaging the muscles of the pelvic floor.

When dealing with adult athletes, core training will be drastically improved by asking the athlete to engage the pelvic floor while performing any stabilization exercise in quadruped or in a bridge position. It is enough to tell an athlete to mimic the action employed when one realizes he had to use a bathroom, but the line was very long. This usually is enough to get the message across.

Quadruped Draw-In

This has become the position of choice for teaching clients how to fire the deep abdominal musculature. Although in the past I have recommended a supine position with visual feedback, the weight of the internal organs makes working in quadruped neuromuscularly more efficient. Clients tend to feel this exercise more than any of the other positions previously advocated.

Start the client on all fours, relaxed, allowing the weight of the internal organs to distend the abdominal wall. Kneeling next to the client, place one hand on the client's back and the other hand on the now-relaxed and distended abdomen. Ask the client to lift the abdominal wall off your hand without moving the spine. Have him hold this position for five seconds and allow the abdominal wall to again drop into your hand. *The key is to be able to lift the abdominal wall without moving the spine.*

Repeat for five contractions lasting five seconds each.

After the client has developed this skill, ask him to exhale as he draws in the abdomen. It is not necessary to actually hollow, but clients must learn to feel this draw-in, or, more appropriately, draw-*up* action.

This exercise teaches the client the stable position necessary to perform any of the exercises that follow.

Quadruped Hip Extension Over Bench

This exercise is done to eliminate lumbar movement by blocking pelvic shifting using a bench. This is not the least bit real-world, but will force the athlete's understanding of glute isolation and glute firing.

Don't use a stability ball for this exercise, as the ball will deflect and the surface needs to be rigid.

To perform the exercise, the hip bones begin in contact with the bench. Have the client draw in using the quadruped draw-in described previously, and extend the hip with a bent leg. The bent leg eliminates the contribution of the hamstring and forces more glute activation. The bending of the leg shortens the hamstring, making it a less effective hip extensor and placing more emphasis on the glute.

Use the same sequence as above with five reps held at the top for five seconds.

It is critical the client concentrates on squeezing with the glutes for the entire five seconds.

You should see no pelvic movement whatsoever. Movement should be limited to the hip. Any lumbar extension is compensation for poor glute function.

Quadruped Hip Extension
Bent-Leg, Dowel Parallel

The quadruped hip extension exercise progression is simple, but we have made one significant change to improve the effectiveness of this movement: The non-working leg is placed on an Airex pad.

This allows the hip to be extended without having to produce the small amount of rotation necessary to actually get the knee off the ground while in a quadruped position.

The hip is extended and held in the position for five seconds before alternating sides for each subsequent rep.

Level One

This is done while balancing a dowel or stick along the spine. The objective sounds simple, but it is actually difficult to accomplish. Have your client extend the hip without disturbing the dowel or allowing the lumbar spine to move away from it. Any change in lumbar curve can easily be seen as an increase in the space between the dowel and the lumbar spine. With proper control of the lumbar spine via the deep abdominals and multifidus muscles, the hip should extend without extension of the lumbar spine.

Progress from five to eight and then to ten five-second holds. Again, the leg is bent to deliberately shorten the hamstring and make the glute the primary hip extensor.

Level Two

We move this to a level two exercise with the addition of two-and-a-half-pound ankle weights.

Quadruped Hip Extension
Bent-Leg, Dowel Perpendicular

Level Two

After your athlete masters the bent-leg version of the quadruped hip extension with the dowel parallel to the spine, the dowel is shifted to a position perpendicular to the spine over the hip bones.

The same hip extension is performed, but now the objective is to eliminate any rotational compensation in the lumbar spine.

Level Three

Again, the addition of ankle weights changes the exercise intensity.

Quadruped
Alternating Arm and Leg

Level Four

The last and most difficult step in the progression is an alternate arm and leg action from the quadruped hip position. This is an advanced exercise often used far too early with beginners.

All the preceding exercises are held for five seconds and progressed using a 5-8-10 rep progression.

Supine Progression

The supine progression may be the most important part of the overall torso training program. The supine or bridging progression teaches athletes to fire both the glutes and hamstrings while maintaining the core position with the deep abdominal muscles.

In addition, the progression now moves to a position with the feet in contact with the ground, a more real-life motor pattern than quadruped. The supine progression also targets the back via the multifidi.

The supine exercises train or retrain the multifidi while improving glute function. The multifidus muscles, along with the transversus abdominis, have received much attention due to research being conducted in Australia. This research has shown the multifidi and transverse abdominis experience rapid atrophy after a back injury and must be retrained by anyone who has experienced back pain.

The multifidus muscles are the deepest of the spinal erector group and act to resist flexion and anterior shear during forward bending. The multifidi are also responsible for rotational stability between the individual vertebrae.

One possible way to exercise the multifidus muscles is to apply a rotational stress to the spine. By resisting this rotary force, the multifidi are stimulated. Training or retraining the multifidus muscles is often neglected in many torso and low back rehabilitation programs.

Although great attention has been lavished on the deep abdominal musculature, the ability to stabilize the spinal column itself is potentially more important. The supine progression teaches the movement patterns necessary to safely and correctly perform supine exercises, facilitates the glutes and targets the multifidi. The supine progression begins to transfer the improved glute function achieved through the quadruped exercises into the slightly more specific bridge position.

Cook Hip Lift

Level One

This is an invaluable exercise that provides a triple emphasis on the glutes, hamstrings and on the torso. The Cook hip lift develops glute and hamstring strength and function, and also teaches the critical difference between hip and lumbar spine range of motion.

The ability to distinguish between hip motion and lumbar spine motion is one of the most important goals of the supine exercise progression. In many exercises that target the hamstrings and glutes, it's easy to mistakenly use more range of motion at the lumbar spine than at the hip. It's also easy to extend the hips with the hamstrings versus using the glutes.

The Cook hip lift is both an exercise and a test. If an athlete performs the Cook hip lift and experiences cramping in the hamstring, the athlete has a weak glute or glutes, or inhibited glute function. Athletes who cramp in the hamstrings with the Cook hip lift must place additional emphasis on learning to fire the glutes. This is probably best done in quadruped in the initial re-learning stages.

In hip extension with the knee bent, the hamstring should be a weak synergist. Due to its shortened nature, the hamstring should provide a small measure of assistance to the glutes in hip extension.

However, in the absence of good glute function — McGill's gluteal amnesia — the hamstrings are forced to become the prime mover. Attempting to be the prime mover while shortened causes the muscle to overwork and cramp.

To perform the Cook hip lift, have your client lie supine in the hook-lying position, then pull one knee tightly to the chest to limit movement at the lumbar spine. To ensure the knee stays tight against the chest, place a tennis ball near the bottom of the rib cage and have him pull the thigh up to hold the ball in place. The ball must not fall out during the set.

The opposite knee is bent ninety degrees, and the foot is placed with the heel down and the toe up. The action of pushing through the heel stimulates the hip extensors. Pushing through a flat foot will often result in athletes with poor glute firing using the quadriceps to substitute for the hip extensors.

Your client should draw in the abdominals to stabilize and extend the hip by pushing the heel down into the floor. Don't be surprised if the range of motion is initially limited to a few degrees.

This exercise serves two main purposes:

• It teaches the difference between range of motion of the hip and range of motion of the lumbar spine.

• There's a gain of additional flexibility in the psoas due to the reciprocal nature of the exercise. It's not possible to contract the glute and hamstring without relaxing the psoas.

Follow the bodyweight progression, three sets of 10, 12, 14 reps on each leg.

Key point: The tennis ball must not fall out. If the athlete extends from the lumbar spine instead of the hip, the ball will fall to the floor. What this means is the athlete is inadvertently substituting lumbar spine motion for hip extension.

Gray Cook popularized this exercise to teach athletes how to separate the function of the hip extensors from the lumbar extensors.

Most athletes are unaware of how little range of motion they possess in the hip joint when the range of motion in the lumbar spine is intentionally limited. You will quickly realize the range of motion in this exercise is only two or three inches.

The range of motion can be increased significantly by relaxing the grip on the opposite knee, but this defeats the purpose. Relaxing the hold on the leg substitutes lumbar spine extension for hip extension.

Hands-Free Cook Hip Lift

Level Two

In the hands-free version of the Cook hip lift, the exercise is performed exactly the same, except the ball must now be held by the contraction of the hip flexors. In this situation, the glutes must contract while the opposite-side psoas maintains an isometric contraction.

Isometric Supine Bridge

Level One

This level-one exercise requires the athlete to transfer the knowledge gained about hip range of motion from the Cook hip lift and from the quadruped exercises to a bridge position. Begin with the athlete in a hook-lying position, and then raise the hips to create a straight line from the knee through the hip to the shoulder. You're looking to create and maintain this posture with the glutes and hamstrings, not by extending the lumbar spine. Any drop in the hips drastically reduces the effectiveness of the exercise. At the top point, have the athlete draw in the abdominals and maintain this position.

Before attempting this exercise, it is important to learn the difference between hip movement and lumbar spine movement through an exercise such as the Cook hip lift. Athletes who do not understand this distinction arch the back to attempt to extend the hip.

Program three thirty-second holds.

Isometric Single-Leg Supine Bridge

Level Two

The single-leg supine bridge takes the concepts learned through the quadruped draw-in, the double-leg bridge and the Cook hip lift, and begins to progress to a higher level of function. At this point the exercise moves from a four-point stability base to a three-point base. This change in base of support and stability will now begin to target the multifidi as rotary stabilizers of the spine to a greater degree.

To teach the isometric single-leg supine bridge, have your client in a hook-lying position, draw in the abdominals to stabilize, perform a double-leg bridge and then extend one leg. This should create a straight line from the knee through the hip to the shoulder. This single-leg position is maintained by pushing the heel down and squeezing the glute. Have the client squeeze the glutes as if trying to make a hard fist.

Have your client do three fifteen-second holds on each side.

Bridge with Alternate March

Level Three

The next step in the progression is to add a small alternate march action to the isometric bridge: Alternate lifting one foot then the other off the ground. This is a march, not a leg extension.

A yardstick across the crests of the hip bones acts as a level to remind the athlete not to let the opposite hip drop when the foot is lifted. With this exercise, the progression may better target the multifidi due to the rotational stress applied to the spinal column as a result of moving from four support points, the shoulders and feet, to three support points, the shoulders and one foot.

This is a transitional stability exercise that will greatly increase the level of difficulty. Have the athlete push through the heel and activate the glute on the same side as the supporting foot.

Program one set of five-second holds, five on each leg. Progress this to eight and eventually ten holds.

The key to developing a torso program is to properly combine the movements described into a progressive program.

The Superficial Core

You can do a million sit-ups and crunches and they will have no effect on abdominal definition. When people ask me the best exercise for abs I tell them table push-aways. It usually takes a few minutes for them to get it, but it's not a joke; it's the truth. If you want better abs, eat less and train more, but don't just train your abs.

The idea of working abs to get abs is one of the oldest misconceptions in training. This goes back to the idea of spot reduction. Spot reduction has never worked and will never work. The research has been done over and over, and the answer is always the same: We can't decrease the fat layer on a particular area by working that area. That means the guys doing sit-ups to lose abdominal fat and the lady sitting on the adductor machine are all wasting their time. Good total body work was, is and always will be the key to fat loss.

Does your client want better abdominal definition? Finish every workout with some hard interval training instead of extra sit-ups or crunches. Interval training is the real key to fat loss and the resulting definition. Interval training burns more calories than steady-state aerobic training, and because it is a sprint program, your client will get a sprinter's body.

Abdominal training may reduce the diameter of the waistline, but will not do anything to reduce bodyfat. The truth is there are lots of good reasons to do core training. A strong core is one of the keys in the prevention of back pain. A strong core will help you look better and improve performance in a host of sports, but sit-ups or any other abdominal exercise will not reduce bodyfat.

A good abdominal or core program is a lot more than crunches. A great deal of your core programming should be isometric exercises such as our quadraped and supines series just described.

One of the major functions of the core musculature is the prevention of motion, meaning the abdominals are great stabilizers. Work on the stability function, not just on flexion and extension.

The Hips

Understanding the Hips
Hip Flexion
The Psoas and Iliacus
Back Pain
TFL Cramping

Weakness in the Hip Muscles
Dysfunctional Hip Flexors

Hip-Dominant Exercises
Hamstring Group

Hip-Extension Exercises

Understanding the Hips

Gray Cook often makes this point: Hip mobility is something we lose. We are all born with exceptional, probably excessive hip mobility, and as we age, it goes away. You won't find a single baby who can't get his foot in his mouth, and you won't find very many adults who can.

The big thing with understanding hips is we need more static flexibility work, more direct hip flexor work, and more attention to mobility.

In the standard Janda idea, the muscles on the backside were said to be long and weak, and the muscles on the front, short and strong. As we look at the hip, we realize someone who spends a lot of time in a flexed posture is going to have long, weak glutes and short, weak hip flexors. The fact that those muscles are short does not make them strong.

We now do direct hip flexor work because we've found we need to strengthen that group, and while we were doing a lot of work above ninety degrees in hip flexion, we've started doing things from the bottom up in addition to the work above ninety.

In terms of things being too short and too tight in the hip, we've got soft tissue mobility and restrictions — muscular restrictions and capsular restrictions.

And then we've got muscular mobility issues, limited active range of motion – the ability of the iliacus and the psoas to flex the hip and the ability of the glute to extend the hip.

There are two types of limitations, one being passive structures, one being active structures. We need static stretching and activation work — low-load training, a term more applicable than activation, because muscles don't actually become inactive. Muscles can't be shut down. They simply have diminished capacity; they're down-regulated.

We need to stabilize the region between the ribcage and the pelvis, and move at the hip joints. That's the key, getting core stability while we gain active hip mobility.

If you can get core stability and active hip mobility in your clients, they're going to be moving well, performing better and on the way toward pain-free.

Hip Flexion

Increased knowledge of the biomechanics of hip flexion is one of the most valuable things I have learned since the release of *Functional Training for Sports*. The problem with understanding hip flexion in general and the psoas muscle in particular is we use the term hip flexor as a generic term to apply to five muscles, four of which have distinctly different leverage positions from the other.

My reading of the work of physical therapist Shirley Sahrmann has changed my understanding of hip flexors, as it has about many other muscle groups.

Our understanding of the motion of hip flexion comes from looking at the anatomical leverages of the different muscles involved. The five muscles capable of assisting in hip flexion are the tensor fascia latae (TFL), the rectus femoris (distinct in that it is both a member of the quadriceps group and a hip flexor), the iliacus, the sartorius and the psoas.

Three of these muscles possess something in common; two are distinctly different. The TFL, rectus femoris and sartorius all have insertion at the iliac crest. This means all of these muscles are capable of hip flexion up to the level of the hip, a function of the principles of mechanical leverage.

The Psoas and Iliacus

The psoas and the iliacus are different. The psoas has its origin from the length of the lumbar spine, while the iliacus originates on the posterior of the ilium. This creates two distinct dissimilarities.

The psoas acts directly on the spine, both as a stabilizer for the iliacus and as a flexor. The psoas and the iliacus are the only hip flexors capable of bringing the hip above ninety degrees.

In the case of a weak or under-active psoas or iliacus, the femur may move above the level of the hip, but it is not from the action of the psoas and iliacus, but rather from the momentum created by the other three hip flexors. With this knowledge, our understanding of back pain, hip flexor strains and quad pulls is drastically expanded.

To assess the function of the psoas and iliacus, we use Shirley Sahrmann's simple test: In a single-leg stance, pull one knee to the chest and release. Inability to keep the knee above ninety degrees for ten or fifteen seconds indicates a weak psoas or a weak iliacus.

Other signs are:

• a cramp at the iliac crest in the region of the TFL

• an immediate backward lean to compensate

• a large pelvic shift to the right or left

• a quick drop from the top with a catch at the ninety-degree point

Any of these indicate the client is attempting to compensate for the weak or under-active muscles.

If the tester is concerned the subject is a skilled compensator, we have a better test developed by strength and conditioning coach Karen Wood that has also become our favorite psoas and iliacus exercise. Have the client stand with one foot on a plyo box to place the knee above the hip; twenty-four inches works well for most people.

With the hands overhead or behind the head, have the client attempt to lift the foot off the box and hold it up for five seconds. Inability to lift and hold is indicative of a weak psoas or iliacus, or both. To add resistance and use this test as an exercise, lateral resistors or bands can be used to increase the difficulty of the isometric.

Any test of the psoas originating from below the hip is inherently invalid as the iliac-originated hip flexors are now at a leverage advantage.

Understanding the unique functional contributions of the psoas and iliacus illustrates how a weak or under-active muscle can be a factor in both back pain and in quadriceps strains.

Back Pain

You also need to realize the hip and the lumbar spine are linked. When talking about the hip, we're talking about the lumbar spine; when talking about the lumbar spine, we're talking about the hip. We can't think of one without considering the other.

The reality is we work the hip to protect the spine. When the hip doesn't work properly, when the hip doesn't move the way we need it to, either actively or passively, we're going to get spinal motion, and then we're going to have back problems.

The solution to low back pain isn't found in the back, it's in the hips.

If we think about the postures of an athletic body or a deconditioned client, we often see excessive anterior tilt.

Follow the logic:

Weak external obliques allow anterior tilt;

Anterior tilt allows the psoas to shorten;

The short psoas inhibits the glutes;

The weak glutes and tight psoas prevent hip extension.

The result is lumbar extension substituted for hip extension, and subsequently low back or anterior hip pain.

Hip mobility requires the right muscles moving the hip joint to decrease the movement of the lumbar spine as a substitute. This means core stability is directly related to hip mobility. You can't separate the two, because if the hips don't move, the spine will.

Often with back pain, inability to flex the hip past ninety degrees will often cause many clients to flex the lumbar spine to give the illusion of flexing the hips. Watch how many of your clients immediately flex the lumbar spine when asked to bring the knee to the chest. There is a clear distinction between bringing the knee to the chest and bringing the chest to the knee.

Attempting to bring the knee toward the chest and above the level of the hip forces the client to use the psoas and iliacus. If they are unable to do this, one or all of three things happen.

The athlete will flex the spine and bring the chest to the knee. At first observation this appears the same, but from a back pain perspective, it could not be more different. Flexion of the lumbar spine is the leading cause of disk degeneration. Those who substitute back motion for hip motion get back pain, and perhaps eventually surgery.

In the quadraped bent-knee leg raise, we see a similar example of how this happens with extension, rather than flexion. If the hip does not move and if we can't properly use the glutes, there's going to be lumbar extension to replace the lacking hip extension. You see this all the time in gyms, people moving the lumbar spine both in quadraped exercises and in movement. As you begin to watch people who move inefficiently, you'll be shocked at how much they move the lumbar spine to avoid moving the hip or to make up for the inability to move the hip.

The ability of the glutes to work is critical, because if the glutes can't work, there will be low back pain. When you look at Stuart McGill's work, it's very clear:

Weak glutes, bad back.

Interestingly, a bad back often means a strong back, because the back extensors are overused. People with bad backs tend to have greater extensor torque than people with healthy, pain-free backs. These people are constantly using their lumbar erectors as hip extensors instead of using the glutes.

People with bad backs will often have disappearing glutes, the no-butt look. When you see that, you know the solution. The solution is squatting. The solution is single-leg work. The solution is to get those glutes doing their jobs, get those hips moving. When you get the hips moving and get the glutes working, in most cases the back pain will go away. And for this you'll be real popular with your clients.

TFL Cramping

People will also use the TFL and the other ischial hip flexors to flex the hip. In this case your athlete will complain of a low-level strain in the TFL. This is a result of overuse of a synergist, and will feed into a synergistic dominance of the TFL and further psoas and iliacus dysfunction.

A muscle cramps when attempting to shorten in a disadvantageous position. With the hip flexed above ninety, the TFL is already shortened and unable to produce the necessary force to hold in this position of poor leverage. The attempt results in cramping, much like a hamstring cramp in bridging when the glutes are under-active.

These same effects are often seen when attempting hanging knee-ups, an exercise we almost never do as it teaches compensation, except the cramp or strain is in the rectus femoris.

This is what we see in our hockey athletes who use a flexed athletic posture. The athlete will use the rectus femoris to create hip flexion. This can result in the mysterious quad pull seen in sprinters or on forty-yard-dash day in football.

The etiology is the same as above, only the culprit is now the rectus femoris instead of the TFL. It should be noted most quad pulls or quad strains are limited to the multi-joint rectus femoris. Soreness will generally be near the insertion point of the rectus femoris into the quadriceps, at about the halfway point of the thigh.

Weakness in the Hip Muscles

The psoas and iliacus are to the anterior hip as the glute is to the posterior hip. As seen in the discussion of glute activation and the core, a weak glute max will cause synergistic dominance of the hamstrings and extension of the lumbar spine to compensate for hip extension. This will lead to back pain, anterior hip pain and hamstring strains. On the opposite side, a weak or under-active psoas will cause back pain from flexion rather than extension, TFL strain and rectus femoris strain.

Another Sahrmann point: *Use of the hamstring as the primary hip extensor changes the lever arm of the femur and can cause anterior capsule pain.*

Dysfunctional Hip Flexors

The plan of attack for a client with a weak or under-active iliacus or psoas is reasonably straightforward. In order to properly execute the plan, you will need to enlist the help of good manual therapist, who can sometimes be hard to find. This may be a massage therapist, chiropractor or physical therapist, but the key is the ability to get the hands into the tissue. Don't get hung up on which profession; just find someone with good hands.

The following is the protocol.

Soft Tissue

Treat the soft tissue, done by a good manual therapist who can get into the psoas. This has to be done manually. Foam rollers, or even more targeted work with a tennis ball, can't get into a deep area like the psoas.

Stretch

The Thomas position is popular for psoas stretching. This is a physical therapy test used to measure hip flexor length, but people use it for a stretching solution in addition to testing.

Position the client on the table with one knee to the chest and the sacrum on the table end. Push down lightly on the extended leg. Half-kneeling psoas stretches will also work, but the Thomas position works best, as the iliacus and psoas can be difficult to self-stretch.

This difficulty is partially solved by my new favorite anterior hip self-stretch, a half-kneeling hip flexor stretch with the down leg on an Airex pad and the forward leg elevated on a twelve-inch box.

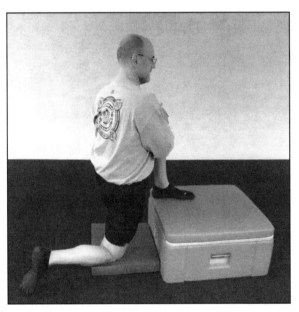

The body position is oriented about forty-five degrees toward the box; it's not straight-on. The athlete's torso is facing out, toward the forward-leg side rather than straight ahead. The athlete will need to maintain this hip rotation, which is going to stress the psoas as the foot goes up. There's a significant amount of internal rotation created when the foot is placed on the box.

Advanced clients should lift the stretched-side arm overhead.

Remember, keep the lumbar spine stable. The psoas inserts on the lumbar vertebrae. Arching the back shortens the psoas the exercise is designed to stretch.

This is the best self-psoas stretch we have found; if you've been spending a lot of time wrestling around with your athletes in the Thomas position, teach them this one instead.

Anterior hip mobility is the most difficult area to stretch and an area we neglect. Don't skip this stretch.

Strengthen

We do a seated psoas contraction into hip flexion with the hands behind the back to maintain lumbar curve. The athlete must be seated on something high enough that the feet don't touch the ground. Begin with three ten-second holds and progress to ten times in ten seconds.

Hip-Dominant Exercises

A section on hip-dominant exercise could actually be an extension of the core chapter, because if you think about it, when does bridging cease to be an exercise for core stability and glute activation, and become a strengthening exercise for the hip extensors? The line between core strength exercises and hip-dominant exercises is impossible to draw.

Many of our core stabilization exercises are actually foundational movements that morph into hip extension exercises. The concept of glute activation created in the bridging exercises carries over directly into all of the bent-leg hip-extension exercises. In fact, bent-leg hip-extension exercises are merely progressions from bridging done in a concentric and eccentric manner.

The training of the entire posterior chain becomes more critical as we begin to further our knowledge of functional anatomy. The posterior chain works in conjunction with the quadriceps to control all locomotor movement from walking to running.

Dr. Vladimir Janda referred to the systems of the posterior chain as the deep longitudinal subsystem and the posterior oblique subsystem, and demonstrated how critical these muscles are in transferring force from the ground to the upper body.

When the foot hits on the ground, the ankle is stabilized by the anterior tibialis and peroneals. This allows force to be transmitted through the hamstring into the glute max. If we do not perform single-leg hip-extension exercises, we will again miss a critical part of force transmission and of ankle stability. The exercises must begin at the ground with the peroneal group and anterior tibialis, and proceed up the chain through the lateral hamstring and into the glutes.

The use of the thoracolumbar fascia as the crossing point of movement through the lumbar spine reinforces our core training concepts, as both the transverse abdominus and internal oblique act on the same thoracolumbar fascia. Movement is literally linked from the feet to the shoulders by the core muscles and fascia.

The muscles that extend the hip, primarily the gluteus maximus and hamstring group, are often neglected in training programs. When we view the systems from a functional anatomical perspective, hip-dominant exercise is as important as knee-dominant exercise, or potentially more important.

Many coaches mistakenly believe squatting is enough exercise for the entire lower body. These programs are characterized by a leg day consisting primarily of squat movements with a token single-joint hamstring exercise such as a leg curl. This places excessive emphasis on the knee extensors and neglects the hip extensors. This can be a major problem, particularly if glute function is inhibited. Athletes with inhibited glute function will present with large quadriceps in relation to the glutes, possibly even able to squat large amounts of weight. Most often these quad-dominant, glute-deficient athletes will prefer a narrow, knee-dominant squatting style.

In recent years, the Olympic lifting community has advocated doing variations of the straight-leg deadlift. This exercise has been called the Romanian deadlift and is a hip-dominant deadlift done with a limited knee bend. Many US powerlifters used this lift for years prior to the introduction of the term Romanian deadlift.

While this exercise addresses the need for hip-dominant exercise, it does not address the need for unilateral hip-dominant exercise. If you study the subsystems carefully, it's obvious unilateral exercise is critical to proper function of the posterior chain.

Hamstring Group

To make matters worse, the hamstring group, a secondary hip extensor, is still mistakenly trained as a knee flexor. Although some anatomy texts describe the hamstring group as knee flexors, we now know the hamstring is actually the second most powerful hip extensor, as well as a stabilizer of the knee.

Hamstrings are only knee flexors in nonfunctional settings. In any locomotor activity, the function of the hamstrings group is not to flex the knee, but to extend the hip. As a result, lying or standing leg curls are a waste of time for athletes. Exercises like leg curls train the muscles in a pattern never used in sport or in life.

The training and retraining of the hamstring muscles in nonfunctional patterns may explain the frequent recurrence of hamstring strains in athletes who rehabilitate with exercises such as leg curls, or through the use of isokinetic machines such as Cybex. More importantly, strengthening the hamstrings in the absence of proper glute function is training a synergist to do the job of a prime mover.

Most hamstring injuries are actually the result of poor glute function. If the glutes function poorly, the hamstrings become what Janda called synergistically dominant. In other words, we have a synergist attempting to perform the task of a weak prime mover. Over time the hamstrings will tire and eventually strain. If the solution to the hamstring strain is more hamstring strengthening, as is often the case, the cycle will continue. Any time you see a hamstring strain, look for a weak glute.

Note a favorite Shirley Sahrmann quote:
"When assessing the factors that contribute to an overuse syndrome, one of the rules is to determine whether one or more of the synergists of the strained muscle is also weak. When the synergist is weak, the muscle strain is probably the result of excessive demands."

This may explain the frequent complaint heard by athletic trainers and therapists, "I can't believe he pulled his hamstring again; he has great strength."

The reality is hamstring weakness was never the problem. The problem was a weak prime mover. We now know to look for a weakness causing a strain, and to strengthen the weak muscle instead of the strained muscle.

Lateral Hamstring

It's important to promote tissue length in the lateral hamstring, an area prone to shortening. We use a table-top hip opening stretch for the lateral hamstrings.

When we're teaching our athletes the table-top lateral hamstring stretch from a standing position with one foot on a table and the other on the floor, we don't want them rotating from the lumbar spine, we want them rotating from the hip.

The bottom foot is neutral or internally rotated, and so is the top foot. People with poor hip mobility will externally rotate the top foot, and externally rotate the bottom foot.

Be very particular when lining up your athlete on the table. Make sure you see the foot straight ahead on the down leg, and the foot of the up leg straight up, with maybe a little bit of internal rotation.

The initial stretch is a common hamstring stretch. To move laterally, have the client rotate in at the hip, keeping both feet in the straight-forward positions. Stress the idea of turning the pelvis in and out

and in and out, not getting a lot of lumbar spine motion, whether it's lumbar flexion or lumbar rotation. Avoid both, really get the athlete to turn at the hip joint.

Thing about the pelvis as the attachment point for the lower body muscles. Minimize back motion and concentrate on pelvic motion.

We're trying to open and close the door of the hip joint.

Hip-Extension Exercises

We break hip-extension exercises into two distinct movement patterns: straight-leg hip extension and bent-leg hip extension. Movements from both categories should be used to properly train the posterior chain muscles. Although some experts claim bent-leg hip extensions isolate the glutes, this is not true for closed-chain movements.

When the foot is in contact with a surface — ground, slideboard top, stability ball — both the glutes and hamstrings work to some degree. Depending on the starting length of the hamstring group, the hamstring will emerge as either the prime mover or the synergist.

Both straight-leg and bent-leg hip extensions target the glutes and hamstrings. The difference lies in the concept of length and tension relationships. Length-tension basically dictates muscles will work best at normal length. If they are shortened or overstretched, they will not develop optimal tension.

It is not possible to truly eliminate one muscle group's contribution, only to lessen it. Straight-leg hip extension unquestionably targets the hamstrings to a greater degree because the hamstring begins at normal length, but all of the bent-leg hip-extension exercises also involve the hamstrings as synergists.

The difference with bent-leg hamstring exercises is the hamstring is deliberately shortened to decrease its contribution and to increase the contribution of the glutes. With the knee bent, the length-tension relationship of the hamstring is now poor, and the glutes will be forced to do more work.

Hamstring cramps during bent-leg hamstring exercises clearly demonstrate the client has poor glute firing or activation, because in spite of the poor length-tension relationship, the hamstring is still attempting to compensate for the weak glute. Due to the shortened state of the hamstring, the need to shorten an already deliberately shortened muscle causes the muscle to cramp.

The key to any of the hip-extension movements is to instruct the client or athlete to think glutes first. Improvement of glute firing must be a conscious effort.

Exercises such as squats and squat variations affect the glutes and hamstrings only as they relate to knee and hip extension involved in achieving a neutral standing position. In squatting, the hip never moves into full extension. Quad-dominant athletes can become effective squatters with minimal glute involvement, particularly if they are allowed to squat to positions above parallel.

To properly work the glutes and the hamstrings, the movement must be centered on the hip and not on the knee. To understand this concept, envision a front squat. The hip moves through approximately ninety degrees range of motion in concert with the knee movement. Generally there is one degree of hip movement for each degree of knee movement. The focus of the exercise is shared equally by the knee and the hip extensors.

In an exercise such as the modified straight-leg deadlift, the hip moves through a ninety-degree range of motion, but the glutes are assisted by the hamstrings. A well-designed program must include both straight-leg, hip-dominant exercises and bent-leg hip-dominant exercises to balance the lower-body muscles.

Most of the exercises in this section will initially use the 8-10-12 bodyweight progression, meaning bodyweight is used for the first three weeks, with the number of repetitions increasing each week from eight to ten to twelve reps. External resistance may be used when appropriate, or obstacles of greater difficulty may be substituted.

Cook Hip Lift

The Cook hip lift is covered in depth in the core section, but it is important to remind you to begin by distinguishing between hip range and movement of the lumbar spine. Don't skip this step.

Foot-Elevated Hip Lift

The foot-elevated hip lift is an excellent progression from the Cook hip lift and has become a staple in our program. The foot-elevated hip lift is just a single-leg bridge. This is a great example of the blurry line between core stabilization and posterior chain strength — an exercise that began as a core movement becomes a strength exercise for the posterior chain.

The foot can be elevated on an aerobic step, a balance board, a foam roller, or a medicine ball to increase the difficulty of the exercise. Aerobic steps in four- and six-inch heights allow a good progression. For a level-two exercise, a four-inch step is used. For level three, a six-inch step or balance board is used. For level four, a foam roller works well.

A two-dimensional unstable surface such as a foam roller causes the hamstrings to be worked in two separate and important functions. The hamstrings assist in hip extension, while also working eccentrically to prevent knee extension.

To progress to level five, substitute a medicine ball. The medicine ball is the most difficult due to the three-dimensional instability it introduces at the hip. The hamstrings must work at two joints, while the hip stabilizers work to prevent hip adduction and abduction. The key is the athlete must be instructed to think about raising the hips by squeezing the glute while keeping the abdominals drawn in.

For all these hip-lift exercises, use the 8-10-12-rep bodyweight progression.

Modified Straight-Leg Deadlift

The modified straight-leg deadlift (SLDL) is the predecessor of the popular Romanian deadlift and ranks with the squat among frequently maligned, misunderstood, and poorly executed lifts. Squats and deadlifts and their variations are often called unsafe and dangerous. In truth, these lifts are safe and beneficial when performed correctly with an appropriate load.

However, the squat and the SLDL can be dangerous when performed improperly or with too heavy a weight. The unfortunate reality is most athletes perform both of these exercises with questionable technique and too much weight.

I'm not a fan of the double-leg versions of the SLDL or the Romanian deadlift, as they are difficult to teach and difficult to learn. Flexing from the hips with the spine stable, what physical therapists call a waiter's bow, is one of the most difficult exercises to teach in strength and conditioning.

As a result, I now use only single-leg options of these exercises. Single-leg versions impact the back significantly less, and impact the glutes and hamstrings significantly more. In addition, the muscular systems discussed earlier are trained far more effectively in the single-leg versions. If we can obtain better muscular specificity and less lumbar load, it's an improvement.

The old-school purists will say, "What, no deadlifts?" I will always go back to the same point: If we can improve performance and have less chance of injury, it's a good idea. However, in point of fact, we do use the trap bar deadlift in some of our programs.

Single-Leg Straight-Leg Deadlift

The single-leg SLDL is a variation that develops the entire posterior chain, enhances balance and decreases both load and stress on the back. Beginning loads will be less than fifty percent of the comparable load of the two-legged version.

This exercise is far safer and is also more challenging. One of the obvious benefits is the tremendous proprioceptive work at the ankle. The deep longitudinal subsystem is engaged in this exercise, so the peroneals and anterior tibialis must both work extremely hard to provide stability to the ankle and consequently to the hip. Single-leg hamstring work is more functional than double-leg hamstring work, and single-leg hamstring work that challenges balance and proprioception is the most beneficial. This is another exercise that can be used as a part of the warm-up or as a loaded strength exercise.

In previous years our single-leg SLDL was done with a perfectly straight leg. Paul Chek said for years we need a ten- to twenty-degree knee bend to effectively recruit the glute, and we weren't doing it. We were going with a much straighter leg, and much lighter loads. We've now switched to the Chek style, slightly bent knee, semi-straight-leg deadlifting.

With the hip-dominant pattern we need that twenty-degree knee bend, and we need much heavier loads than I originally thought. Five years ago, we were probably using fifteen-pound dumbbells to do these, and we were getting a lot of hamstring soreness. When we flex the knee twenty degrees, we can use significantly more load, and we get a lot more glute soreness. The straight leg really negates the ability of the glute to be a hip extensor. That leg being bent a little bit was a huge change for us, and has had a big impact on our glute training.

And I love kettlebells for single-leg SLDLs, even with the eight-pound-jump limitation. Kettlebells really allow a much better vertical loading pattern. They're easier to hold onto, and in this situation they're far superior to dumbbells.

One-Leg, Two-Arm Straight-Leg Deadlift

The one-leg, two-arm SLDL is another excellent single-leg alternative to the double-leg versions of the Romanian or straight-leg deadlift.

Charles Poliquin frequently uses the idea of varying the exercise without changing it. The one-leg, two-arm SLDL is an excellent example of allowing some variability without having to teach an entirely new movement pattern. The essence of the exercise remains the same, but the exercise is changed enough to allow different loads and slightly different neurological patterns.

The one-leg, two-arm SLDL moves from a dumbbell exercise to a straight bar or two-dumbbell exercise, and alters the loads at both the scapulo-thoracic joint and the thoracolumbar fascia. It allows greater loads than the single-arm version and will provide greater stress to all of the trunk extensors and scapulae retractors.

This makes the exercise an excellent progression from the single-dumbbell version. From a functional standpoint, however, the two dumbbells or the straight bar may actually make the exercise less functional. This is not of great concern, as the greater loads on the hip extensors offset the loss of the linkage from glute max to the lat across the thoracolumbar fascia.

The important point is the client is able to move to a level two exercise with an increased load from the level one movement.

Reaching Single-Leg Straight-Leg Deadlift

One of the things we often struggle to teach is the hip hinge action so essential for one-leg straight-leg deadlifts. This inability led to the reaching one-leg straight-leg deadlift. This exercise was already a part of our warm-up, but I had not considered it as an exercise in the strength program until recently.

The one-arm, one-leg SLDL had been our primary exercise for an accumulation or hypertrophy phase, while the two-arm, one-leg SLDL was used for the higher loads of an intensification or strength phase as athletes got stronger.

The reaching single-leg straight-leg deadlift is more suited to the lighter loads of the accumulation phase and is an excellent exercise for beginners.

The key is that the action of reaching allows the coach to give cues like "get long." Our instructions are to reach forward with the hands toward the front while reaching back with the leg. Reaching turns on the thoracic extensors and prevents the shoulders from rounding.

Athletes can begin with any weighted med ball. We usually begin with two or three kilos. Any of the med balls with handles are excellent for this exercise. The truth is a dumbbell works just as well.

Repetitions should remain in the eight to ten range to keep the loads on the spine low.

Slideboard Leg Curl

The slideboard leg curl is an exercise stronger athletes can use as a level one exercise, or it can be used as an eccentric-only exercise for beginners. The slideboard leg curl has quickly become a favorite exercise even though it seems to violate the no-single-joint exercise rule. In fact, the slideboard leg curl is not a single-joint exercise even though there is only one joint moving.

The slideboard leg curl works in a similar manner to the hip-lift exercises. In the hip-lift exercises, the glute is the prime mover, while the hamstring assists in hip extension. In the slideboard leg curl, although only the knee joint is moving, the glutes must act to keep the hips in extension while the hamstring works to both eccentrically resist leg extension — a primary hamstring function — and to concentrically produce knee flexion. This is a complex and functional exercise when performed correctly.

Some authors describing leg curls using a stability ball make the exercise a simultaneous hip-flexion and knee-flexion exercise by allowing the hips to drop. This method of performance takes what could be a great exercise and reduces it to an average exercise. The key to the slideboard leg curl is to force the glutes and hamstrings to maintain hip extension, while also using the hamstrings as both eccentric resistors of leg extension and then finally concentric knee flexors.

Eccentric-Only Version

Many clients, particularly those who have glute-firing issues, will not be able to switch from the eccentric portion of the exercise to the concentric portion of the exercise while maintaining the glute contraction. In this case, the hips will drop and flex during the concentric portion of the exercise. If this happens, program eccentric-only reps to improve both strength and function.

Start your client with the toes up and the heels on the board as in a double-leg bridge. Have the client draw in the abdominals and place both hands on the glutes to feel the contraction. With both hands on the glutes and the stomach drawn in, count five for the slide out from the hip-flexed bridge position to a position with the legs out-stretched.

From that point, have the client relax down, return to the bridge position, and repeat for three to five reps.

Concentric Version

These are performed as above maintaining the glute contraction, but curling back to the start position. It is critical there be no bend at the hips.

TRX Leg Curl

The TRX leg curl is an excellent progression from the slideboard leg curl.

The biggest drawback to the TRX leg curl is it may be too difficult a progression. The concept remains the same as in the slideboard: The glutes must stay engaged to get the benefit of the exercise.

This is an example of a TRX exercise I discounted without trying it. As I often say, it is important to give exercises an honest trial before you decide they are not useful.

Stability-Ball Leg Curl

The stability-ball leg curl is a level-three exercise because it requires using the glutes and spinal erectors to stabilize the torso while the hamstrings perform a closed-chain leg curl. This exercise develops torso stability while also strengthening the hamstrings.

Technique Points

• Heels are placed on the ball, and the body is held with the hips off the ground.

• The ball is curled under the body using the heels while the body is held straight.

Cardiovascular Training

Conditioning for Athletics
Fiber Type
Work Capacity Model
Physiological versus Performance Testing
Using Physiological Testing

Specific Conditioning for Athletics
Off-Season Conditioning
Preseason Conditioning

Long Cardio versus Interval Training
Interval Training Research

Interval Training Programs

Interval Training Methods
Work versus Rest
Heart Rate
Karvonen Formula

Implementing Interval Training
Beginning the Program
Interval Training Modes

Running and the Female Athlete

Training Endurance Athletes
Pain Site versus Pain Source
The Endurance Athlete's Program

Even though most sports are not aerobic in nature, aerobic capacity for players is stressed because people believe an efficient aerobic system promotes faster recovery.

An efficient aerobic system *will* facilitate faster recovery, but are we enhancing the recovery ability of an athlete we have made slower? At what cost are we developing the aerobic system and how are we going to do it?

Physiological principles tell us muscle fiber responds to training. Are we taking explosive anaerobic athletes and making them slower in our zeal to enhance their recovery ability?

Aerobic training is it is easy to perform and implement, particularly when compared with training for speed and power. It is much easier to demand volume and effort than for coaches to learn the finer points of speed and power development.

Most team sports have a highly anaerobic component that puts a tremendous stress on the adenosine triphosphate (ATP), phosphate creatine (ATP-PC) and lactic acid (LA) systems. During most games, players perform a series of three- to five-second sprints. Very rarely is a player actually running at a steady pace for any length of time.

It would appear the aerobic demand of the previously described sequence would be fairly low. However, the demands on the athlete's speed, speed endurance and acceleration would be high.

One of the major drawbacks of slow aerobic training is it may compromise speed at the cellular level. The adaptation of the muscle to aerobic training is in direct opposition to the primary needs of most athletes. Charlie Francis, in his book *Training for Speed,* makes a number of thought-provoking points regarding the training of the sprinter, and it's my contention all team sport athletes are really sprinters.

He wrote, "Enough power-related work must be done during the early years, ages thirteen to seventeen, to maintain genetically determined levels of white or power-related muscle fiber and promote the shift of transitional or intermediate fiber to white, power-related muscle fiber."

Francis further states, "Endurance work must be carefully limited to light or light to medium volumes to prevent the conversion of transitional or intermediate muscle fiber to red endurance muscle fiber."

This may be one of the most important statements about the training of an athlete you will ever read. These concepts have formed the essence of my cardiovascular philosophy for the last fifteen years, and are key to the long-term development of athletes both young and old.

For many players, particularly young developing players, any emphasis on aerobic conditioning through steady-state exercise is counterproductive.

Here's the key to making a kid lousy at sports: early endurance training. If you want a child to be slow, start endurance training as soon as you finish reading this. Older players, too, may be training themselves out of their sports by adhering to the aerobically oriented off-season programs of many sports' coaches.

A highly skilled player may not be as adversely affected as a marginal one. Marginal players at most levels generally have lower vertical jumps and lower anaerobic power than their more skilled counterparts. These players are already at a disadvantage that will only be magnified by an aerobically oriented training program.

We understand muscles are made up basically of three types of fibers: fast-twitch anaerobic, slow-twitch aerobic and intermediate. The ratio of fast-twitch fibers to slow-twitch fibers is one of the primary determinants of success in most sports. The best way to estimate fast-twitch capability is through vertical jump testing and ten-yard-dash testing.

Francis notes, "Young athletes who do not achieve high levels of oxygen uptake during a treadmill test but who perform well over ten- to forty-meter sprints probably have inherited a high proportion of white power-related muscle fiber."

Current theory leads coaches to assume athletes with low maximum oxygen consumption (Max VO2) values are out of shape. In fact, these athletes probably possess the exact quality coaches are looking for. At Boston University, many of our talented hockey players who went on to long NHL careers were the worst performers in tests used to evaluate aerobic capacity.

An athlete with a high vertical jump and poor aerobic capacity will be a better prospect for team sports than one with great aerobic capacity and poor explosive power. Athletes with predominantly fast-twitch fiber will excel in sprint-oriented sports, but will struggle in aerobic activities. Those with predominantly slow-twitch fiber will excel at endurance-oriented sports.

What happens to the intermediate fibers is a result of the training program chosen, *and a program emphasizing long aerobic workouts will cause the intermediate fibers to adapt to the characteristics of slow twitch.*

One emphasizing interval sprints from five to sixty seconds with longer recovery will promote the movement of intermediate fibers toward the anaerobic, fast-twitch fiber.

Conventional aerobic training — long, slow distance — should be done only as frequently as is absolutely necessary. Instead, the aerobic system should be developed as a by-product of anaerobic training. Anaerobic interval training will generally keep the recovery heart rate in the aerobic range of over 120 BPM if the intervals are done intensely enough.

This type of training will develop aerobic capacity, but as a by-product of the anaerobic work. This is obviously a more sport-specific method of training the aerobic capabilities of an anaerobic athlete.

Work Capacity Model

The conventional model of training espouses the development of conditioning in a pyramidal concept. Many experts in the fields of training believe the peak of conditioning can only be as high as the base allows. The base in theory is the development of a level of aerobic capacity onto which a series of anaerobic blocks could be placed. This is an architectural model based on a mechanical system that probably does not apply to exercise.

In all of my programming since the early '80s I have indicated the concept of aerobic base is flawed and the development of an aerobic base is counterproductive. Numerous studies have proven this over the past ten years, yet many continue to advocate a period of general aerobic training to develop the aerobic base.

What I propose is an inverted pyramid based on a work-capacity model. If our goal is to be able to go at a hard pace for thirty seconds, the model that makes sense is shown below. Although times could be changed to forty-five or sixty seconds, the concept would not change. It is far better to start small and develop conditioning than to endure the potential overuse injuries and negative fiber-type adaptations associated with endurance training.

It is significantly easier to get an explosive athlete in shape than it is to make an in-shape athlete explosive. The first will take weeks, the second may take years. Think about this statement as you design your conditioning programs.

Mark Verstegen likes to refer to conditioning as energy system development or ESD. In energy system development, we see the beginning of sport-specific training. When it comes to conditioning, training truly should be as sport-specific as possible. At a bare minimum, conditioning should at least be specific to groups of sports. When developing sport-specific conditioning programs, the key is to look at the field, the substitution patterns and the energetics of the game. It's not how far athletes run in a game, but at what pace and over what time period.

Work Capacity Model for Energy System Development

	Number of rep/repeats						Total time elapsed
Week 1-3	30 seconds	30 seconds	30 seconds				1:30 minutes
Week 2-4	30 seconds	30 seconds	30 seconds	30 seconds			2:00 minutes
Week 3-5	30 seconds	30 seconds	30 seconds	30 seconds	30 seconds		2:30 minutes
Week 4-6	30 seconds	30 seconds	30 seconds	30 seconds	30 seconds	30 seconds	3:00 minutes

Physiological versus Performance Testing

The unfortunate consensus in much of the sports world assumes the overall fitness of an athlete is based on his Max VO2. MVO2 is a standard measure of aerobic capacity originally intended to evaluate the condition of athletes involved in endurance sports. In the areas of conditioning and fitness testing, the influence of exercise physiologists is heavy, and this information tends to trickle down to all levels of sport.

There is at least one fatal flaw in using physiological data to evaluate the performance of athletes. Physiological data like MVO2 or various thresholds are measures of physiological variables, *not performance variables*. Physiological testing tells us something about the inner workings of the athlete, but not nearly enough.

Energy systems expert Paul Robbins, also of Athletes' Performance, refers to MVO2 as a measure of what someone *might* do. In sports conditioning and in the testing of conditioning, success is as much mental as it is physical. Our most aerobically fit athletes don't get the highest scores on performance tests. This means whether we use the yo-yo test, the 300-yard shuttle run or a two-mile run, we do not see any correlation to the physiological variables.

All testing should be performance-based for athletes because we want to see what they are capable of in head-to-head competition. I don't care if one athlete can use more oxygen or accumulate less lactate than another athlete; I want to see who will come in first when we line them up and test them. Athletes find physiological testing both frustrating and confusing because it rewards physiology over performance. If you are going to evaluate athletes, give them a chance to do what they do best, which is to compete.

In a physiological testing of our 2004 Boston University hockey players, the athlete who lasted the longest in the treadmill VO2 test scored a fifty-two. There were athletes who ran half as long and scored in the sixties. Do I tell the first athlete he is in poor shape when he watched the test and saw he ran twice as long as the guy who tested in better shape?

Hockey Conditioning Case Study
June 2004

Player one, 27 years old, five-year NHL vet, 5'10" 202 pounds
Player two, 28 years old, eight-year NHL vet, 5'10" 190 pounds

	Player One	*Player Two*
Peak VO2	51.5	53.1
Peak HR	172	181
AT VO2	48.4	41.5
AT HR	165	163
% Efficiency	93%	77%
One-minute Recovery	50 BPM	25 BPM

You may think I believe physiological testing to be a complete waste of time. On the contrary, we use the oxygen analyzer to perform VO2 testing on all our athletes. The better VO2 testing units on the market will provide an indication of anaerobic, lactate and ventilatory threshold, plus an actual maximum heart rate.

The entire concept of lactate as a factor in fatigue is very much in flux. Many top physiologists are unsure if what we see at threshold is actually the onset of anaerobic metabolism. In any case, we do know a ventilatory threshold occurs and this threshold signals some type of metabolic change.

Physiological testing has value, just not to evaluate fitness. The key seems to be not a high VO2 max, but rather a high threshold. This is a measure of efficiency. The question is not how much aerobic capability exists, but rather how much *usable* aerobic capability.

That evaluation is left to competitive testing in which the success or failure is obvious. The person who comes in first is in the best shape.

The case study on the previous page is an excellent illustration of my point.

This is an illustration of how VO2 stats can be misleading. Player one is clearly significantly more fit than player two, even though player two has a higher Peak VO2.

If we just looked at the Peak VO2 number, we would conclude player one was less fit than player two. However, player one is 93% efficient, while player two is only 77% efficient. Player one recovered fifty beats per minute in the first minute following the conclusion of the test, while player two recovered only twenty-five beats per minute.

This physiological data prompts a lot of questions. When asked, player two acknowledged doing a great deal of long steady-state training to raise his VO2 and lower his bodyfat. Player one trained cardio almost exclusively via interval training. The results in terms of thresholds and recovery speak for themselves.

Using Physiological Testing

Physiological testing, provided it is actual gas analysis, yields excellent data that can be used to help the athlete understand the cause and effect of training, and to design better training programs. It just should not be used as the measure of how fit or prepared an athlete is to play a sport.

The common target heart rate concept uses yet another flawed physiological assumption. For my eighteen- to twenty-two-year-old collegians, a theoretical target heart rate would be a max of 198-202. Our true range when tested was 180-211. When we do heart-rate-oriented training, the formulaic assumption of 220 minus age would result in overtraining for some and undertraining for others, a variance of up to twenty-two beats per minute. This is detailed more in the interval section on page 142.

Another trendy idea is to do blood lactate values. This also is a physiological measure and not a performance measurement. Athletes become frustrated when they perform well on performance testing and are then told they are out of shape based on a physiologist's analysis of data.

The key to your programming is to look at the demands of the sport and not just do what everyone else is doing, but to envision what would be the best test for your athletes at their levels. If you are working with young athletes, be even more careful because of the intermediate fiber type characteristics discussed earlier.

A final problem with testing of any type: *Athletes will train for the test.* If you want your athletes to train for speed and power but you test for aerobic capacity, you can rest assured your athletes will be training for aerobic capacity and not speed.

Specific Conditioning for Athletics

The areas of conditioning that need to be emphasized are muscular specificity and movement specificity, however very few programs address changes of direction as a vital component of sport conditioning. Most of the programs detailed in this section address change of direction as a key component of conditioning.

The ability to tolerate the muscular forces generated by accelerating and decelerating, and the ability to adapt to the additional metabolic stress caused by acceleration and deceleration are the real keys to conditioning. Deficiencies in these components are often why athletes feel they're not in game shape.

Many athletes train by running or worse, riding a stationary bike a set distance in a set amount of time with no thought to the additional stresses provided by the need to speed up and slow down. These are old-fashioned conditioning programs that operate on the oversimplified assumption that thirty seconds of exercise is always the same. Ask any athlete to perform a linear interval like a 220-yard run and a 150-yard shuttle run on a twenty-five-yard course. Then ask the athlete to compare the feeling. Most athletes will describe the shuttle run as being much more difficult.

Conditioning Injuries

Athletes are frequently injured in training camp settings even after following the coach's prescribed pre-camp conditioning program to the letter.

This is usually due to a program that ignores the three vital components of the conditioning process.

- Acceleration

- Deceleration

- Change of direction

Programs that force athletes to increase speed, decrease speed and change direction drastically reduce the incidence of early-season groin and hamstring injuries, and better prepare the athletes for the demands of an actual game or event.

Off-Season Conditioning

Tempo Runs

Begin an off-season running program with tempo runs. I have our athletes run 110 yards — the length of a football field from the end line to the opposite goal line — and then walk the width of the field. When the athletes reach the opposite sideline, they run the 110 yards back.

In tempo runs we expect them to run at seventy-five to eighty percent of the pace they would use if sprinting 110 yards. This pace would be about eighteen to twenty seconds for a hundred yards.

Over a three-week base phase, we begin at ten times 110 and work up to fourteen. Tempo runs get the body ready for the more aggressive intervals to follow. Running is essential in the off-season to counteract the negative postural changes of a full season spent bent over and forward flexed in many sports positions. Stationary cycling, on the other hand, reinforces the negative changes of the sports season by keeping the body in a flexed posture and not allowing the hips to extend.

Shuttle Intervals

Next in the off-season conditioning program is the progression to shuttle runs. The fundamental difference between tempo runs and shuttle runs is we begin to increase the muscular effect. Shuttle runs involve three key injury-prevention features: acceleration, deceleration and direction change.

One of the failures of track-based interval programs like 220s and 440s is these do not incorporate two of those three injury-prevention features. Injuries are most often associated with the muscular stresses caused by speeding up, slowing down or changing direction. Shuttle runs add a muscular component to the energy system program.

Begin with:

• 150 yards at twenty-five or thirty seconds, followed by a sixty-second rest. This can be done on either a twenty-five- or fifty-yard course. A twenty-five-yard course is more difficult, as it doubles the direction changes and the resulting acceleration and deceleration.

• Progress to 300 yards done in less than sixty seconds.

Bike Training

Interval training on the bike can be effective for older players who are unable to run due to wear and tear. Younger athletes tolerate running well, while older players' bodies are less conducive to running. Running will always be the preferred method, but the bike can be an adequate substitute.

Our athletes ride for twice the time interval as running. If the workout calls for six 150-yard sprints, approximately six thirty-second intervals, we substitute a bike program of six times one minute. In our case, we use Schwinn Airdynes to capitalize on the dual-action of upper and lower body, and ride half-miles.

Preseason Conditioning

Although I am generally opposed to training on a stationary bike in the off-season, my opinion changes in the preseason period. This may seem like a bit of a flip-flop, but in actuality it's logical. In preseason, the concern shifts to avoidance of muscle strains and overuse injuries. At this point, additional work may best be done on a stationary bike if the athletes are also training on the field, ice or on the court.

The rationale for not using a bike, or any incomplete hip-extension apparatus, is the hip extensors and flexors are not properly prepared for the rigors of high level movement such as running. Very often athletes who train on a bike, stairclimber or elliptical trainer will have the energy system ability to finish a session, but not the muscular ability. Most exercise machines do not require or even allow hip extension past neutral, and athletes who do not run don't properly develop the hip flexors or extensors.

On the opposite side, most of the recovery of the swing leg in biking is of a passive nature. The result of off-season training centered around a piece of exercise equipment instead of running is often a groin or hamstring strain during play. The muscles are simply not properly prepared for the stresses placed on them.

The same concept holds true with patella tendon issues in basketball. Most basketball players flirt with patella tendon or patella–femoral pain throughout the year. Additional running will aggravate these conditions. When levels of stress are high for either muscles or joints, as in preseason, additional conditioning may best be done on an alternative piece of equipment.

When training in the off-season, the opposite is true; training should center around running whenever possible.

Slideboard Training

The slideboard as a training tool was made popular in the 1980s by Olympic speedskater and current USA Hockey orthopedic surgeon, Eric Heiden. Speedskaters have been using the slideboard for a number of years to develop skate-specific conditioning and mechanics when ice surfaces are unavailable. In the past ten years, hockey players and other athletes began to use the slideboard as part of their off-season and preseason training.

All of our athletes, regardless of sport, perform lateral conditioning on the slideboard two times per week during a four-day work week.

The real use of the slideboard is to provide an excellent anaerobic endurance workout. You should manipulate the work-to-rest ratios to meet your athletes' needs.

Suggested Guidelines

Work interval: *15-30 seconds*
Number of intervals: *Begin with five*
Rest interval: *45 seconds to 1:30 minutes*
Length of workout: *10-50 minutes*

Work intervals longer than thirty seconds usually result in loss of technique and are recommended only for advanced athletes with great leg strength. Rest intervals should be two or three times the work interval.

We generally increase the number of work intervals or decrease the rest time rather than lengthen the time interval. A simple two day per week slideboard program is illustrated on the next page, and you'll find more detail in the slideboard training section on page 181.

Sample Slideboard Conditioning Program
Two Lateral Interval Days per Week
Number of intervals, work duration, then rest duration

	Day One	*Day Two*
Week 1	5x:30-1:30	6x:30-1:30
Week 2	7x:30-1:30	8x:30-1:30
Week 3	9x:30-1:30	10x:30-1:30
Week 4	7x:30-1:00	8x:30-1:00
Week 5	9x:30-1:00	10x:30-1:00
Week 6 *	7x:30-1:00	8x:30-1:00
Week 7	9x:30-1:00	10x:30-1:00

*At week six, add a ten-pound weight vest to all intervals

Dual-Action Bikes

For additional in-season conditioning work, I like the dual-action bikes from Schwinn or Ross for the following reasons.

• Dual-action bikes are excellent as they tend to mimic the combined arm and leg action of running or skating.

• The combination of arm and leg action produces a higher heart rate than pedaling alone.

Dual-action bikes provide directly accommodating resistance. This is another often overlooked aspect of the dual-action bike. The fan system delivers an equal and opposite reaction to the effort of the rider. There is no need to tighten a screw or to adjust the workload of the bike. The bike simply responds to the effort of the rider with greater air resistance.

The dual-action bike tells the rider not only how long he has ridden, but also how far. This allows for competitive opportunity in a team or small-group setting.

Twenty-Percent Rule

Conventional long, slow distance aerobic training may be done once or twice per week as an easy alternative to the more strenuous interval work. Time should not exceed forty minutes on these days. This is an excellent opportunity for athletes with joint problems to substitute the bike for a run. As has been clearly stated, do not spend extensive time periods developing the aerobic base. Training time and recovery ability is short, and most athletics are interval activities, not aerobic sports.

Coaches must look at the demands of the sport and the fitness of their players when implementing a conditioning program. We can't make blanket recommendations; training for athletics should be adjusted to prepare each player for the demands of the specific game.

One final thought when developing conditioning programs: Do not increase the total time or total distance run by more than twenty percent from week to week. A twenty-percent increase will keep your athletes continuing to improve conditioning without an increased risk of injury. In order to monitor this, it is important to calculate both total distance and total time.

Example
5 x150-yard shuttle run = 750 yards

Total time is approximately 2:30 of actual work time based on an estimate of thirty seconds per 150-yard shuttle.

In order to stay within the twenty-percent rule, the distance cannot increase by more than 150 yards, and the time by more than thirty seconds. This means you could either add an additional 150-yard shuttle or have your athlete perform one 300-yard sprint and four 150s. This would give a total time of three minutes and a total distance of 900 yards.

This twenty-percent rule is the key to injury prevention when designing conditioning programs.

Long Cardio versus Interval Training

Long, slow distance sounds like a torture method, "You've been sentenced to one year of long slow distance." I despise long, slow distance aerobic training. It is bad for women and it's bad for almost all athletes other than those who race for long periods of time or over long distances.

Most running injuries are of the overuse nature. Very little trauma occurs in the endurance world save the infrequent untimely meeting of runner and motorized vehicle. And when overuse is the problem, less is always the answer.

Conventional aerobic training is only good to get a person fit enough to tolerate interval training, or to serve as a break from interval sessions. Steady-state aerobics may be nothing more than the necessary precursor to any interval program.

Does that mean we've been lied to all these years? I think unintentionally, yes. The whole aerobic craze was a mistake. Long aerobic training is popular because it is easy to implement and because the media glorified it.

Interval training is hard. Interval training is uncomfortable. *Interval training is superior.*

Interval training develops aerobic capacity better than aerobic training. The fastest way to raise VO2 max, our standard measure of aerobic fitness, is through interval training. Look at the research; ask a physiologist: If you want to be more aerobically fit, steady-state aerobics is not the best way to get there.

Another benefit to interval training is the positive changes in the body that come about from interval work. Bottom line, sprinters have leaner bodies with a more aesthetically pleasing appearance than those who only do steady-state aerobic training. Those engaged in interval sports almost inadvertently develop a better body. In fact, sprinters generally have less bodyfat than the thinner distance athletes.

If that's true, why would anyone do long aerobic training? The truth is, I have no idea. I can't see the benefit, and that is why my athletes and clients almost never do aerobic training.

Interval Training Research

A recent study done on strength training showed resistance exercise reversed the genetic fingerprint of elderly people. "The genetic fingerprint was reversed to that of younger people — not entirely, but enough to say their genetic profile was more like that of young people than old people," wrote Simon Melov, director of genomics at the Buck Institute in Novato, California. Although this study actually looked at strength training, the concept could also apply to interval training. Interval training stresses not only the energy system, but also the muscular system.

Another study known as the Tabata study again demonstrated the benefits of interval training. Dr. Izumi Tabata compared moderate intensity endurance training at about seventy percent of VO2 max to high intensity intervals done at 170 percent of VO2 max. Dr. Tabata used a unique protocol of twenty seconds work to ten seconds rest, done in seven or eight bouts. This was basically a series of twenty-second intervals performed during a four-minute span.

Again, the results were nothing short of amazing. The 20/10 protocol improved the VO2 max and the anaerobic capabilities more than the steady-state program.

Further evidence for the superiority of higher intensity work can be found in the September/October 2006 issue of the *ACSM Journal,* wherein at the conclusion of his research Dr. David Swain stated:

> *"Running burns twice as many calories as walking."*

Do the math. Swain says a 136-pound person will burn fifty calories walking a mile, and proportionally more as the subject's weight increases. In other words, a 163-pound person — weighing twenty percent more — would burn twenty percent more calories; the expenditure goes from fifty to sixty calories, a twenty-percent increase.

Swain goes on to explain that running at seven miles per hour burns twice as many calories as walking at four mph. This means a runner burns a hundred calories in roughly eight-and-a-half minutes, or about eleven calories a minute. The walker at four miles per hour burns fifty calories in fifteen minutes, the time it takes to walk a mile at four miles per hour. That's less than four calories per minute of exercise.

Canadian researcher and sport scientist Martin Gibala, Associate Professor of Kinesiology at McMaster University in Canada, published a study in the *Journal of Physiology* comparing interval training to steady-state training. The study, although conducted over only a two-week period, looked at a twenty-minute interval program versus steady-state work ranging from 90 to 120 minutes. The interval work consisted of thirty-second sprints followed by four minutes of slow pedaling.

This would amount to two to two-and-half minutes of high-intensity work during a twenty-minute session as compared to 90-120 minutes in the heart rate zone for the distance group. The remarkable result: Subjects got the same improvement in oxygen utilization from both programs. What is amazing is the twenty-minute program only requires about two minutes and thirty seconds of actual work.

The study concluded both methods showed roughly the same improvement in the chosen marker of oxygen utilization. Each group worked out three times a week; the interval group exercised for a total elapsed time of one hour per week with six to seven-and-a-half minutes of intense exercise during that hour. The steady-state group exercised between four-and-a-half and six hours a week, yet the aerobic benefits were the same.

If time is an issue, interval training is the answer. The Gibala study only looked at aerobic capacity and not caloric expenditure or weight loss, but it's another huge boost for those who believe in the superiority of interval training. Athletes have known this for years; unfortunately, the fitness and medical communities continue to beat the long, slow distance drum.

Interval Training Programs

In the simplest sense, interval training is nothing more than a method of conditioning using alternating periods of work and rest. The complicated part of interval training is figuring out the rest and work ratios for individual athletes.

Athletes in team sports have used interval training for years to prepare for their sports, while the rest of the fitness world embraced conventional steady-state aerobic training. Savvy personal trainers are using concepts previously reserved for athletes to improve results in their fitness clients. Every day more people discover they don't need thirty or forty minutes a day on a piece of aerobic equipment to get lean or to get fit. Even better, the data actually shows less is more.

The popularity of interval training has even given it a new name in the literature, often referring to as High Intensity Interval Training (HIIT), and it is now the darling of the fat-loss and conditioning worlds.

Many modern fat-loss articles espouse the value of interval training for fat loss. In my normal process of professional reading, I read both Alwyn Cosgrove's *Afterburn* and Craig Ballantyne's *Turbo Training*. What struck me immediately was what these experts were recommending for fat loss looked remarkably like the programs we use for conditioning.

At the time I was reading these programs, I was also training members of the US Women's Olympic ice hockey team. All of the female athletes I worked with used steady-state cardio work as a weight-loss or weight-maintenance vehicle. I was diametrically opposed to this idea because steady-state cardiovascular work undermined the strength and power work we were doing in the weightroom. My policy became if they wanted to do extra work it would be only intervals, not as a fat-loss strategy, but rather as a slowness-prevention strategy.

A funny thing happened: The female athletes we prevented from doing steady-state cardiovascular work also began to get remarkably leaner. I didn't put two and two together until I read the Cosgrove and Ballantyne manuals and realized we were doing exactly what the fat-loss experts recommended: We had the women on a vigorous strength program, and they were doing lots of intervals.

The biggest side benefit of interval training is there's a tremendous aerobic workout without the boredom of long, steady-state bouts of exercise. We see superior results in both fitness and fat loss by incorporating interval training.

If the heart rate is maintained above the theoretical sixty-percent threshold proposed for aerobic training, the entire session is both aerobic and anaerobic. This is why we do almost no conventional aerobic training. All of our aerobic work is a by-product of our anaerobic work.

My clients get their heart rates in the recommended aerobic range for fifteen to twenty minutes, yet in some cases they do only five to seven minutes of actual work.

There are three major reasons people don't interval train.

• One, the media has drastically oversold the benefits of aerobic training in the same way they oversold the high-carb, low-fat diet.

• Two, intervals are hard. Aerobic training may be long and boring, but you don't end up lying on the floor panting for air.

• Three, people don't know where to begin with interval training.

Numbers two and three present the greatest problem even if we can overcome number one. The data on interval training sells interval training over aerobic training if anyone bothers to look. It's getting people to realize interval training doesn't initially have to be devastatingly hard, and describing how to construct an interval program that's difficult.

To understand how to perform HIIT in our programs, we need to understand exactly what interval training is. In the simplest sense, interval training is nothing more than a method of exercise that uses alternating periods of work and rest.

How much work do we do? How hard should we do it? How long should we rest before we do it again?

The field of exercise science is in a state of flux unlike anything we have seen in the last thirty years. There is a distinct lack of clarity in the former bedrock of exercise physiology. In the past, we had firm belief in concepts like anaerobic threshold and lactate threshold. But now, it seems the more we know, the more we don't know. The fact is we still know very little about exercise physiology.

Heart-Rate Elevation

Here are some things I do know that will help you with designing interval programs.

Shorter intervals produce less heart rate elevation, yet can feel as difficult as longer intervals. In other words, it's not simply about HR elevation.

Intervals of less than a minute don't elevate HR as significantly as longer intervals. This does not mean they are not beneficial, it only means the heart needs time to elevate.

Strangely enough, your athlete may not recover as rapidly from a shorter interval as from a longer interval when the recovery is viewed as a multiple of the work interval. In other words, a thirty-second sprint may require a one-minute recovery (2:1 rest to work) where a one-minute sprint might only require an additional thirty seconds (1.5:1 rest to work).

Shorter intervals of fifteen to sixty seconds have a higher muscular demand and a lower perceived cardiovascular demand. The cardiovascular demand may be perceived to be lower based on less elevation in heart rate.

Even though I am recommending heart rate as the best way to dictate interval training, heart rate may not tell the whole story.

Interval Training Methods

There are two primary methods of performing interval training. The first is the conventional work-to-rest method, and the second is heart-rate based using a monitor.

Work versus Rest

This technique uses a set time for work and a set time for rest. Ratios are determined, and the athlete rests for generally one, two or three times the length of the work interval before repeating the next bout. The big drawback to the work-to-rest method is time is arbitrary. We have no idea what is actually happening inside the body; we simply guess.

Rest-to-Work Ratio

The longer the interval, the shorter the rest as a percentage of the interval. In other words, short intervals with a high muscular demand will require longer rests when viewed as a percentage of the interval. Fifteen-second intervals will need at least a two to one (2:1) rest-to-work ratio. Three to one (3:1) will work better for beginners.

Interval rest recommendations are as follows:

- Fifteen seconds work — Beginners rest at least forty-five seconds (3:1), more advanced rest thirty seconds (2:1)

- Thirty seconds work — Rest one to one-and-a-half minutes (2:1 or 3:1)

- Sixty seconds work — Rest one to two minutes (1:1 or 2:1)

As the intervals get longer, the recovery time does not need to be as long as it relates to the interval. In other words, a two-minute interval may only need to be followed by a two-minute rest.

Heart Rate

With the mass production of heart rate monitors, we are no longer required to guess. The future of interval training lies with accurate, low-cost heart rate monitors. We don't look at time as a measure of recovery as we formerly did in our rest-to-work ratios; we are now looking at physiology.

It's important to understand the close relationship between heart rate and intensity. Although heart rate is not a direct and flawless measure of either intensity or recovery status, it is far better than simply choosing a time interval to rest.

To use the heart rate method, we select an appropriate recovery heart rate. In our case, we use sixty percent of theoretical max heart rate using the Karvonen method.

There's a big problem with the commonly used 220-minus-age maximum heart rate formula: At least seventy percent of the population does not fit into our theoretical calculations. Older athletes are even less inclined to fit the formula. It's not unusual to see our thirty-five-year-old athletes work in excess of 185 beats per minute. Assumptions based on the old formula can create significant program design issues if used to create conditioning programs.

The old formula doesn't fit a significant portion of the population, and it is not based on research. Even the developer of the famous formula says his thoughts were taken out of context.

The more accurate method is known as the Heart Rate Reserve Method, also called the Karvonen formula.

Karvonen Formula

The Karvonen formula looks at larger measures of fitness by incorporating the resting heart rate and is therefore less arbitrary. It looks like this:

Maximum heart rate minus resting heart rate times percent, plus resting heart rate (RHR) equals theoretical heart rate (THR)

Example: (200-60) x.8 +60 = 172

After a work interval of a predetermined time is completed, the recovery is set by the time it takes to return to the recovery heart rate.

When using heart rate response, the whole picture changes. Initial recovery in well-conditioned athletes and clients is often rapid. In fact, rest-to-work ratios may be less than 1:1 in the initial intervals. An example of a typical workout for a well-conditioned athlete is shown below.

Interval 1
Work 60 seconds, rest 45 seconds

Interval 2
Work 60 seconds, rest 60 seconds

Interval 3
Work 60 seconds, rest 75 seconds

Interval 4
Work 60 seconds, rest 90 seconds

In a conventional 2:1 ratio time-based program, the rest would have been too long for the first three intervals, rendering them less effective. The reverse may be true in a deconditioned client. I have seen young, deconditioned athletes need rest periods up to eight times as long as the work interval. I've seen clients who needed two minutes rest after a fifteen-second interval.

Implementing Interval Training

Most people visualize interval training as a track concept, but our preferred method of interval training is the stationary bike. Although running is the theoretical best mode of interval training, the facts are clear: Most adults are not fit enough to run.

In fact, statistics estimate sixty percent of those who begin a running program will be injured. In a fitness or personal training setting, that is entirely unacceptable. Women, based on the structure of the female body — wider hips, narrower knees — are potentially at even greater risk. Physical therapist Diane Lee says it best in her statement, "You can't run to get fit. You need to be fit to run."

Interval training can be done on any piece of cardio equipment. However, the most expeditious choice is a dual-action bike like the Schwinn Airdyne. An athlete can work really hard and not be injured on a stationary bike.

Fit individuals can choose any training mode, however the bike is the safest choice. In my mind, the worst choice might be elliptical trainers. Charles Staley has a concept he calls the 180 Principle: Staley advocates doing exactly the opposite of what you see everyone else doing. Walking on a treadmill and using an elliptical trainer seem to be the two most popular modes of training in a gym; my conclusion, supported by Staley's 180 Principle, is neither is of much use.

Many athletes avoid running due to knee problems. However, most knee pain is caused by distance running, not interval training. Interval work is usually tougher on the muscles and mind than on the joints. Many athletes who can interval train with no knee pain find the repeated foot strikes of jogging problematic. If for some reason the program calls for a steady-state run, which it rarely should, athletes with patella-femoral pain would be allowed to ride a stationary bike or use an elliptical trainer.

Although heart rate recovery is an excellent way to gauge fitness, recovery is clearly a variable based on intensity. Recovery is fairly consistent regardless of the length of interval if the interval is done at the same relative intensity.

Shorter, more intense intervals provide a greater stress to the recovery system while providing an apparently lower stress level to the cardiovascular system.

For shorter intervals heart rate is a somewhat imperfect indicator of intensity. The heart rate takes time to elevate, and a thirty-second sprint is not sufficient to push the heart rate of a trained individual to maximal levels.

This does not mean these intervals do not have value, only that the effect on the cardiovascular system may be different. Shorter intervals produce lower heart rates, yet seem to require a greater recovery period. This is an area that needs further study as we learn more about heart rate training.

Our knowledge of interval training, particularly as it applies to team sports, is in its infancy. We need to do additional work with heart rate monitors to begin to develop better interval protocols.

However, some simple recommendations can be made.

Resting time should increase slightly after each interval. A simple system would be to select a theoretical rest-to-work ratio and work up to it. A workout previously done with a time-based rest-to-work of two to one (2:1) would theoretically be as follows.

Interval 1
1:1 (30-second sprint, 30-second rest)

Interval 2
1:1.25 (30-second sprint, 38-second rest)

Interval 3
1:1.5 (30-second sprint, 45-second rest)

Interval 4
1:1.75 (30-second print, 53-second rest)

Interval 5
1:2 (30-second sprint, 60-second rest)

It is obvious this would not be practical.

A practical modification would be:

Interval 1
30-second sprint, 30-second rest

Intervals 2 and 3
30-second sprint, 45-second rest

Intervals 4 and 5
30-second sprint, 60-second rest

Beginning the Program

Deconditioned clients may need three weeks to a month of steady work to get ready for intervals. This is okay; plan for it and don't wipe out a beginner with interval training. Begin with a quality strength program and some steady-state cardiovascular work. This is a good use for steady-state work, preparing an athlete or client for the intervals to come.

For most sports, the majority of conditioning should be interval training done on a field, a slideboard, or for athletes with injury problems, a bike. Conditioning program effectiveness is tremendously increased if a heart rate monitor is used.

For our hockey players, we have gone to a system of self-paced interval training based on individual heart rate response.

The athletes are told:

- How many intervals to perform

- Whether or not they are attempting to train above their anaerobic threshold, as determined during their VO2 test

- How many beats of recovery heart rate they are to use

For an athlete with a threshold in the 160- to 170-beat-per-minute range, we recommend a forty-beat-per-minute recovery. For athletes with thresholds above 170, we recommend a fifty-beat-per-minute recovery period. Each athlete recovers at his own ability based on the reaction of his heart to training. This means some athletes may perform the majority of the workout at a 1:1 rest-to-work ratio, while others will be 2:1 or even 3:1.

Each athlete performs a self-paced workout, but cannot cheat due to the presence of the heart rate monitor. This insures we will not overtrain unfit athletes or undertrain fit athletes.

Think about an old-fashioned interval workout. Everyone would be told the distance to run, the time to run the distance, and the rest time. This is incredibly arbitrary. The assumption is the time of the work interval is all that matters.

In reality, the more fit athletes may be having an easy day, while the less fit athlete is actually working too hard. Basing the workout on actual recovery versus an arbitrary ratio of rest to work is more logical.

Interval Training Modes in Detail

Running

Running is the most effective, but is also the most likely to cause injury.

A combination of shuttle running (intensive) and tempo running (extensive) are best. Both can be done in standard rest-to-work format or with a heart rate monitor.

Shuttle runs have both high muscular demand because of acceleration and deceleration, and they also have a high metabolic demand.

Running is relative. Running straight ahead for thirty seconds is significantly easier than a thirty-second shuttle run.

Treadmill Running

The treadmill is a close second to ground-based running in both effectiveness and injury potential.

Getting on and off a moving treadmill is an athletic skill and an error can result in serious injury. Treadmill interval running is probably not for the average personal training client.

Treadmill speeds are deceiving. For example, ten miles per hour is only a six-minute mile, yet can feel very fast on a treadmill. However, ten MPH is not a difficult pace of intervals for a well-conditioned athlete.

- High-quality interval treadmills should go to fifteen MPH.

- Lack of true active hip extension may undertrain the hamstrings.

In treadmill running, the belt moves, while the athlete just stays airborne. Treadmill times do not translate well to running on the ground. This may be due to lack of ground-contact time.

Time-based: Try fifteen seconds on, with forty-five seconds off at seven MPH on a five-percent incline. When safety is a concern, decrease the speed and increase the incline.

Heart-rate based: (max HR of 200 used for example) — Use a fifteen-second sprint and rest until the heart rate returns to 120 beats per minute.

Rest is rest; don't allow the athlete to walk or jog, or the heart rate will lower more slowly.

Non-Motorized Treadmills

Another alternative is the non-motorized treadmill, like the new Woodway Speedboard. The concept of a treadmill that has no motor is not new, but the idea is gradually gaining acceptance in the performance world.

A company called Sprint manufactured a line of non-motorized treadmills that were well before their time; the Speedboard may still be before its time, however intelligent coaches will immediately see the value in non-motorized treadmills.

The non-motorized treadmill takes the major flaw out of treadmill running. The runner must now actively extend the hip to move the belt. This is a big leap forward for those in the Northeast who are forced indoors during tough winter weather.

Stationary Bike

- Probably the best safe tool

- Requires limited skill, low potential for overuse injury

Dual-action bikes like the Schwinn Airdyne produce a higher heart rate due to the combined action of the arms and legs. There is no better affordable option than the Airdyne. Although they require periodic maintenance, these are the perfect interval tools as they do not need adjustments to belts or knobs during training. The fan is an accommodating resistance device, meaning the harder the push, the more resistance in return.

If you have large-fan Airdynes, purchase and install windscreens. Most athletes dislike the large-fan Airdynes as they are unable to work up a sweat without the optional windscreen.

Use the same time recommendations as for the treadmill. Do not go all-out because this will seriously undermine the ability to repeat additional intervals. Levels should be adjusted down for fitness level and up for body size. Larger athletes will find the bike easier.

Large-fan Airdynes will have slightly different work levels than the newer, smaller-fan models.

Slideboard

The slideboard is the best bang for the buck after the Airdyne. Some question the effect of the slideboard on the knees, however there is nothing more than the anecdotal reports of a few writers to support this as an issue.

In a fitness setting there is a skill requirement. Clients must be warned they may fall and potentially be injured. This may sound stupid, but be sure to inform the client the board is slippery.

The slideboard provides the added benefits of a standing position and hip abductor and adductor work.

Slideboards are also great for groups. No adjustments between athletes are needed; you just need extra booties. We order four pair for every board.

Climbers and Ellipticals

The key to using any climbing device is to keep the hands and arms off of the equipment rails. This is critical: Put a heart rate monitor on your client, keep the hands off the rails and watch the heart rate skyrocket. If the client complains about lack of balance, slow the machine down and develop balance, but don't allow the client to hold on.

The StepMill is the least popular, and is the most effective. Conventional stairclimbers are easier to abuse than the StepMill. Many users ramp up the speed while allowing the arms to hold much of the bodyweight.

The elliptical machine is the most popular because it is easiest. This is nothing more than human nature at work. Discourage your client from using an elliptical trainer.

Running and the Female Athlete

Women who run successfully for long periods of time are structured to run. They look very much like male runners; good female runners generally do not look like plus-size models and they are usually not tall. It's not a question of cause and effect; it's a question of natural selection. You can't run to get a runner's body. It's actually the reverse: You have to have a runner's body to survive running.

This is simple anatomy and physics. No matter how hard you try or how well you eat, you can't change your skeleton. The problem with most women and the activity of running comes down to the Q angle, which boils down to this: Wider hips make for narrowness at the knees. Q angle looks at the inclination of the femur relative to the pelvis. The increased Q angle seen in most female athletes predisposes them to issues not found in male athletes. IT band issues, patella-femoral problems and problems with the plantar fascia can all be magnified by an increased Q angle.

This angle of hip to knee creates problems, and those are magnified by the number of steps taken. The average person gets about 1,500 foot strikes per mile; do the math on a five-mile run. Running produces forces in the area of two to five times bodyweight per foot contact. Do we need more math than that?

Let's go back to our elite female runner. Look at her body. You will generally see two things: She has narrow hips and she has small breasts. There may be exceptions, but at the elite level I doubt it. One thought process may be, "Great, my hips and breasts will decrease in size if I run." The other view is more logical: Women with larger breasts and wider hips don't make good runners. It's the same reason there are no large gymnasts or figure skaters... physics. Bigger people rotate slower. Natural selection rules.

What happens when a normal-sized woman begins to run? She becomes a statistic. She becomes a physical therapy client as she tries to shovel you-know-what against the tide. Her wider hips cause her to develop foot or knee problems. Her larger bodyweight causes greater ground reaction forces. Greater ground reaction forces stress muscle and breast tissue. The end result might be hurt and saggy instead of lean.

This is not a popular position, but the bottom line is distance running is not good for most women. If your female clients want higher intensity exercise, give them intervals on a stationary bike. Schedule them for a spin class, put them on rowers or stairclimbers, but don't send them out for a run.

The reality is in women *or* men, endurance training can lead to overuse injury. My point is the female bodytype puts women at greater risk.

Research has shown that six out of ten females who begin a distance running program will eventually be injured.

A study of Army recruits suggests greater amounts of running not only results in greater risks of injury, but in some instances may also impart no additional increase in fitness, a finding consistent with an earlier study of civilian runners.

On a typical women's basketball team, this translates to nine out of fifteen athletes potentially injured by a program of distance running. Factor in the size and weight of the typical female collegiate basketball player and we can safely assume this number goes up, not down.

It is tough to look at something you enjoy and realize it may not be good for you. As you have this conversation with some of your female athletes, they may not be happy to hear it. The purpose of this section is to promote a cautious, thoughtful attitude, not to stop those who are running pain-free from continuing the activity.

However, it is clear the majority of the women who take up running do so as a weight-loss or weight-control method. Running may be a poor exercise choice for weight loss as a participant and even worse, a poor recommendation for your client if you are a trainer.

Training Endurance Athletes

Training endurance athletes can be a gold mine for personal trainers and strength coaches if they understand the mentality. Endurance athletes have a lot of qualities that make them desirable clients. They are generally motivated, in need of help and often affluent. In addition, triathletes, runners and rowers far outnumber team sport athletes in the adult population.

The first question you need to ask yourself in order to understand the endurance athlete is why the client is an endurance athlete in the first place. The answer generally comes in one of four parts.

- Genetic predisposition, always been good at endurance activity

- Mental predisposition, always been a Type A personality

- Endurance training provides a competitive outlet for adults

- A combination of the above

This matters because personality characteristics and genetic predisposition are at first a positive factor, but can rapidly become a negative. High levels of motivation and drive can initially produce great results. However, often they also produce injuries.

Endurance training isn't good for adults, but no endurance athlete wants to hear that. This is what they do, and they are not about to change because you think the risk of injury is too high. If you can't change them, you might as well help them.

In order to train endurance athletes, you need to understand how they think. This involves something I call *The Endurance Cycle*.

The Endurance Cycle

Train... Injury... Rehab/PT...
Train... Injury... Rehab/PT...
Train... Injury... Rehab/PT...
Train... Injury... Rehab/PT...

The cycle is simple. Train hard until you get hurt. Call your physical therapist, who by now is a family friend, rest and repeat. This is so prevalent I have coined another term, The Endurance Conversation. This is a typical conversation overheard between two endurance athletes.

Endurance Athlete One:
"Are you training or injured?"

Endurance Athlete Two:
"Well, I just got over ____itis, and I've being running in the pool."

This may seem like a strange conversation, but between two endurance athletes, this is as common as others talking about the weather. Endurance athletes view injury as a reasonable expectation, and are not surprised when it happens.

The entire physical therapy profession owes a great debt to the early aerobic proponents of the '70s. As a kid growing up and playing sports, I had never heard of a physical therapist. Physical therapists were put on the map by endurance athletes and their conditions ending in *'itis*, what we now recognize as the chronic use injuries of *'osis*. Endurance athletes fueled the physical therapy boom, and today they continue to be some of the physical therapist's most regular patients.

Injury Progression, The Three *Is*

- *Ingestion*— Oral anti-inflammatories (no change in training)

- *Injection* — Anti-inflammatories like cortisone (no change in training)

- *Incision* — Surgery, the "let's take a look" option (followed by a mandatory long layoff)

When dealing with endurance athletes, the truth may be hard to say and even harder for them to hear: All non-traumatic injuries are training-related. All *'osis* conditions are caused by overuse. If you didn't fall off something or get hit by something, you did something wrong in training.

Ask an endurance athlete, and rarely will one admit he just did too much, too soon. Instead, blames goes on the shoes or some other inanimate object.

Pain Site versus Pain Source

The way our medical system is structured makes dealing with overuse injuries very difficult. Most doctors are trained in what could be called the trauma model. They repair a dislocated shoulder or reconstruct a damaged knee. Injuries like these are generally the result of an outside trauma impacting the joint.

With the endurance athlete, the pain develops over time, often as a result of a problem far removed from the site of the pain. Our current sports medicine system is still attempting to apply the trauma model to the overuse injury, with limited success.

In the trauma model, we use the three *Is* to attack the pain site. This results in lots of preventable knee, hip and back surgeries.

With endurance athletes, you need to understand pain is often felt at the attachment points like the patellar tendon and Achilles tendon, but the stress may be coming from somewhere else.

The solution for most endurance athletes is usually far removed from the point of pain. Poor glute function can make the front of the hip hurt. Foot and ankle problems can cause knee, back and hip problems.

As described more fully in the previous joint-by-joint section, we illustrate this for our athletes with a simple band example. Place a long elastic band around the athlete's neck and pull gently. Ask the athlete what he feels. What he feels will be pressure on the back of the neck. Now release the band. *Voilà!* The pain is gone. A pain in the neck disappears by letting go of a band being pulled from the front.

This example demonstrates why we should treat the pain *source* instead of the pain site. The big key in training an endurance athlete is to discover where the pain is coming from. Where it hurts is obvious, but if the athlete did not get hit, chances are the pain site and the pain source are separated by at least a foot's distance.

Reality Therapy

Reality therapy for an endurance athlete is tough but necessary. The first thing I say to an injured endurance athlete is the answer to the question *Does it hurt?* is yes or no. Any answer other than no is a yes. *It loosens up after a while, Not if I warm up properly*, or *Only at the end of my run/bike/swim* are all yes answers and are indications something is wrong.

An endurance athlete will never get better if he runs or bikes or swims with pain. This is the reality therapy so necessary with endurance athletes. *If it hurts, don't do it.*

You will never change an endurance athlete's personality, but you may be able to change the method of training.

Time and Money

A very wise man once told me you are going to spend time and money on your health. What endurance athletes need to understand is it's up to them to decide how and when. An endurance athlete can pay for a strength coach or personal trainer to develop a training program, or pay for physical therapy after the injury. The athlete can take a small layoff before something becomes a major issue, or take six weeks off after surgery. Healthy or hurt, the athlete gets to decide.

Speed limping is done at a price of both time and money.

The Endurance Athlete's Program

If I could make one change in every endurance athlete's training program, it would be to add more interval training. Endurance athletes love long, slow distance work. However, as discussed in depth earlier, interval training develops aerobic capacity better than long aerobic training.

The unfortunate truth is too much steady-state work yields too little benefit and too many injuries.

In endurance training, the emphasis is usually high on the quantity side and low on the quality side. This is the main mistake of endurance athletes in training.

With this being the case, why do endurance athletes continue to do large volumes of steady-state work? There are three basic reasons:

- They're good at it.

- It's easy to do.

- They've always been told they need to build an aerobic base.

Many endurance athletes avoid interval training because it is much harder. It's easy to throw on the shoes and do the same run done a hundred times before, or jump on the bike for the same ride. That does not make it the best way to train.

If I could make more changes, I would get my endurance athletes to buy a foam roller to work on tissue quality. Most endurance athletes' bodies are a mess of trigger points and other overuse injuries just waiting to arise. Regular soft tissue work followed by regular stretching would be time much better spent than logging more and more miles.

As noted in the soft tissue section, the key to understanding foam rolling and stretching is understanding the qualities of muscle tissue. Muscle tissue does not just get short, it also gets dense. Dense tissue must be manipulated by rolling or massage prior to stretching to get the maximum effect. In fact, stretching without rolling is like pulling on a knot in a shoelace. It only gets tighter.

The last, and maybe the most critical change, would be to get the endurance athlete on a strength program. For an endurance athlete, two days a week on well-designed strength work can be life-changing.

Vital for a strength coach or personal trainer is to realize the endurance athletes view strength training much like going to the dentist: They do not look forward to it.

Keep the program brief and basic. Think about what you read earlier in the joint mobility section; create mobile ankles, hips and thoracic spine through mobility work in the pre-workout warm-up. Work to stabilize the knees and lumbar spine through a good core and lower-body program. Keep strength work specific. Work on single-leg exercises primarily.

Lower-body lifting is key. Don't fall into the *running is enough for the lower body* trap. This could not be further from the truth. In strength training, I would rather see an endurance athlete neglect the upper body than the lower body.

A word of caution: *Make changes slowly.*

- Replace one weekly endurance session with an interval training session

- Get the athlete on a roller

- Add some stretching

- Start a strength program

Think about time spent versus potential benefit. Don't work on strengths. Think about volume versus intensity, quantity versus quality.

Final point: If you work with endurance athletes and haven't read Christopher McDougal's *Born to Run*, you really need to get a copy. If nothing else, it'll get you to pull your athletes out of their shoes.

Developing Athleticism

Power Development with Olympic Lifts
Technique Points
Coaching the Olympic Lifts
Cleans versus Snatches

Teaching Snatch Variations

Alternatives to Olympic Lifting

Testing Elasticity versus Power

Developing Elasticity

Training for Speed

Sprint Speed

Accuracy in Sprint Times

Speed or Acceleration?

Start Tips and Drills

Increasing Sprint Speeds

Sport-Specific Training

Balance and Instability Training

Losing Power with Age

Power Development with Olympic Lifts

Coaches are always looking for the best and safest method to develop power in their athletes. Power translates into faster, more explosive athletes. Meanwhile, evidence continues to mount showing the Olympic lifts are an effective way for athletes to rapidly improve power output.

Unfortunately, while growing numbers of coaches and athletes want to use the Olympic lifts or their variations, very few have the expertise necessary to teach or do the lifts well.

Teaching the Olympic Lifts

As strength and conditioning coaches working with high school, college and professional athletes, my associates and I use the Olympic variations almost every day with most athletes over the age of fourteen. When speaking at clinics for athletic trainers or high school coaches, we always start with one simple concept: Before adding any Olympic movements to your program, learn to perform the movements yourself, and then learn to teach them.

If you can't teach and supervise the Olympic lifts, don't use them. Just because the Olympic lifts are popular doesn't mean you should blindly insert cleans, snatches and push presses into your program. Instead, get your high-velocity training from medicine balls and plyometrics.

Although the Olympic lifts will result in impressive development of the musculature, this is not the primary objective. The Olympic lifts are most effective when used to train the nervous system to ultimately produce faster contractions, in addition to training the muscular system.

The objective is not just to move weight, but to move weight in a fluid and powerful manner. Don't just pile on weight, focus on technique.

The physiological characteristics that make great Olympic weightlifters — good lever system, mesomorphic body type, great hip flexibility — are not present in many of the athletes we deal with on a regular basis.

Your objective as a coach is to develop better athletes, not to develop Olympic lifters. Olympic weightlifting should be a means to an end, not an end in itself. Don't get caught up in designing a program for Olympic weightlifters; design a program in which athletes utilize Olympic lifts and their variations for power development.

Technique Points

Technique always comes first. When in doubt, reduce the weight, move a step back in the progression or select a simpler exercise.

Remember, if the back is flat, nothing bad can happen. Either too much rounding or too much arch can be a problem.

You are in charge; you select the weights, you terminate sets when exercises are done poorly.

Always stop at technical failure. This is not the point at which another rep cannot be done, but rather the point at which another perfect rep cannot be done.

Be picky: Require perfect form. An athlete lifting the proper amount of weight should have perfect form.

If you are unfamiliar with an athlete, start with a weight that can be done easily. It's easy to get athletes to go up in weight, hard to get them to take a step back. If you are going to make a mistake, make a conservative one.

For athletes who lack good postural musculature, first attend to technical development.

Watch for failure of stabilizers. Stabilizers will frequently fail before prime movers. Common mistakes are the loss of back position in squatting and the inability to return a cleaned weight to the hang position.

There is a thin line between conservative coaching and holding athletes back. Some athletes, usually men, will dislike being told to terminate a set at technical failure. Ingrain this concept early. Hold back in areas like squats and hang cleans that have large potential negative repercussions.

The key is to pick a weight heavy enough to require hip action, but light enough so the athlete doesn't muscle it. It really is a learned art.

Understand the difference between acts of omission versus those of commission. An act of omission is something you don't do; an act of commission is something you do. In exercises like squats and hang cleans, we don't want to commit errors. There is limited opportunity to correct a back injured by poor technique or poor weight selection.

Our progressions are based on time, with an understanding of mastery. Athletes or clients do not move forward without mastery.

Coaching the Olympic Lifts

These are logistical points to improve your ability to coach on the floor.

Always coach from behind the athlete when coaching Olympic lifts. If you are behind the athlete, you can reposition him with your hands and not be in danger of getting hit by the bar.

I like our coaches to be behind the lifter on the right-hand side, and to use their hands to draw the shoulders back, to reinforce lower back arch or to push the athlete forward to get the shoulders over the bar.

Coach squats from the side. This will allow you to see depth and back position, the two major keys in squatting.

Correct small errors. Be attentive to the details. Watch how the athlete picks up the bar or returns the bar to the blocks or the rack. Often a good set is spoiled by the athlete losing back position when returning the bar.

Reinforce constantly.

For explosive exercises, athletes should start and land in the same position. Inability to land in the start position indicates the exercise is too difficult, or the athlete lacks eccentric strength, or both.

Teaching Guidelines

Think safety first. Training plates and light bars make teaching the Olympic lifts easy.

Practice proper technique. This is basic: If it doesn't look right, it probably isn't. The objective is not just to move the bar from point A to point B. The objective is to move the bar from point A to point B in a technically correct manner. Compromising this point could compromise the safety of your athletes.

Emphasize speed of movement over the weight on the bar. Most of the technical mistakes made in teaching and learning the Olympic lifts are the result of one thing: too much weight. The battle between ego and common sense must be refereed by the trainer. Your best correction is often the most obvious: Reduce the weight.

Anyone can teach Olympic weightlifting if they possess common sense and the ability to recognize the fundamental positions. To be a good teacher of Olympic lifting, you must provide daily feedback in a positive manner, and you must be willing to consistently ask people to continue to improve their technique.

If you can't teach a lift, don't use it in your programs. This applies to all areas of your program, but particularly to Olympic lifting. If you can't teach the Olympic lifts, don't use them. Period. Work with your athletes on developing great technique and great bar speed and put less emphasis on the amount of weight lifted.

Using lifts you are not able to successfully teach is a classic coaching mistake. The reason many sports medicine professionals and many sport coaches think the Olympic lifts are unsafe is because coaches frequently place these exercises in the program without proper instruction and without constant supervision.

Get your high-velocity hip-extension training from medicine balls and plyometrics if you cannot teach and supervise your athletes in the Olympic lifts. Learn to balance theoretical benefit with practicality and safety. Before adding any explosive movements to your program, learn to teach the movements. Don't worry about weight, worry about technique.

Many coaches encourage athletes to Olympic lift or squat in an unsupervised environment, and athletes get injured. The squat or the clean is no more responsible for an injury than a car is for a car crash. Cars are safe when driven as directed; squats, cleans and snatches are safe when done as prescribed. The problem always lies in the instructions and implementation, not the exercises.

Olympic lifting requires constant supervision. Even if you are capable of teaching the Olympic lifts, ask yourself how much time you can spend in the weightroom teaching. If you are prepared and have the time to teach, by all means add Olympic movements to the program.

Your athletes will see great gains in power and will probably learn to enjoy the athleticism of Olympic lifting more than they enjoy conventional strength work.

Cleans versus Snatches

My opinion on teaching the Olympic lifts has changed significantly over the past few years. Although I am a big proponent of the hang clean, we see more and more athletes at the college and pro levels who do not have enough upper-body flexibility to properly rack the bar in the clean position. This results in very sloppy attempts to perform the hang clean and clean variations.

One solution proposed by some strength and conditioning coaches is to use dumbbell cleans for athletes who do not possess the flexibility to properly rack or catch the clean. My position is dumbbell cleans don't allow an athlete to handle the appropriate amount of weight. In addition, a dumbbell clean teaches a reverse-curl bar path not desirable in quality Olympic lifting.

Instead, we often use the dumbbell and barbell close-grip snatch with greater frequency for athletes who are inflexible through the wrists and shoulders.

Many coaches are afraid of the snatch because they have never performed it and have only seen it performed by Olympic weightlifters. When performed with a wide grip, the snatch can place the athlete's shoulder joint in an abducted and externally rotated position that could be compromising.

For this reason, I am an advocate of a modification of the classical snatch: Our athletes initially learn a one-arm dumbbell snatch and then a close-grip snatch, and we have never experienced shoulder problems from them.

The one-arm dumbbell snatch is actually an exceptional exercise to prevent shoulder injury. It develops unilateral shoulder stability as well as trunk stability, and it is probably the easiest of the Olympic lifts to teach and learn.

Many coaches disagree with the idea it's easier to teach athletes to snatch than clean. The coaches who disagree have often never tried to teach their athletes to snatch, and don't use snatches in their program.

Many athletes, particularly those who have been on a mirror-oriented program, will have decreased flexibility in the shoulder, elbow and wrist. To perform the close-grip snatch, they don't need to be very flexible in the shoulders, elbows or wrists; they simply need to be able to get their arms overhead.

When I encounter an athlete who cannot get into the proper catch position for the clean, I go right to teaching the snatch and forget about the clean.

Often if I have athletes who have experienced low back pain, I only use snatches for power work. Snatches will generally use loads of fifty to sixty percent of the athlete's hang clean, and as a result will place much less stress on the low back.

For many athletes the finish position of the snatch places less stress on the low back than the stress placed on a tight athlete trying to raise the elbows into the proper position to catch the clean.

Teaching the One-Arm Dumbbell Snatch

Step One

The start position for the dumbbell snatch is the basic pulling position. The athlete stands with the feet slightly wider than shoulder-width apart, knees slightly bent. The dumbbell is between the knees, chest over the dumbbell. Wrist is curled under, arm straight, and the elbow is turned out.

Step Two

From the start position with the dumbbell between the knees, have the athlete jump, shrug and catch the dumbbell in the overhead support position. It's helpful to cue the athlete with the instructions *Try to hit the ceiling with the dumbbell* and *Pull it as if you were going to let go.*

Teaching the Close-Grip Barbell Snatch

The close-grip barbell snatch uses a grip identical to that of the hang clean. The wide grip generally taught for the snatch is discouraged, as its only true purpose is to allow the athlete to lift more weight.

Have your athlete practice the overhead support position with a shoulder-width grip. Keep the bar over the back of the head, knees bent and back arched. While executing the snatch, again have the athlete visualize trying to pull the bar up to hit the ceiling.

Begin by teaching the one-arm dumbbell snatch and proceed to the close-grip snatch with the bar, and you'll be amazed at how proficient your athletes will become at a lift you may have initially felt was too difficult.

The easiest way to teach the Olympic lifts is from a hang position, with the bar above the knees. This position eliminates a great deal of the lower back stress often associated with the Olympic lifts. Many athletes have difficulty learning the lifts from the floor, but any athlete can become a great technician from the hang position.

The Hang Clean and Close-Grip Snatch

The hang clean and close-grip snatch are the easiest variations of the two true Olympic lifts to learn. Other similar maneuvers are variations of these two basic lifts and can easily be taught after these have been perfected.

Before proceeding, first review with the athlete how to properly pick up and put down the bar. Most importantly, the back should be arched and tight. Then review the basic positions of the hand and overhead positions and put it all together.

Now the athlete is ready to perform the hang clean. To move into the hang clean from the start position, have the athlete slide the bar down the thighs, stressing trunk flexion, not knee flexion. Next, instruct the jump, shrug and catch, with the bar ending in the front squat position.

The final exercise is the close-grip snatch. By this point, the athlete should have an excellent sense of the overhead support position. To execute the snatch, have the athlete envision trying to throw the bar up to hit the ceiling. Completing the move, the athlete should keep the bar over the back of the head with a shoulder-width grip, knees bent and back arched.

Finally, work with the athlete on returning the bar properly to the floor or blocks. Make sure the back is arched when putting the bar down. The lift doesn't end until the bar is on the floor.; we regularly stress this important point.

Hang Clean to Bodyweight Relationship in Men

Excellent	Good	Fair	Poor
1.5 x BW	1.3-1.4 x BW	1.1-1.2 x BW	1 x BW

Hang Snatch to Bodyweight Relationship in Men

Excellent	Good	Fair	Poor
.9 x BW	.8 x BW	.7 x BW	.6 x BW

These numbers may be less accurate for larger athletes like football linemen. Football linemen generally do not have great strength-to-bodyweight ratios or power-to-bodyweight ratios. Another area to consider is the strength-to-power ratio. Many athletes will have a large strength focus and a poor strength-to-power ratio.

Strength to Power Ratio (Hang Clean to Front Squat)

Excellent	Good	Fair	Poor
.75	.7	.6	.5

Alternatives to Olympic Lifting

Many coaches are not comfortable teaching their athletes to Olympic lift, but athletes need increases in hip and leg power. For these coaches, jump squats may be an answer. Jump squats have been popular for years with European track-and-field athletes. They provide a great deal of the hip power many athletes seek from Olympic lifting, and are perfect for coaches who have reservations about technique or for athletes with shoulder or back problems that prevent them from Olympic lifting.

The jump squat is simply a jump from a position slightly above full squat depth. Beginners can land and stabilize between jumps, and advanced athletes can utilize a plyometric response off the floor.

The most important issue for jump squats is load selection. Authors and researchers have recommended using a percentage of the back squat one-rep max as a load, most often twenty-five percent.

However, this method of loading is potentially dangerous as it does not take into account the athlete's bodyweight. The following example illustrates this point.

If one athlete has a one-rep max in the back squat of 500 pounds and a second athlete also has a one-rep max of 500 pounds, both would use 125 pounds for jumps squats using the guideline of twenty-five percent of the back squat max.

Now assume athlete one weighs 200 pounds and athlete two weighs 350 pounds. Obviously, athlete one has a strength–to–body weight ratio far superior to that of athlete two. Loading athlete one with 125 pounds may be reasonable, but athlete two, who weighs 350 pounds, would probably have difficulty executing a technically sound jump squat with an additional load of 125 pounds. Athlete two may even have difficulty performing jump squats with just bodyweight due to his strength–to–bodyweight ratio.

Instead of a one-rep max percentage, use the following formula.

Squat plus bodyweight times .4, minus bodyweight equals jump squat weight

Athlete one: [(500 + 200) x .4] – 200 = 80
Athlete two: [(500 + 350) x .4] – 350 = –10

The example shows the 350-pound athlete gets sufficient loading from performing jump squats with bodyweight, but would be overloaded by the 125 pounds of the one-rep-max percentage guideline. For athlete one, a load of eighty pounds is sufficient.

Consider the total weight an athlete can squat as the combination of his bodyweight plus the weight on the bar, and use this number to calculate the load for jump squats. This guideline can be used by both weaker athletes looking to develop power and by larger athletes who have strength-to-bodyweight issues.

Whether you choose to develop leg power through Olympic lifting or by performing jump squats, the use of external loads to train the legs and hips can be the fastest way to achieve gains in speed or jumping ability. The beauty of Olympic lifts and jump squats is the athlete can develop power without necessarily developing large amounts of muscle. The emphasis is on the nervous system, not the muscular system, making this an excellent training method for all athletes.

Many athletes and coaches have the mistaken impression explosive lifting is for football players only. This could not be further from the truth. Olympic lifting and its variations are suitable for athletes in all sports and of all sizes, and are of particular interest to athletes looking for total-body strength without increases in size.

Olympic lifting is fun, safe and challenging when done correctly and supervised aggressively. Work on developing great technicians. This will lead to improvements in power and athleticism you may not have guessed were possible.

Testing Elasticity versus Power

What I'm about to describe has changed the design of my training programs with regard to the elasticity and power elements vital in athletics.

In evaluating power in athletes, an article about five-jump testing led me to look at the information that came with my Just Jump vertical jump testing device. The Just Jump is a force platform of sorts that measures time in the air and converts the time figure to a vertical jump number. The longer the time between the two contacts, the higher the athlete went vertically; there is complex math involved of which I am blissfully unaware.

I like the Just Jump more than the Vertec, another commonly used vertical jump testing device, primarily because it is faster and easier to use. However, the Just Jump, like the Vertec, has its drawbacks. Athletes will quickly learn to cheat on the Just Jump, just as they do on the Vertec. Still, it's a relatively valid and reliable tool when used correctly.

Although the article referenced five jumps, the software in the Just Jump only includes a four-jump test, which provides three pieces of data. The first is a measure of contact time, how long the athlete is on the mat. The second is what the manufacturer calls the ELPF, or Explosive Leg Power Factor. This is a measure of the athlete's power output.

The third piece of data is the average jump over the four trials. The power factor is calculated by dividing the time spent on the mat by the time spent in the air. The shorter the contact time and the higher the jump, the higher the power output.

I tested my athletes with no real expectations, but with the hope the data would lead to some useful information. Instead, the information obtained made me rethink how we train for power and will greatly impact the future training of our athletes. This became what I now believe will be another quantum leap in athletic training.

To supply some background, the athletes tested were Division 1 hockey players. The average vertical jump in the group was approximately twenty-five inches. I was curious why some of our best players and best skaters, athletes who were explosive on-ice, were below average in the vertical jump.

One player, who in my mind was one of our most talented, had a season-ending vertical jump of twenty-one-point-eight inches, not exactly Division 1 material at first glance. This is where the data gets interesting. One of the things I hoped I would see from a four-jump test was an explanation of why some of these athletes with what seemed to be poor power outputs could still be exceptional performers.

Example Athlete

Vertical jump, 21.8

Four-jump average, 19.5

Elasticity rating, .89%

I divided the athletes' vertical jumps by the average jump score of the four-jump test to get an elasticity rating, basically a measure of efficiency. What I am calling the elasticity rating is a measure of how well an athlete uses explosive power.

Due to equipment and testing constraints, we have been forced to estimate power in sports that feature multiple ground reactions by measuring one ground reaction.

We then surmised this power output — basically a vertical jump or standing long jump — was indicative of reactivity as well as power.

Mark Verstegen uses the term elasticity to describe what I previously called power. When I think elastic in an athletic sense, I think of an explosive athlete. I then assume a high vertical jump, the assumption being an athlete with a high vertical jump is both explosive and elastic.

Our new data seemed to indicate otherwise. Some of the athletes were explosive, but not elastic. These athletes were able to produce a single powerful explosive contraction when given an unlimited amount of time to produce force.

Surprisingly, this did not necessarily transfer well to a multi-jump, multiple-ground-reaction situation. Other athletes were not as explosive, but were far more elastic. The athlete I described above as athlete one was not powerful, but was elastic. He was able to store and release his somewhat limited power with great effectiveness.

Much like a ball bouncing, this athlete was able to react positively to the ground in a repeated fashion.

Developing Elasticity

The take-away point of that Just Jump testing is we must simultaneously train for both power and elasticity, because power does not equal elasticity. Obviously, those with greater power have more capacity for producing greater elastic response, but in keeping with our specificity concept, these are related but not synonymous.

The key is to meld the training we use to develop power with the need to learn and practice elasticity.

The solution for us is to use the Just Jump as a training tool as well as a testing tool. I purchased three additional units; twice a week in addition to our plyometric progressions, we now do elasticity work with instantaneous feedback provided by the jump tester.

Prior to obtaining this data, our athletes performed an Olympic movement for power development every day. We now perform our Olympic exercises twice each week, and twice weekly we train by in effect taking the four-jump test.

The athletes are encouraged to work to increase the ELPF — the explosive leg power factor — and to improve elasticity as well as power. In essence we now have two power days and two elasticity days.

We do this for the first two phases of our off-season program. This is done because the primary emphasis of our first two plyometric phases is on eccentric control in jumping.

My goal is to have the athletes better prepared for phases three and four of plyometric training by developing elasticity with the four-jump test. In phase three and four of our plyometric program, we begin to train for elasticity.

Bottom line: Test some athletes. Take a look at those who are succeeding with what you might consider limited explosive power based on numbers like vertical jump or one-rep-max Olympic lifts. Then check the elasticity of these athletes and see if they are more elastic than explosive. You will be convinced we need to train for power and elasticity as separate but related concepts.

Training for Speed

At our facility, when we test speed, regardless of sport, we test the ten-yard dash. To be specific, what we really evaluate with tests like the forty-yard dash is acceleration. The best sprinters in the world accelerate for up to sixty meters. This means in a world-class sprint race, each ten-yard split continues to get lower up to sixty meters. A forty-yard dash is a test of acceleration ability not speed if we want to get our physics right.

Our only athletes who ever run a forty-yard dash are NFL Combine or Pro Day athletes. Even these athletes only run the forty at the actual events. We never run a forty in training. In fact, over eighty percent of our training is done for ten yards, working to increase power and decrease steps. Less than twenty percent is done for fifteen or twenty yards.

In over twenty years of training athletes for the Combine, I have never had an athlete run a forty-yard dash prior to being tested by a pro scout. In spite of this, or perhaps because of it, my athletes have routinely tested well at the Combine, and many years we have had the fastest athlete at a given position. My hesitance to run a forty prior to the Combine or the Pro day was based on a simple concept: If an athlete is injured, he can't run the forty on the day it really matters. In the NFL evaluation process, injuries at the wrong time can be career-killers.

One problem arises with this philosophy. Athletes want to know what they will run in the forty. In order to increase the ability to project forty-yard-dash times from ten-yard-dash times, I studied the segmental breakdowns of the forty from past NFL Combines to see if there was discernible pattern, analyzing the data to see if there was a consistent formula to apply.

The results were surprising.

Initially the ten-yard dash was the focus of our training primarily because the most frequent injury seen in athletes doing Combine or Pro Day prep work is a hamstring strain. In fact, hamstring strains are the most consistent injury seen in all sprinters. These hamstring strains are almost always the result of running repeat forty-yard dashes in preparation for the testing. I have never seen a strain occur in a ten-yard dash; the ten-yard dash is a great test and close to one-hundred-percent safe.

In addition to the injury reduction angle, we have always concentrated on the ten-yard dash for the simple reason the first ten-yard segment — the start, if you will — is the easiest area to improve. The first ten-yard segment, although equal in length to each following ten-yard segment, takes more than one-and-a-half times as long to run.

This may seem obvious as this is the zero-to-sixty phase of the vaunted forty-yard dash. To really understand the significance, it is important to look at some data.

Below is a comparison of two athletes from the 2003 NFL Combine in the forty-yard dash. Athlete one is 188 pounds and ran a very respectable 4.59. Athlete two is 236 pounds and ran a 4.70, also a respectable time for a 236-pound athlete.

2003 NFL Combine

Distance	Athlete One Bodyweight 188	Athlete Two Bodyweight 236
10 yard	1.59	1.70
10-20	1.06	1.05
20 yard	2.65	2.75
20-40	1.94	1.95
40 yard	4.59	4.70

The data gets significantly more interesting when broken down into ten-yard segments, doesn't it?

When looking at the data, one thing immediately jumps out. Both athletes ran from ten to twenty, twenty to forty and ten to forty in nearly identical times. Athlete one obtained the entire differential in the times — eleven tenths — during the first ten-yard segment. Athlete one may not be faster; he simply accelerates better. His speed is no greater; however, his initial acceleration is significantly better.

This graphically demonstrates how critical the initial rate of acceleration was in the race. Athlete one obviously has less inertia to overcome and as a result accelerates faster, but this faster initial acceleration corresponds exactly to the difference in forty-yard-dash times.

This definitely reinforces my feeling about the importance of the start and of the first ten-yard segment, and the result reinforces the importance of strength development in improving forty-yard-dash performance.

You may think this is a generalization, and it is, but it's a generalization based on common sense. Smaller athletes with exceptional acceleration have run as low as 2.8 from ten to forty, while exceptionally large athletes, those above 300 pounds, were shown to run as high as 3.4. However, these were extreme cases.

In general, to estimate forty-yard-dash times from ten-yard times, you can calculate it as follows.

• For athletes under 200 pounds, assume a low of 2.8 seconds and a high of 3.0 seconds added to the ten-yard time.

• For athletes from 200-250, add 3.0 to 3.2 seconds to the ten.

• For athletes 250-350, add 3.0 to 3.4 seconds to the ten.

In any case, the data clearly shows working on the initial ten-yard segment of the forty-yard dash is both the safest and the fastest route to lowering the forty time.

Sprint Speed

Speed is the stuff of urban legend. Deion Sanders supposedly showed up at the NFL Combine, ran a 4.2 and went home. We routinely hear of high school kids who purportedly run 4.3s and 4.4s. The stories of reported speed have gotten out of control. This would not be a problem in and of itself. Most of us could look at it and say, "So what? People lie or embellish. "

The real problem is the lies seem to be setting the standards. One of the reasons I don't like to train athletes for the NFL Combine is the unrealistic expectations of athletes and agents based on these stories, or resulting from the occasional freakish performance like Vernon Davis.

Davis measured 6'3" weighing 263 pounds, and ran a 4.38 forty and vertical jumped forty inches. Those are insane stats.

Every year it seems there is some freakish performance by an athlete who raises the bar of expectation. I would have less of a problem if these expectations were not trickling down to high school kids. My intention is to set the record straight with facts. In order to prove this, I pored over the NFL Combine results for the six years I had on file. The statistics on the following page are taken directly from Combine results.

Although the Combine times are considered electronic, they are closer to handheld than electronic. This is an important factor in the speed legend stories.

There are three potential timing options.

Electronic Start, Electronic Finish

This should be the standard, but unfortunately it's not. The start is done with a touch pad and the finish with a photocell. This is the most accurate, and as a result yields the slowest times. An electronic start, electronic finish time has been shown to be twenty-two tenths of a second slower than a handheld forty-yard dash.

Hand Start, Electronic Finish

This is a system used uniquely at the NFL Combine. A hand start, electronic finish will be approximately a tenth of a second slower than a handheld forty-yard dash. In the Combine, the use of a hand start will be particularly evident in the faster ten-yard-dash times.

Athletes will run ten-yard times much closer to a handheld, but times at each following split will be closer to the electronic time.

Hand Start, Hand Finish

This results in the fastest and least accurate times. Handheld times are clearly more prone to human error. Many of the legendary times were handheld timing, combined with human error or human expectation.

Accuracy in Sprint Times

At the NFL Combine in 1996-1998, 2001, 2003 and 2006, no one ran a 4.2. No one. Not one person.

In 2001 Ladainian Tomlinson ran one 4.36, and five in the 4.4s. 2003 was a fast year, yet still produced no 4.2s. Ten athletes ran 4.3s in 2003. The heaviest was a 223-pound running back. The Combine track is always said to be slow, but the truth is it is simply accurate. All of the supposed fast times seem to be run at times when no independent verification is available. Seems a bit curious, doesn't it?

Here's another angle on the whole speed thing. Ben Johnson and Carl Lewis ran split times of 4.67 for forty meters. The split times are below.

1.84 Ten meters

2.86 Twenty meters (1.02 split)

3.8 Thirty meters (.94 split)

4.67 Forty meters (.87 split)

Forty meters is 43.74 yards. This would make the distance approximately ten percent farther. We could reduce the time by approximately thirty-six tenths to account for the additional 3.7 yards. This would mean in constant acceleration mode the best sprinters in the history of the world — *using blocks* — ran 4.31 for forty yards.

Does it seem plausible high school football players can run faster times without blocks?

In 2006 of nineteen running backs listed in the unofficial internet Combine report, Maurice Drew of UCLA had the only 4.3 and he ran a 4.39. In other words, one running back ran under 4.4, and he did it by one one-hundredth. Four wide receivers out of thirty-one ran under 4.4; in fact, five ran over 4.6. This means more wide receivers ran over 4.6 than under 4.4.

2006 was an exceptional year for defensive backs with nine sub-4.4s. The key, again in 2006, was there were no 4.2s in the results I saw. In 2005 I believe one athlete actually ran a 4.2, although I did not have those stats available. One athlete in a decade.

As coaches, we need to stop perpetuating the myths. We need to tell our athletes what the average at the NFL Combine was and not what the best freak times were. We need to further explain to them it is unrealistic to expect to even meet the NFL averages. As with everything in our society, we have raised the bar unrealistically high. Let's be honest with ourselves and with our athletes.

The reality is most athletes are looking to reduce the forty-yard-dash time by as little as one- or two-tenths of a second.

In an elite-level race that takes from 4.3 to 5.3 seconds to complete, the first ten-yard segment takes the longest time and by default is the easiest to impact. Ten-yard dash times range from one-and-a-half to two seconds, each proceeding ten-yard segment taking roughly one to one-point-one second to complete. By simply improving performance in the initial ten-yards, we can easily take off the elusive tenth of a second from our athletes' times.

First Step or First Push

The forty-yard dash should be run in approximately seventeen steps. Simple. An athlete with a normal stride length will measure out at about seven-and-a-half feet. This means a reasonably good sprinter will cover fifteen feet, or five yards, every two steps.

The big key to the forty-yard dash is to get the athlete to develop stride length in the first ten-yard segment by pushing, not overreaching. The first five-yard segment should take three steps; the remaining seven segments would take two steps each for a total of seventeen steps. Is seventeen the magic number? No. The key is to teach athletes to push, not reach, and to minimize stutter steps.

Speed or Acceleration

In the year 2000, *The Journal of Applied Physiology* published research in an article called *Mechanical Basis of Human Running Speed*. The article synopsis begins with the line, "Faster top running speeds are achieved with greater ground forces, not more rapid leg movements." This became known as the Weyland study after the lead researcher, Peter Weyland.

To further validate Weyland's work, think about the term "having a great first step." In reality it should be *has a great first push*.

Get yourself in a starting position. Take a step. Don't push, just step. Do you really go anywhere?

First step is really a function of first push, not vice versa. This is nothing more than physics. Those who can produce the greatest force into the ground — the action — will yield the greatest benefit from the ground — the reaction.

Weyland's research clearly indicates front-side mechanics and what many work on with high-knee drills are not nearly as relevant as what happens behind the body as force is transmitted into the ground.

• We try to get our athletes to master three steps for five yards and five steps for ten yards, and to do it without a reaching action.

• We continue to emphasize stride length as a function of back-side action-reaction and not front-side reach.

• We teach push, with no emphasis on stride length from the front-side mechanics.

• We never do B-skip-type drills, as these teach improper mechanics and are not appropriate for forty-yard sprinters.

Most track coaches and unfortunately, many performance coaches, spend an inordinate amount of time on A and B drills. We use these strictly as warm-ups and have really minimized the time spent on mechanics. I have replaced the block of time usually spent on trying to teach pretty running with really heavy sled work, which we refer to as a sport-specific leg press.

I have seen lots of slow people with great sprint mechanics who do not have the capability of putting force into the ground. There is a reason for the strong correlation between vertical jump and sprint speed: *Both are a function of force into the ground.* A strong athlete with poor mechanics will usually beat a weak athlete with great form.

Here are the keys to the first ten yards.

Is the athlete moving quickly or does he look like he's moving quickly?

Many athletes come out of the start with great turnover and go nowhere. Often these athletes look fast and run slow. Generally these are fast-twitch athletes who do not like the weightroom.

The great accelerators often look slow coming out because they are producing great force and minimized steps. Running is all about action and reaction. Force placed into the ground produces forward motion, very simple. The start is clearly not about turnover or frequency, but about force into the ground.

This is the reason there is such a strong correlation between the vertical jump and forty-yard-dash times. When an athlete applies force into the ground, the ground returns force back in an equal and opposite manner. More force, more vertical displacement.

Have you timed your athletes for a ten- and twenty-yard dash?

Try being objective versus subjective. Time your athletes not just in the forty, but also in the ten and twenty. One-and-a-half seconds handheld is fast for adult men. One-point-eight is average for a ten.

Next, video the ten-yard dash and the twenty-yard dash.

See how many steps it takes the athlete to run ten and twenty yards. This will tell you if you have an athlete who is moving the feet but not applying any force. A good sprinter will run the ten in five or six steps and the twenty in nine or ten steps. Don't tell the athlete to cut down steps; telling an athlete you are counting steps will cause over-striding. Tell the athlete to push the ground as hard as possible.

Look at the video and analyze the first step.

Does the athlete gain ground? Here's a good indicator of a powerful start: The foot taking the second step does not touch the ground while the front foot is still on the line.

In other words, after step one you should not see two feet in contact with the ground.

You will be amazed at how many athletes *step out* of the start instead of *pushing out* of the start. Just as we confuse speed and acceleration, we often confuse first step and first push. A quick first step does nothing; it is the push that creates the action-reaction, not the step. What you want is great push, not a great step.

This also relates to stride length. Stride length is accomplished by great forces placed into the ground, not by things like knee lift.

Another indicator the athlete is beginning to understand powerful starts is the appearance of falling forward out of the start, almost out of control. I tell my athletes to drive themselves out of the start so aggressively they almost fall flat on their faces. I cheer if they look like they are about to fall, as it shows me an aggressive push.

Time each test three times.

Either average all three or take the middle, throwing out the high and low. You don't want to record a mistake.

Electronic timers don't make mistakes unless there is a malfunction. Throw out scores that are obviously wrong.

- The weight is on the front hand and foot. This is not track. There is no block. The back foot is minimally helpful.

- The hips are low; don't let the athlete raise the butt. It's not possible to push out from straight legs.

- Never take instructions from a track coach on forty technique. They use blocks, and your non-track athletes don't have them.

- Eyes are between the hand and the foot. Make sure the athlete doesn't look up. The head should be in a normal anatomical position.

- Weight should be so far forward that if the athlete doesn't run, he'd fall.

These drills will improve what you already have. They are teaching drills. The real key to speed lies in increasing force production. To really improve speed, these drills and cues must be combined with a lower-body strength and power program that emphasizes maximal strength. Don't underestimate the value of force production in the forty.

Dive Starts

Have the athlete dive into a crash pad from the start position. This is a great drill for teaching first-push power.

Timed Tens

I love timed tens. I try to watch the start and count the steps. We use a Speed Trap timer and don't watch the clock. We time every week, sometimes twice a week.

A Few Rules

- Tell the athlete only three attempts per day. This leaves time for the athlete to ask for one more at least twice. I really want to time five sprints, but always say three.

- Try to get the athlete to forget about the timer and concentrate on the technical things: big push out of the start, great hip extension.

- The use of a timer is an excellent way to reduce anxiety about being timed. My athletes are very comfortable about being timed by the time the Combine or Pro Day comes around.

Athletes will choke and revert to old patterns as soon as a timing device is present. Timing early and often allows the athlete to see the changes in patterns like stepping out of the start or stuttering. The timer also demonstrates these behaviors result in slower times, not faster.

Frequent use of the timer does what the book *The One Minute Manager* calls catching someone doing something right. We focus on execution, not time. Great execution will lead to better times, which will ingrain proper habits.

Three for Five, Five for Ten

This is a tough drill as you constantly have to emphasize stride length coming from push, not reach. The goal of the drill is to get the first five yards in three steps, eventually progressing to getting ten yards in five steps — three for five; five for ten. Be careful with this drill; I view it as an advanced drill, and one that must be monitored constantly. Success is not accomplished as much by the number of steps or strides, but by the quality of strides. Overstriding defeats the purpose.

One-Leg Starts

This is another great drill to teach the athlete how to use the front foot in the start. Simply ask for a series of timed tens from only the front foot. This will teach the athlete how to focus on exploding off the front leg. Often our athletes will move from abysmal at this drill to being able to run as fast as from a three-point start.

Increasing Sprint Speeds

Great sprint coaches are few and far between. I still find myself almost twenty years later quoting Charlie Francis. It's been a long time since I've read a fresh take on speed. I have watched track coaches spend countless hours making pretty runners using neuromuscular drills, while totally neglecting strength and power capabilities. I have watched track coaches try to develop an aerobic base with their sprinters, what I consider more foolishness.

The end result in track is failure, failure the leads to a common solution — longer races. When track coaches fail to make an athlete faster, they move the sprinter up a distance. Can't improve your 400-meter time, try the 800. We know we can work on maintaining your apparently un-improvable speed over longer distances with more work.

Speed development takes effort and thought. Aerobic and anaerobic capacities take primarily effort. It takes years to make an athlete fast, and months to make him fit.

Gary Winckler, head women's track and field coach at the University of Illinois has said, "Sending sprinters on long runs is a death march."

Ask yourself how many times you have heard a track coach talk about putting in miles to develop a base. Any talk of aerobic base is misguided, particularly if you are trying to develop speed.

To succeed in increasing sprint speed, an athlete needs to get stronger and more powerful.

Mass is a necessary and desirable by-product of training in most team sports, particularly those that involve contact or collisions.

My areas of interest tend to be ice hockey and football. Both of these sports most often require increases in speed concurrent with increases in size. The key is to develop mass that either creates speed, prevents injury through collision tolerance or allows for more powerful collisions.

In other words, we need to develop what I classify as propulsive mass. We train with weights to develop strength and power, and I really think in the sports environment we train for strength only so we can develop more power.

The ideal result of a training period: increased lean body mass, an increase in vertical jump and a decreased ten-yard-dash time. This would mean we have developed more mass and can move that mass with greater speed.

A good result of a training period: increased lean body mass while maintaining the same vertical jump and ten-yard-dash time. In this case, the physics are still favorable. If momentum equals mass times velocity, this outcome still produces more momentum. We have a better athlete as the athlete moves greater mass with the same speed.

A poor result: increased lean body mass with a decrease in vertical jump or speed. This is the worst-case scenario, but is not always fatal. For smaller athletes who tend to get pushed around, a small loss of relative speed and power may not be a poor trade.

In football we have used the Lewis Power Formula to determine if athletes who gained significant amounts of bodyweight lost or gained power. Remember, with linemen, inertia matters. Size is a necessary evil for offensive and defensive linemen, even when it is non-propulsive.

Sport-Specific Training

Strength training is and always will be a major part of the conditioning process for athletes. Nothing helps sports performance more than the development of strength and power. This is great news for those of us who have made a career of helping athletes reach those goals.

Even though we all agree about the importance of strength training, and even though there's general consensus of the best ways to improve athletic strength and power, debates rage about the specifics. One particularly contentious debate is over the very idea there are specifics for training players in individual sports.

Athletes and their parents or coaches love to hear a particular exercise is good for a specific sport. It makes strength and conditioning specialists sound like we know what we're talking about, and it gives athletes confidence in our abilities to help them with their individual needs.

It's in my best interest to tell people sport-specific training and sport-specific exercises actually exist. But is it true?

Say I'm training two high school kids. One's a cornerback on the football team, and one's a centerfielder on the baseball team. Both are fast and would benefit by being even faster. Both would benefit by being stronger and developing more power. Both want to add some muscular size, but not at the expense of speed or agility. Do I train them differently, even though their goals are basically the same?

In the most fundamental sense, the answer is no. The best methods to develop speed and power are somewhat universal.

However, there is a catch. Although it's dubious to say certain exercises are better for certain sports, it's fair to say some exercises are worse for athletes who play particular sports.

Those in the hard-core crowd love to bang square pegs into round holes, one size fits all. If the squat is a great exercise, it must be great for every athlete in every situation. I was one of those guys for years, forcing my basketball players to squat, and searching endlessly for ways to help them learn the right technique.

Then I figured something out: There's a limiting factor in squatting we call segmental proportion. Athletes with long femurs relative to the length of the torso will be lousy squatters. These guys were almost always forwards or centers, six-feet-five or taller.

But it's not just about height — some tall basketball players are actually very good squatters.

The problem is an athlete with these proportions needs an extreme forward lean when squatting, making it look like he's doing a good morning. This athlete will generally be frustrated with the inability to do the exercise correctly, and may even suffer back pain.

Eventually I could identify these athletes before we got anywhere near the squat rack. Basketball players with exceptionally long femurs always look short sitting down. I remember sitting next to a player and realizing that despite the fact he was eight inches taller than me, we were eye-to-eye when seated in chairs.

My advice to fellow coaches: If an athlete is built proportionally and can squat with good form, go for it. If the athlete is all legs, be careful: You're looking at a square peg.

The problem of segmental proportions isn't exclusive to basketball players. In the past five or six years I've seen a growing number of offensive linemen in football who have what I call basketball builds. They tend to be 6'5" or taller, with long legs and relatively short torsos.

Everyone believes football players in general, and linemen in particular, should squat early and often. But this square peg, round hole training methodology leaves a lot of the taller linemen with back and knee problems.

Good Solutions for Bad Leverage

Physics rule in all sports. The reason there are so few short NBA players is the same reason there are so few tall Olympic lifters. It's much easier for a short person to do an Olympic lift from the floor than it is for a tall person. Keep this in mind if you train tall athletes.

The diameter of a plate is constant; it gives short athletes good leverage and puts tall ones at a disadvantage.

To offset leverage, try these options:

• For strength, use front squats, belt squats, single-leg squats, single-leg squats with the rear foot elevated (Bulgarian split squats) or trap-bar deadlifts.

• For power, try Olympic lifts from the hang position above the knees, along with Vertimax jumps.

Balance and Instability Training

Over the past few years, my training philosophy has changed in regard to the number of times per week we perform a lift. The old philosophy was a heavy–light system in which a specific lift, such as the front squat, was done twice per week, once with a heavy load and once with light load. Light days were difficult to enforce and regulate. Now instead of light days I often opt for unstable days or unilateral days.

Unstable days serve two purposes.

- Unstable-surface training forces the athlete to lift lighter, while also developing balance and proprioception.

- The unstable surface also requires the athlete to concentrate on technique and weight distribution to be successful.

Unstable-surface training has become controversial over the past few years with the explosion of stability-ball training and the use of other unstable environments.

Opponents of unstable-surface training tend to be old-school powerlifters or Olympic lifters who feel the old ways are the best ways. The advocates of unstable-surface training believe it adds additional proprioceptive demand to the exercise, a long-held position of rehab specialists.

The science here is undeniable. Physical therapists have designed exercises to increase proprioceptive demand in a rehab setting, and would never think of discontinuing this practice. The application of this concept to healthy athletes as a preventative measure is sensible.

The opponents of unstable-surface work frequently cite studies indicating it does not cause additional activation of the prime movers, and they may be right.

However, those of us who advocate unstable surface training are not doing it to add additional stress to the prime movers, but rather to add additional stress to stabilizers and neutralizers.

Unstable surface training is actually used in our programs to decrease the stress on a prime mover, while increasing the stress on that prime mover's synergists.

Many of the opponents of unstable surface training are denying the concept without actually understanding its purpose.

Losing Power with Age

Training older clients for power is not just good idea, it's essential. Check out these stats lifted straight from Professor Joe Signorile's presentation at the NSCA Caribbean Clinic in 2003: *Between the ages of 65 and 89, explosive lower-limb extensor power has been reported to decline at 3.5 percent per year compared to a one to two percent per year decrease in strength.*

This means even though we are losing strength as we age, we are losing power almost twice as fast. Interpretation: We're really screwed if we need to move fast.

In elderly men, maximal anaerobic power has been reported to decline 8.3 percent per decade from age twenty to age seventy.

Note: *That said anaerobic, not aerobic.*

Loss of power is a huge issue. Power is one of the major performance variables associated with independence, fall prevention and rehabilitation following injury.

Research has confirmed training is speed-specific, and therefore increases in power and speed of movement require both strength and contractile speed be addressed. This means your older clients who train for power will be more independent, fall less often, and get better faster after an injury.

We need to set aside our primary focus on safety in our older clients, and start to figure out how to train all of our clients for power.

Does this mean cleans and plyometrics for Grandma and Grandpa? Probably not. What it does mean is we must introduce a velocity component to our training not just for athletes, but for all of our clients. The big question is not if we should, but *how* we train adults for power.

There is no better way to train for power than to use equipment specifically designed for power development. The Keiser equipment line was created by Dennis Keiser to allow training at speed with complete safety.

The Total Gym and the Shuttle MVP both allow for elements of power training, as does an old staple, the medicine ball. The med ball may be the least expensive tool for power training, with a huge return on investment. Med ball training is covered in the next section.

Power is relative. What constitutes a power exercise for an athlete is an exercise in insanity for the average adult. The converse is also true: What might be a power exercise for an older client could be a dynamic warm-up for the athlete.

The important point is we need to train as fast as our clients are physically capable of going if we want to delay the loss of power so prevalent throughout our aging process.

Equipment Choices

Slideboard Training
    Slideboard Technique
    Setting Up Workouts
    Off-Season Training

Medicine Ball Training
    Rotation Progression

Sled Training for Athletics

Sled Pushing

TRX Suspension Training

Kettlebells
    Suitcase Carry
    Bottoms-Up Kettlebell Walk
    Get-Up

Manufacturers will continue to try, but no one will ever build a machine that works better than a free weight. Free weights always have been and always will be better than machines. The only machines we need are cable pieces that allow us to perform exercises we can't do with a bar or dumbbell.

The one exception might be the new Keiser units that give power outputs. Keiser may revolutionize training with this equipment. If you're a powerlifter, see if you can test the Keiser Power Rack and try your dynamic effort work like Westside bands and chains with an air system.

Other than that, we don't use a lot of equipment or tools in our facility. The few we use in addition to free weight are described in this section.

The slideboard may be the best, most cost effective conditioning mode available for athletes exclusive of actually running. No other piece of equipment can do all of the following:

- Place the athlete in a sport-specific position, almost regardless of sport

- Positively stress the abductor and adductor muscles

- Allow athletes to work in groups of three to four on one piece of equipment

- Provide work capacity training in an interval format with no adjustments, all for under $600

Think about all the sports that put athletes through lateral movement of the lower extremities; there are very few sports that do not include such lateral motion. Now think about training devices that accurately mimic lateral motion and positively stress the muscles involved — few, if any.

A slideboard has a smooth, flat surface about twenty-four inches wide, ranging in length from seven to nine feet. Commercial slideboards come with special slippers athletes use while training, and the only maintenance required is the occasional application of no-wax furniture polish to the slideboard surface.

It's a rare device that accurately addresses the specific lateral movements for sports such as ice hockey, field hockey, football, soccer and baseball.

Strength and conditioning coaches who deal with multiple sports can easily tailor each slideboard workout to specific sports and to specific positions within a sport.

For example, when we are training ice hockey players, we put the forwards and defensemen on a slideboard adjusted to nine feet, or about one-and-a-half times the athlete's height. This one-and-a-half height rule applies to all but a few positions. For hockey goalies, we work with a shorter, seven-foot board to reflect the fact the net is only six feet wide on a standard hockey rink.

The realistic movements produced by slideboard exercises reduce a player's chance of incurring a groin injury during pre-season workouts and drills. This is because the motion of the slideboard positively stresses the abductor, adductor and hip flexor muscles, which is something that does not occur on a bike or on a commercial climber. Consequently, the specific muscle groups used in lateral movements can be conditioned before the stresses and strains of the actual in-season sport come into play.

From a budgeting perspective, top quality commercial-grade lubricant-free boards cost less than $600, and several athletes can share a single slideboard.

Since the most effective training intervals include generous rest periods, groups of three or four athletes take turns using the slideboard without interrupting a workout.

Technique

The basic movement on a slideboard is a push-glide motion similar to skating down a rink. On a slideboard, an athlete pushes the inside leg from one side of the board to the other by pushing off with the outside leg. When working out on a slideboard, athletes should maintain a knee bend ranging from 120 to 130 degrees and work to eventually perform one push-off per second.

Emphasis should be placed on extension of the ankle, knee and hip joints. When the athlete reaches the end of the board, the knee of the pushing leg should touch the calf of the leg that has just arrived at the bumper.

The hips should stay at the same level the entire time the athlete is on the board. We tell our athletes if they could plot the position of their hips on a graph, it would ideally be a straight line.

Athletes are also instructed to not bring their non-weighted foot behind their bodies when pushing off.

Setting Up Workouts

Begin with five work intervals, making each one five to thirty seconds long, depending on the conditioning and conditioning requirements of the athlete. Use rest intervals lasting fifteen to ninety seconds between each work interval. The entire workout should last ten to twenty minutes.

Note: All of the rest intervals are longer than the work intervals. The longer rest intervals are due to the intensity of working out on a slideboard.

When creating a slideboard workout for your athletes, consider that work intervals longer than thirty seconds will quickly exhaust an athlete and usually will result in a loss of technique. As your athletes become better-conditioned, try to increase the number of work intervals or decrease the rest times rather than increasing the length of time for each work interval.

All of our athletes, regardless of sport, perform lateral conditioning on the slideboard two times per week during a four-day work week.

Our athletes condition every day. The difference is in a four-day off-season program, our athletes will do lateral-movement conditioning twice and linear conditioning on the other two days.

For three-day programs, we simply alternate linear and lateral. This means we get three linear days and three lateral days every two weeks.

When combined with a program of plyometrics and land sprints, the slideboard can become a major part of improving the lateral movements of any sport. Try adding a slideboard workout to your off-season or summer program. Your players will see and feel the difference at the start of their competitive seasons.

Off-Season Training

It is important to emphasize the slideboard should be used only for off-season workouts, not for workouts during the competitive season. We avoid slideboard training during the competitive season because the intensity of a good slideboard workout can result in overuse injuries. During the competitive season, we must be careful to avoid creating stresses on the hip flexors, adductors and abductors beyond what an athlete receives in normal practice and play.

Slideboard training programs can be developed using typical interval-training concepts. Athletes should begin a slideboard program with some introductory workouts in which rest intervals last three times as long as work intervals.

For example, to familiarize an athlete with the concepts of interval training on the slideboard, the athlete begins by working on the board for fifteen seconds followed by a forty-five-second rest interval, with eight to ten repeats. This generally results in heart rates of 160 to 190 beats per minute. Such a program provides an aerobic benefit as long as the heart rate is maintained above 120 beats per minute during the recovery period.

However, the main purpose of the slideboard is to provide an excellent anaerobic endurance workout. The anaerobic and aerobic emphasis of a slideboard workout can be changed by the manipulation of the work-to-rest ratios as described in the section on interval training.

A high work-to-rest ratio of 1:2 would be useful for an athlete who needs to increase anaerobic conditioning. Conversely, a low work-to-rest ratio of 1:1 would provide more aerobic and endurance benefits and would be a typical slideboard exercise for a sport such as soccer, where the player is constantly running.

By changing work-to-rest ratios and altering the length of work and rest periods, a coach can create specific lateral-movement workouts for individual players and positions in sports.

A good example is to compare a slideboard lateral conditioning workout for a hockey forward with that of a baseball shortstop. Both the shortstop and the forward need anaerobic conditioning for speed, and we might create a high work-to-rest ratio of 1:3 for both athletes.

However, the hockey forward requires a much higher level of conditioning than the baseball shortstop. As a result, both athletes would get a work-to-rest ratio of 1:3, but the length of the intervals would be different: The shortstop would work fifteen seconds and rest forty-five, while the forward would work thirty seconds, then rest ninety.

Review the interval training program design beginning on page 136 for the specific lateral work setup we use at MBSC.

Medicine Ball Training

Medicine balls can be a great tool for power development in clients who lack the confidence or desire to Olympic lift. In addition, medicine balls are really one of the only tools available to develop torso power for striking sports like golf or tennis.

A medicine ball is simply a weight until you throw it. The reality is you can lunge or step up with any object that has mass and get the same effect. The uniqueness of the medicine ball is in the user's ability to develop specific power by throwing it, and more importantly to take advantage of the eccentric or concentric development gained by throwing toward a wall.

Medicine ball training has become an integral part of training for any athlete interested in power development. The development of a wide range of both elastic and non-elastic medicine balls has re-popularized this long-lost technique.

The opportunity to develop rotational power is one of the primary benefits of med ball training. In both plyometrics and Olympic lifting, power development is traditionally uni-planar with no trunk focus. Medicine balls become a tool like Olympic lifting and plyometrics for the trunk musculature, sort of like Olympic lifting for the core.

Med balls provide a safe method to train for power for almost all ages and levels of training. In fact, no other training mode provides the specific strength and power potential of the medicine ball.

The new rubber medicine balls and a masonry wall are excellent for these applications due to the elasticity of the ball. The older-style non-elastic balls are excellent to develop the concentric power of the throws.

For years I was fascinated by the ability to perform medicine ball drills off the wall with a rubber ball. Later I discovered I could really improve the concentric force production of our athletes by switching to a non-elastic ball like the Dynamax. Non-bouncing balls force the thrower to create far more concentric force to produce any rebound off the wall.

For overhead athletes like pitchers, tennis players and swimmers, the med ball provides great eccentric training for the rotator cuff while developing power in the core muscles.

Total-body power in all athletes can be developed through throws with heavy balls. Total-body throws should be done in a large open area and are great to simulate the actions of the Olympic lifts. These are particularly useful for athletes who are unfamiliar with Olympic lifts or have injuries that prevent them from performing exercises like cleans or snatches.

These throws also allow coaches uncomfortable with teaching the Olympic lifts to get hip and leg power work in a resisted situation.

Balls like the Dynamax ball and the D-Balls are excellent for these applications because they don't bounce. Dynamax is closer to leather and has a little more bounce than the D-Ball. Both are non-elastic.

The Dynamax balls are also great for exercises like medicine ball bench presses. Medicine ball bench presses are excellent for upper-body power for larger athletes since they do not stress the rotator cuff and shoulder like plyometric push-ups and other bodyweight upper-body plyometrics. The Dynamax balls can also be caught with minimal stresses on the wrists due to its soft density.

Some suggested throws for total-body power are from a squat position forward, a scoop-type throw from a squat position, and throws from the lunge position. The limit to the uses of the medicine ball is really the coach's imagination.

Athletes should not attempt to catch a dense medicine ball thrown by a partner. Catching heavy medicine balls can be dangerous to both the shoulders and fingers of the athletes.

Medicine ball throws should be treated like any other strength and power exercise. Twenty to thirty of each type of throw in two or three sets of ten can be done twice a week. As the athlete moves from kneeling to half-kneeling, and eventually to standing, the link between the hips and hands will show rapid improvement.

Keep volumes low to moderate and tell the athlete to throw the ball aggressively, as if to break it.

Rotational medicine ball throws are the key to developing torso power for athletes involved in just about any sport.

For rotational throws it's best to find an area with a masonry wall. In rotational throws the athlete can throw as hard as possible against the wall with balls in the four- or five-kilo range to develop true power in the core and hips. Excellent imitative drills for throwers can be developed once the athletes master the basics.

The rotational progression begins with the athlete in a half-kneeling position. Half-kneeling is a position with the athlete kneeling on one knee with the hip extended. Beginning in a kneeling position eliminates the ankle- and knee-joint movements and exposes weaknesses and compensation patterns that may not be visible in standing throws. Half-kneeling also teaches the athlete to use the glutes.

Rotation Progression

- Half-kneeling side twist, ninety degrees to the wall, two or three feet away from the wall

- Standing, front and side

- Standing with step

- Single-leg

In addition to developing rotary power, the same progression of positions can be used for overhead throws. Overhead throws should be done with two- or three-kilo balls, as care must be taken when providing stress to the rotator cuff.

Throwers should perform rotational throws a minimum of two days per week and a maximum of three. For throwers, the medicine ball may be our most underrated tool to develop rotational power.

Sled Training for Athletics

Sport is about acceleration, not speed. Coaches consistently use the wrong term when discussing the quality they covet most. As coaches, our interest is not in top speed, but rather in acceleration, the zero to sixty of the auto world. How rapidly an athlete accelerates, not the athlete's absolute speed, will determine success in team sports. This idea was developed in the section on developing speed on page 167.

A great deal of the research on speed development focuses on speed in the track and field context and not in a sport context. In track the shortest event is the fifty-five meters; in sport the long event is a forty-yard dash, although baseball goes to sixty. The track influence may have limited application in sport due to sports' frequent use of acceleration mechanics versus speed mechanics.

In training for track, running coaches reference pulling and work on drills to develop a pawing action against the ground. In sport the action is primarily pushing, with the center of gravity slightly ahead of the feet, kind of a reverse Michael Johnson. This may mean much of what we currently view as speed development may have limited application to team sport athletes.

Numerous studies have discredited the weighted sled as a tool for speed development, citing the sled's limited effect on top speed. The evidence that weighted sleds may not improve top speed running does not apply to acceleration and may have led us to undervalue a potentially important piece of equipment. Many authors who said the weighted sled did not improve speed indicate it will improve acceleration. Our problem has been we misinterpreted the results of the research.

Most coaches spend time working on running form and technique to improve speed. These same coaches also include lower-body workouts to improve strength. Although these are both important, there may be a missing link: the development of specific strength.

How often do we see athletes who run pretty, but are not fast? Many coaches attempting to develop speed spend far too much time on technique drills and far too little time developing the specific power and strength necessary to run faster.

Weighted sled drills target the specific muscles used in sprinting and help bridge the gap between form running drills and weightroom exercises like squats and Olympic lifts.

Many athletes can squat large amounts of weight; far fewer athletes are able to run fast. Any student of speed will tell you many of the strength exercises commonly recommended for speed development work hip extension, but not hip hyperextension. In running speed, all of the force production is from hip hyperextension. The ability to apply force to the ground and create forward movement can only occur when the foot is placed under the center of mass and pushed back.

Although squats will train the muscles involved, the training is not specific to the act of sprinting. This may be one reason we see a higher correlation to vertical jump improvement than to speed improvement through strength training.

A weighted sled teaches strong athletes how to produce the type of force that moves them forward. Sports scientists like to break this down into special strength and specific strength. Although minimal, it is important to understand the difference between the two qualities.

Special strength refers to movements with resistance that incorporate the joint dynamics of the skill. Sled marching would fall into the special strength category. Sled marching may even be the best tool available for speed development. An athlete's inability to produce force in the action of sprinting becomes glaringly obvious in sled marching.

Specific strength means movements with resistance imitative of the joint action. Sled running would be placed in the specific strength category.

Coaches have suggested resisted speed development work should not slow the athlete down more than ten percent and should not involve more than ten percent of the athlete's bodyweight. These recommendations seem to be based on motor learning research that indicates excessive loads would alter the motor patterns of activities like sprinting or throwing.

I have always felt there was a missing link in speed development, but until a few years ago this ten-percent rule kept me from aggressively pursuing my gut feeling. I currently think loads up to and exceeding the athlete's bodyweight can be used for special strength work as long as the athlete exhibits a similar motor pattern.

Think of sled marching as a special type of leg press. Athletes incorporate the joint dynamics of sprinting through hip hyperextension against resistance. This can be an extremely heavy movement as long as we get a technically sound march action with perfect posture.

With sled running, the approach moves toward specific strength. In sled running the loads will obviously be lighter, but we still don't follow the ten-percent rule. The main variable in sled training is not the weight on the sled, but the motor pattern.

If an athlete can hold an acceleration position and run without altering mechanics, this is a specific strength exercise for sprinting.

Why should we be limited by arbitrary guidelines like a ten-percent load or a ten-percent decrease in speed? Over twenty yards, ten percent is two one-hundredths of a second.

The key should be to look at the athlete's posture and motor pattern. If the athlete has to alter the mechanics to produce the desired action, the load is too heavy.

Another obvious but overlooked variable that alters the ten-percent rule is the running surface. Loads placed on the sled will be lighter on grass and heavier on AstroTurf; this relates to the coefficient of friction. Less weight produces a larger amount of friction as the sled moves through grass. On Astroturf or a similar surface, the same weight would be too light.

Another variable is a flat sled versus a double-runner sled. A flat sled will again produce greater friction and as a result will necessitate a lighter load on the sled to get a similar effect as that using a sled with runners.

Sled Pushing

If I could only choose one exercise for athletes, I think it would be to push a heavy sled. *Push,* not drag, and heavy.

As I watch someone push a sled, I see a sport-specific, unilateral leg press. I also see the perfect acceleration position for running. Each push is really a closed-chain, single-leg hip extension — great for the glutes, as well as the entire posterior chain, and great for rehab with a lot of the benefits of squats and deadlifts.

Sled pushing uses tremendous core stability fed from a unilateral base. I hate the idea of squatting and deadlifting for core development; no bilateral exercise is particularly good for core development. It's just not the way the muscles work. Simply holding a load while on two legs doesn't activate the core muscles in the way they're used in life or in sport. However, when you push a sled, the base of support changes from side to side.

Sled pushing is also a superb upper body stability workout. Pushing works the entire shoulder girdle.

And then there's the energy system component. GPP, work capacity or conditioning: Any way you slice it, pushing a heavy sled is hard work. And hard work is good for your athletes.

We use the Perform Better Drive Sled. It's a great multi-function sled, lightweight and breaks down to two pieces. However, it's not as sturdy as the Prowler. You need to take care of it.

If you don't have a push sled, pile as many plates as possible on a regular pull sled and have your athletes go for it.

The reality is we may have misinterpreted the message when it comes to resistance training for sprints. Although research shows sled training may not improve the athlete's ability to run at top speed, it certainly will help the athlete get faster.

Sport is about acceleration, not top speed. Very few team sport athletes ever get to what track coaches call absolute speed mechanics. The weighted sled may be the most underrated tool for speed development due to our misinterpretation and misunderstanding of the research and terminology surrounding speed development.

TRX Suspension Training

I thought the TRX suspension strap unit was a silly gimmick, a one-trick pony that was oversold. Now I think it might be the best $149 piece of equipment on the market.

I loved the TRX rows and thought the equipment was worth the price for the "seated row machine" use alone. Actually it's sort of a standing horizontal row, and the TRX eliminates the need for any sort of weight stack cable row apparatus, eliminating a $3000 piece for $149. That should be enough; this just saved you nearly three thousand dollars if you own your own facility.

Most people use the Smith machine or a barbell set low in a squat rack for inverted rows. Today I prefer the TRX suspension straps to allow the shoulder joints to move through their normal spiral-diagonal patterns. Using these implements, we also do rotational inverted rows, pulling up with one arm at a time.

This turns out to be the perfect product, inexpensive with multiple uses. Almost all the exercises I thought were gimmicky are actually excellent variations or progressions. Rear-foot-elevated single-leg squats, leg curls and rollouts are all outstanding on the TRX.

On Alwyn Cosgrove's recommendation, I scheduled two hours of training for our staff members with Chris Frankel of Fitness Anywhere, the company that manufactures the TRX. To say we were all excited with the exercise possibilities of these straps is clearly an understatement.

You'll notice in some of the photos throughout the book we're beginning to use the TRX in a variety of positions. I need to spend more time playing to figure out more cool progressions, but trust me when I tell you to order a TRX and get to a TRX trainer workshop or schedule a TRX expert to train your staff on the variety of its uses.

Kettlebells

I have kettlebells, and I like them for certain exercises in which they're more user-friendly than dumbbells. For example, I love kettlebell swings. I think they're a great power exercise for beginners and older athletic clients who can't handle the wrist stress of the Olympic lifts.

I just don't like them for cleans and snatches because they hurt our athletes.

Look at it from my point of view.

A fourteen-year-old athlete goes home from our facility night after night with bruised and battered forearms. His mom and dad, who are paying good money to have me train their young athlete, ask why his arms look like melted crayons. He tells them how Mr. Boyle has him fling around these cannonball thingies, which on a couple of exercises slam into his forearms... over and over and over again.

Then he tells them, "Mr. Boyle says we should get the hang of it after a few more workouts."

Do you think Mom and Dad will wait to see if Junior gets used to it? Or do you think they'll immediately get on the phone with Mr. Boyle to inquire about his innovative training techniques?

The same goes with our professional athletes: Do I try to explain to a guy who makes $9 million a year he'll eventually enjoy the exercise... after it stops beating up his forearms? Or to keep that athlete in my facility, do I find another exercise that offers the same benefits without the contusions?

Kettlebells are good tools, but not all popular kettlebell exercises are appropriate in our training environments.

Suitcase Carry

The suitcase carry is an example of a kettlebell exercise that in my mind went from a waste of time and energy to a great idea over the course of an hour. At a recent lecture, Stuart McGill espoused the benefits of farmer walks for hip stability.

Previously farmer walks had been viewed as a finisher, a mental toughness exercise and a grip strength exercise. Because of this, I never had much use for them. Suddenly, through the eyes of Stuart I see an exercise, or in fact a whole series of exercises, in a whole different light.

As I thought of farmer walks as a hip stability exercise, I realized Dan John's suitcase carry becomes a standing, moving side plank. Instead of an exercise I had no use for, I suddenly had my next plank progression.

Bottoms-Up Kettlebell Walk

The same applies with the bottoms-up kettlebell walk. During the short span of a few months, both Stuart and Gray Cook espoused the benefits. Stuart likes it for core work; Gray for shoulders.

In either case, when guys like Gray and Stuart talk, copycats like me listen.

I immediately experimented and quickly realized, as usual, they were right.

The bottoms-up kettlebell walk is another great lateral core progression to add to your arsenal.

Getup for Core

And of course we use a kettlebell in the half-getup for core work.

Kettelbell expert Brett Jones has called the getup one of the best exercise you aren't doing, and Gray Cook dedicated an entire two-disc DVD set to it.

The getup is an interesting exercise that will become a bigger and bigger part of our program over the coming months as we discover its subtle benefits.

The half-getup is our phase-three exercise on the way to the full getup. We can progress our straight-leg sit-up into a single-leg flat-foot sit-up and then into a half-getup.

This progression allows us to teach getups to larger groups.

Squats
Gauging Depth

Knee Issues with Squats

Front Squats

Developing a Safe Squatting Style
Pelvic Position during Squatting

Deadlifts
Trap-Bar Deadlifts

Pressing Exercises
Chain Bench Presses

Training the Combine Bench

Overhead Athletes and Overhead Lifts

Strength Comparisons
Strength Charts

Developing Single-Leg Strength
Pelvic Stabilizers

Classifications of Single-Leg Exercise

Progressive Range of Motion

Accelerative and Decelerative Patterns

Posterior Chain Training

Determining Weight for Single-Leg Squats

Facilitating the Glute Medius

Single-Leg Exercises

Single-Leg Stability

Single-Leg Strength

Squats

To examine learning to squat, we must first examine the psychology of lifting weights. There is a macho aspect, particularly with young men, that makes learning exercises very difficult. No one wants to go through the motions with an unloaded bar to groove the motor pattern or develop mobility.

Athletes want to lift and want to be challenged. This presents glaring challenges when teaching the squat.

In the words of Gray Cook, what we are often doing is adding strength to dysfunction. What he's saying in the simplest sense is if you can't squat, don't squat. In other words, an athlete or client who cannot perform the bodyweight overhead squat fairly well should not be squatting. In essence if we allow the athlete with poor technique to squat, we are adding strength on top of dysfunction. The athlete or client still has a poor pattern, but now the poor pattern is demonstrated with external load.

This is a common high school and college football mistake and may be at the root of many athletes' back pain. An athlete who squats poorly is often encouraged by a well-meaning coach to get strong. Instead, the initial emphasis should be to get mobile and perfect the squat pattern. However, very few coaches do this. Instead, they add strength to dysfunction.

Our current approach is to work initially on mobility to obtain or develop the squat pattern. This is now done in our mobility warm-up. The athlete is not in the weightroom wondering how much weight is on the bar and if anyone is watching. From a psychological standpoint, we have removed the barrier to success in learning to squat.

The desire to continually add external load in the weightroom forces the athlete into faulty movement patterns. Working on squat mobility as part of warm-up does the opposite. While we work on squat mobility in our warm-ups, we simultaneously work on single-leg strength.

Many people think they squat to parallel, but aren't even close. It's like grade inflation in school. We get so numbers-oriented, we throw technique out the window. A double-bodyweight back squat done to powerlifting depth without gear is actually a pretty good lift. We've got number inflation from suits and wraps that make everyone shoot for the sky.

Whether you're a front squat guy like me or prefer the back squat, there's only one acceptable depth: powerlifting depth. Three white lights. Period. No parallel, no hamstring parallel, and definitely don't tell me you squat to ninety.

This is all lame, put forth by bad squatters who want to get more weight on the bar, or excuses put forth by those who don't want to work on flexibility and mobility.

When I was a college football strength coach, I'd tell our football coaches when they were recruiting a kid to divide his squat by two. A high school kid who claimed to squat 500 pounds would usually get a little more than half that on test day.

All of the descriptions, parallel, hamstring parallel and ninety degrees, are euphemisms for lousy squats made by lousy squatters or, worse yet, by their coaches. I've had strength coaches tell me, "My guys have trouble getting that low." Well, fix your guys.

Just take weight off the bar and do it right. Squatting isn't an ability you gain; it's an ability you lose. Check out a baby picking something up off the floor. Picture-perfect mobility, perfect squats.

Parallel really means the femur is parallel to the floor. Visualize your client's femur and see if it's parallel to the floor. The difference between the femur parallel to the floor and the bottom of the thigh parallel to the floor is about a hundred pounds in my experience. That means a 500-pound hamstring-parallel squatter is a 400-pound full-squatter. It also means a reduction in mobility and a hundred pounds more compressive load on the spine.

Gauging Depth

To eliminate this, we perform a box squat of sorts, used to gauge depth. We squat to a light touch on the box. No rebound off the box, no sitting. This is clearly not a Westside squat; it's just a consistent depth gauge. I suggest using a twelve-inch box for most athletes.

We have pads to adjust the box up for our taller athletes, but twelve inches works surprisingly well for most of my 5'8" to 6' athletes. We make small adjustments for shorter or taller athletes. You'd be surprised how many will be at a true full squat at twelve inches.

There's more similarity in tibia length than femur length in most athletes. Tibia length really determines the distance needed in the descent, and it actually only varies about two inches from a short to a tall person.

Another thing the box does is encourage sitting down and back. After adding the box technique, I was amazed at how many athletes changed the weight distribution during a set. As fatigue sets in, athletes shift weight onto the balls of the feet, and as a result squat higher.

One nice thing about our box squats: There are no arguments. Either they touch the box or they don't.

Box Squat History

Box squats were first popularized in the 1960s by Olympic hammer thrower and powerlifter, George Frenn. I read about them in an article on squat training in *Powerlifting USA*, back when they were called rocking box squats. The idea was to generate power by rocking back slightly to drive off a box or bench.

They were re-popularized in recent years by the works of Louie Simmons at Westside Barbell, which is why most readers know of them today.

My experiments with box squats go back to the late 1970s and early '80s, and thirty years later I still have the back pain to show for it. That's why I've never used regular box squats with my athletes.

That said, we now use the technique inspired by box squats to help the athletes get the proper range of motion in their squats. It's not a true box squat, since the athletes don't come to a full stop on the box, resting their weight on it to push back off.

It's just a touch to ensure they've gone as deep as they need to go.

Knee Issues with Squats

Anyone who tells you he can't squat because he has bad knees is more than likely full of it. All knee rehab now centers around squats or something that looks like a squat.

What he's really saying is, "I was never a good squatter. I always did them wrong and as a result, my knees hurt." We hear of doctors who say, "No more squats, just lunges." How is a lunge different than a squat? Knee range of motion is knee range of motion.

Is there really any evidence squats are bad for knees? No, none that I've seen. There's actually more evidence for increased patella-femoral compression from leg extensions than there is for danger in squatting.

The idea squats are bad for the knees started with a 1969 book called *The Knee in Sports,* by Karl Klein and Fred Allman. Many squat critics say this book contains strong evidence for squats damaging the knee joint. You know why they think this? Because they never read the book! I have an original copy of it right here beside me and here's what it says:

"If squat type exercises are to be used, the weight should be kept in front. Even though it may not be possible to use as much weight, the exercise is safer and puts much less strain on the back."

The authors continue:

"The depth in the squat should be controlled, with the thighs just breaking the parallel position."

The accompanying photo in the text shows a nice powerlifting-depth squat.

They conclude:

"Much beyond this point, the reaction between the hamstrings and calf muscle begins to act as a pry to force the joint apart, stretching the ligaments."

In other words, Klein and Allman recommended full squats, but didn't advocate breaking parallel. What they cautioned against were what they described as deep squats. Deep squats are squats below parallel as might be seen in the catch portion of the clean and jerk or snatch in Olympic lifting.

This produced a massive overreaction. Those who didn't take the time to read the book or even look at the pictures went on to badmouth squatting, saying it was dangerous and bad for the knees. Some commercial gyms actually went so far as to ban full squats.

The bottom line, although some will disagree, is there's no evidence a powerlifting-depth full squat is bad for the knees, but there's some evidence squatting below parallel — what many like to describe as ATG, ass to grass — could be harmful to the collateral ligaments or to the posterior horn of the meniscus.

Does this matter? Very little. Most people never approach the knee danger-zone in depth anyway.

With my athletes, I'm more concerned with lumbar stress under the bar than with knee stress. We'll develop that thought more as we cover my reasons for switching to single-leg training programs.

Heavy squats and deadlifts may not be good long term. Key point: *long-term.* People who are able to lift heavy for a long period of time are gifted with a good skeleton and good connective tissue and great technique.

Be careful. If you have your clients squat heavy, cycle in belt squats and one-leg squats.

Front Squats

Nearly a decade ago, I came to a conclusion: Athletes I trained would no longer perform the back squat. As a former powerlifter, this was heresy, but I was tired of constantly asking our athletes to keep their heads up and to use their legs, not their backs.

The emphasis of the back squat is always on increasing weight. Unfortunately this is often done by altering technique to improve leverage, not by actually increasing the strength of the muscles so necessary to run or jump.

The decision to discontinue back squats was based on logic that was unfortunately a long time overdue: *Front squats are safer than back squats.*

Whenever one of our athletes sustained a back injury, he was reintroduced to squatting via the front squat prior to the back squat for a number of reasons.

• The front squat keeps the torso upright and decreases the torque that causes problems with the SI joint.

• The nature of the front squat forces the athlete to use a lighter weight than the back squat. This is particularly true with beginners, although our athletes can now front squat nearly a hundred percent of their previous best back squats.

• The front squat places greater stress on the knee extensors and less on the hip extensors. This might seem like a negative, but it actually allows us to perform hip-dominant movements the day after squatting with less overlap.

The reintroduction to squatting via the front squat was always a huge success physically. Mentally, athletes would begin front squatting, but would always be itching to back squat with everyone else. At this point we would cave in to the pressure and allow the athlete to perform the back squat again. This process began the vicious circle of back pain… front squat… back squat… back pain.

Often we hear coaches disparage a form of training or a particular lift as injury-producing. My experience has shown the solution may not be to eliminate lifts entirely, but to change to variations that avoid positions of higher stress.

This is why the front squat makes sense. The front squat produces a better body position by the nature of the exercise. An athlete has a difficult time front squatting poorly. The athlete either front squats well, or drops the bar. There is very little middle ground.

Conversely, in the back squat athletes can squat poorly for weeks, months or years, eventually sustaining an injury.

Knee-Dominant

Another advantage of performing front squats is exercises like straight-leg deadlifts and other hip-extension movements can be done the day after with little fear of overtraining the posterior chain because front squats are much more knee-dominant.

This allows our athletes to in effect train their lower body every workout in a four-day program. Athletes can do knee-extension movements like front squats on one day, and follow up with hip-dominant movements like straight-leg deadlifts the next day.

Something to think about: If the only reason you won't switch to front squats is because the athletes will lift less weight, you really should reconsider.

Flexibility

One of the chief complaints about switching to front squats is athletes have trouble with upper-body flexibility. The use of lifting straps in the front squat alleviates what is often the primary complaint with most athletes.

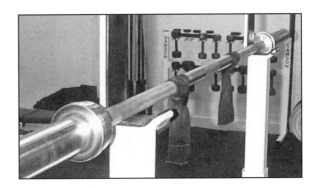

More often than not, athletes use upper-body flexibility more as an excuse. That's why I love the straps: No more excuses.

Developing a Safe Squatting Style

The following steps are critical for developing a technically correct and safe squatting style.

Hands-Free Bodyweight Squat

For the hands-free bodyweight squat, start your client with the arms extended in front of the body at shoulder height.

The key to learning to squat is learning to recruit the glutes. When teaching the squat, place a twenty-inch band or piece of Theratube or a green mini-band just below the knee. Tell the athlete to stretch the band. This really recruits the glutes and forces the athlete out of a valgus squat.

The chest should be up, and the upper and lower back should be arched and tight. Feet should be approximately shoulder-width apart and slightly turned out, about ten to fifteen degrees. The stance may be widened to obtain proper depth if flexibility is a problem.

A one-by-four board, a ten-pound plate, or a wedge may be placed under the heels if the athlete tends to lean forward during the descent, if the heels lose contact with the ground, or if the pelvis rotates posteriorly in the descent.

Although many authorities caution against an object under the heels, athletes at our training facility have experienced great success and no knee pain when using this method.

Pelvic Position during Squatting

Many coaches describe a posterior pelvic rotation as the butt tucking under. When an athlete squats while maintaining a slight anterior pelvic tilt, the hamstrings actually lengthen during the descent.

Athletes with tight lateral hamstrings will reach the end of their hamstring range of motion before they reach full squat depth. As the descent continues and the athlete attempts to get the femur parallel to the floor, the short lateral hamstring will begin to force the pelvis to rotate posteriorly.

Athletes who tuck under should not be loaded until they have developed enough flexibility to prevent the posterior rotation. Our favorite lateral hamstring stretch is found on page 120.

Loading a spine that is moving into flexion is a prescription for disaster. Loading in a posterior tilt can be dangerous.

The spine is meant to be loaded in a lordotic position with a slight anterior tilt.

Coaching
the Bodyweight Squat

- Prior to descending into a squat, have the client inhale deeply to fully inflate the lungs. Fully inflated lungs brace the upper and lower back.

- When descending into the squat, cue the client to sit back, placing the weight on the heels. Bodyweight on the midfoot or toes causes an undesirable forward lean.

- The client should not let the breath out, and the hands should stay level with the shoulders.

- Instruct him to descend slowly until the femurs are parallel with the floor. Insist on the proper depth with light weights for better results.

- In the descent, the knees should be pushed out against the band in a conscious abduction action. This abduction push recruits the glutes and will quickly turn bad squatters into good squatters. Have the client push the knees laterally over the toes.

This is the key to teaching squatting. An abduction force turns on the muscles that control the femur. Very often athletes who have experienced knee pain during squatting will no longer experience pain with this technique.

Teaching squatting with a band to facilitate abduction turns on the femoral control mechanism. Many athletes squat using primarily the wrong muscles.

This ties in with our discussion of glute activation found in the core section on page 91.

- In the ascent, have the client concentrate on driving upward with the chest out, bringing the hips up and forward.

- Tell the client to drive the heels into the floor, and to maintain the abduction pressure on the band.

- He should exhale slowly, letting the air hiss out of the lungs like a punctured a tire.

The squat is a safe movement when done properly. Start with bodyweight to develop proper technique and progress to higher weights after technique is perfect. Injuries occur only when athletes fail to adhere to proper technique.

Hands-Free Front Squat

Again with the arms extended in front of the body, the hands at shoulder height, place a bar across the client's front deltoids. The bar should be in contact with the throat, and should be making the squatter uncomfortable, but not unable to breathe.

The hands deliberately do not touch the bar. This teaches athletes to carry the bar on the shoulders, not on the wrists. Learning to carry the bar with the shoulders will make better squatters and better Olympic lifters. Do not neglect this important point.

Follow the descent and ascent instructions for the hands-free bodyweight squat on the previous page.

Clean-Grip Front Squat

Do not allow a crossover grip in the front squat. Athletes must be able to execute a good front squat to be able to clean properly. The front squat start position is used for the clean catch, the push jerk and the push press.

Even if you elect to use the back squat as your primary lower-body exercise, the front squat is still an excellent way to teach the squat.

- Front squats require perfect body position.

- Front squats develop shoulder flexibility, which is a big plus in the bench press–dominated world of strength training. Flexibility is enhanced if a clean grip is used.

Front squats require less weight and put less pressure on the ego; no one seems to beg for more weight in the front squat.

If you are having trouble developing proper squat technique with your athletes, you are attempting to use too much weight too soon, or your athletes have inadequate flexibility or mobility in the hips and ankles.

The optimal way to stretch for the squat is to sit in the full-squat position, with the elbows on the inner sides of the knees, pushing the knees out over the toes while arching the back.

Make the time for your athletes to master the technique over the first month if necessary, and work hard on the single-leg exercises after your squat workouts.

Deadlifts

Competitive deadlifts are universally ugly. The goal of the competitive deadlifter is only to get the weight from point A to point B. There are no style points or technique requirements. Get the weight from the floor to waist level without a hitch and you get the lift. Flexed spines throughout the lift are the rule, not the exception. Unfortunately, my experiences in competitive powerlifting soured me on a potentially valuable exercise for nearly thirty years.

It took an article by track coach Barry Ross and some experience with de-conditioned personal training clients to change my thought process. Ross's point was simple: The deadlift provides more demand and return than the squat because the weight is in the hands. The muscles of the upper back are forced to work in a way that cannot be imitated in a squat. It was a point that was hard to disagree with, and it forced me to revisit my impression of this valuable exercise.

My argument against deadlifts in our weightroom was always "You can't deadlift heavy and deadlift well." However, I'm in control of technique; in our weightroom technique breaks are my problems as a coach. If we can do squats, we should be able to do deadlifts. Both require a great deal of teaching and attention to detail on both the coach and the athlete's part.

The ah-ha moment for me was realizing how easy a kettlebell sumo deadlift is to teach compared with how hard it is to get someone to squat well. Deconditioned clients and adults in general don't become great squatters right off the bat. However, they all seem to easily conceptualize the sumo deadlift.

In the summer of 2007, we inserted trap bar deadlifts in our program as a priority lower-body strength movement and the results were fantastic. Athletes liked the lift and were able to learn faster and to quickly achieve higher loads. With the squat, loading is more limited by technique concerns, as well as ankle and hip mobility. The trap bar deadlift eliminates most of these issues. The athlete can use higher loads, and the intentional forward lean of the trunk makes it easy for any athlete to get in proper position.

I like the trap bar or hex bar much more than the conventional straight bar. The trap bar deadlift is a great equalizer; in effect the bar is running through the body. The load stays centered, and the movement is very much like squatting with a weight in the hands.

Another benefit of deadlifts is they are not as limited by rules. We don't have to worry about depth in the deadlift. Everyone begins at the ground and comes up. As long as the back remains flat, injury is no greater a concern than in the squat, and in my mind the concern is actually decreased.

With squatting there are two back concerns, flexion and extension. A loss of position can cause a round back and a potential strain on the erectors or a disruption at the SI joint.

This is the same problem in the deadlift, however in the squat, the load on the shoulders and the arched position of the back at the start also predisposes the lifter to extension-based disorders. In essence, the squat is a battle between extension and flexion.

In the deadlift the load in the hands clearly produces a flexion force that must be countered by an extension force. And in the deadlift, the load is positioned at the center of mass rather than near the cervical spine the way it is in the squat. The balancing act is in effect eliminated.

When I look at a squat and a deadlift through the eyes of a biomechanist, the deadlift actually comes out ahead.

The deadlift is a better total-body exercise with more carryover to sprinting and can be done faster, in a concentric-only manner and with less equipment. How wonderfully and refreshingly simple.

Pressing Exercises

It really doesn't matter how much we can bench, however many athletes and coaches have been fooled into believing the bench press is the measure of success or failure of an athlete's off-season workouts. Frequently I see players who are making tremendous progress in conditioning and in lower-body strength, but who are fixated on the bench because their team coach wants them up to two hundred on the bench.

The logic that bench press increases correlate with improvement of sport skill is flawed at best. The bench press is an indicator of one type of upper-body strength, a type that matters little in most sports.

However, this is a book covering strength programs, and if I didn't give the bench press some attention, the critics would howl. Just remember, there are many exercises and many movement patterns that develop strength; don't judge an athlete's success or failure based on bench press results.

Coaches place such emphasis on the bench press because it's an easy exercise to do and an easy exercise to test, much easier in both categories than the front squat or the hang clean. Bench press testing can be done rapidly, and with very little teaching. However, increases in the front squat or hang clean will have a far greater bearing on performance enhancement.

Most athletes like the bench press and are willing to work at it, but they generally like the bench press for all the wrong reasons. They like it because there are rapid improvements; the reason we see such rapid change in the pecs from bench pressing is we literally wake up muscles that don't get used much. We go from atrophy to pecs in a few weeks. Coaches like this instant gratification. They like it when players look better.

Many coaches still have a limited knowledge of strength and conditioning and assume we measure strength by how much an athlete can bench. Have a conversation with many trainers or coaches and any layman about training and the bench question invariably comes up.

Unfortunately, the truly beneficial exercises in strength training, like the front squat and hang clean, are not as easy to learn and take time, patience and coaching. Testing is difficult and potentially dangerous, but not impossible.

Coaches should at least test performance-related factors like the ten-yard dash and the vertical jump, which are readily improved by proper lower-body training. Remember, athletes will train for tests. Make the bench press the big test and you will have athletes with big upper bodies and potentially no improvement in the ability to play their sports.

One thing I can state clearly: Improvements in the ten-yard dash and the vertical jump will correlate strongly with improvements in performance, and bench press increases will not.

Coaches should start their teams on strength programs that emphasize lower-body and abdominal strength and forget the bench. Put your emphasis and your influence in the correct place.

In spite of the above points, clients and coaches still want to know about upper body strength, in particular bench pressing.

Considerations

Horizontal pressing exercises like the bench press and its variations present a few interesting dilemmas. Many young athletes initially experience a rapid strength gain from a bench press program often done three times a week. Due to the lack of use the muscle group gets, progress is rapid and some hypertrophy occurs quickly.

This creates a fundamental problem. The athlete or client associates the success with the frequency and intensity of workouts, not with the concept of awakening a long-dormant muscle group. As a result, the trainee assumes a cause-effect relationship between training frequency and strength gain. This unfortunately leads to a long-term plateau and frustration on the part of the trainee when he's unable to continue to produce rapid results.

As a competitive powerlifter, I tried every program possible to improve my bench press. It was not until I realized there was no relationship between training volume and strength gain that I began to make progress.

In fact, the only relationship I found between volume and strength gain was negative. Most average trainees will gain more on a reduced-volume program. My search for strength led me initially to the same sort of "written by guys on drugs for other guys on drugs" programming, the standard fare of the muscle magazines.

After realizing this training wasn't working for me, I began to read the writings of guys like Dr. Ken Leistner and, later, Stuart McRobert. Both of these authors advocate a hybrid philosophy. Both espouse abbreviated workouts along the lines of the high-intensity, one-set-to-failure school of thought.

However, both are also proponents of basic, multi-joint free-weight exercises. McRobert has written extensively about strength and size development for what he refers to as hardgainers. Reading the work of guys like McRobert and Leistner and combining it with what we know about exercise physiology and human nature led me to the following points.

Keys to Bench Pressing

Schedule the bench press only once per week. When you analyze the workout of the great bench pressers, you'll see most perform the actual lift only once a week.

Use only two upper-body pressing workouts per week. We rarely see strength athletes who still perform three weekly upper-body pressing workouts.

For athletes who bench press less than two hundred pounds, buy a set of Olympic one-and-a-quarter plates. As the athletes progress, the five-pound jumps necessitated by larger plates will be too great. Those who bench press over two hundred can still get away with five-pound jumps, but half that would be better.

Work the assistance exercises hard. Very often plateaus in the bench press can be broken by increasing the strength in the incline bench press or in the close-grip bench press.

The rules on the bench are simple: *It's a touch-and-go lift*. The bar is lowered under control, must touch the chest and return to the rack with no assistance. Any touching of the bar invalidates the lift. Period. No questions, no discussions.

The reason athletes fail to improve their bench press after year one is they don't follow the above rules. It is very difficult to get an athlete or client to stop doing what has provided success, but in strength training less is clearly more as the trainee becomes more experienced.

Push-ups are good for your clients, and in fact they may be better than bench pressing.

Get a set of push-up handles to save their wrists, and a weight vest to add resistance.

When an athlete can do twenty with the vest without looking like a seal, elevate his feet. You'll even train the core muscles and the lats and serratus.

Remember, if your client looks like a seal, he's doing them wrong. Coach tight abs and nose to the floor.

Chain Bench Presses

My initial exposure to the use of chains came in the late '90s. I'd read about Louie Simmons using them at Westside and since I love to try new ideas, I went through the arduous process of putting together my own equipment, which wasn't easy in 1998. I had to find a marine supply company to supply the heavy chains, and then I needed to get lighter chains to attach the heavy chains to the bars.

My hope was this dynamic work would add pounds to my athletes' bench presses. Alas, we never really saw significant changes, and I abandoned the idea soon after. Those old homemade chains are still in the weightroom at Boston University.

Of course, as a coach, I need to do more than increase athletes' strength. Athletics is more about power, especially acceleration.

Fast forward to 2007 when I realized with chains I could introduce a velocity component to free-weight exercises, and do it with maximum safety. The bar could be accelerated at the bottom, and the increasing load of the chain coming off the ground would produce a natural brake.

Thus, in the context of a different goal — power production versus one-rep-max strength — chains proved to be an excellent tool. They allow us to employ a higher speed component in conventional strength exercises.

And, thanks to the increased popularity of Westside training methods, chains are a lot easier to buy and use.

Training the Combine Bench

I can say one thing with confidence about training an athlete to bench 225 for reps: *Throw your coaching techniques out the window.*

For most athletes training for a Combine-type test, the 225-bench press test is an endurance test, not a strength test.

The relationship between strength and endurance changes as the number of reps increases. I have seen athletes who can bench 400 pounds do 225 for twenty reps, and I have seen athletes who bench press 350 do the same number of reps.

The key point: If you want your athletes to get better at reps, have them do reps.

The other reality is up to a certain point we need to develop max strength. In the short run, more strength leads to more endurance. If a guy's maximum bench press is 245, the athlete will be lucky to bench 225 for two. A 400-pound bencher has a far greater chance of doing thirty reps at 225 than a 300 bencher.

We need to work both ends of the spectrum. To get better at the 225-rep test, we must train for both endurance and strength.

The max bench press number determines what the athlete should be capable of. The high-rep practice converts strength to usable endurance. Usually on our first pressing day, we work on max strength and finish with one endurance set; on the second pressing day we work solely on endurance.

But your athletes won't get better at the 225 test by just lifting heavy. For the six to eight weeks prior to the Combine, we performed a set of 225 for max reps at the end of our first pressing day. The goal was to try to get one more rep each week.

Technique matters, but not the technique you're used to.

- I tell our athletes to control the weight at all times... except when benching 225 for a Combine-type test. When benching 225, they go as fast as possible.

- Our athletes lock out every rep... except when repping 225. When benching 225 for reps, you want your athlete to *appear* to lock out the elbows after each rep without actually doing so, a soft lockout.

- Instruct the athlete to switch from concentric to eccentric as fast as possible. In the process of switching, instruct him to go up as fast as possible, allow the elbows to extend almost to full extension and immediately reverse the action and get the bar back to the chest. Bringing the bar back to the chest is less of a controlled eccentric and more of a controlled drop. The bar should descend rapidly, using as little eccentric energy as possible, but not bouncing off the chest.

There are lots of contradictions here, but this a specific event having nothing in common with anything else we teach athletes about strength training. In the Combine bench, we want the athlete to do as many reps as possible, as fast as possible, with technique that is at best borderline. At no other time in training is this acceptable, but the reality is the best performances in this test are done in this style.

Pro scouts will not count reps done with a big bounce, an arch, or an action that comes well short of lockout. However, the judging of this test is entirely subjective and the best performances are always borderline acceptable. The athlete needs to learn to walk the line. This means fast reps with just a hint of a bounce, extending the arms almost to a fully locked position, but not locking out until he needs a rest.

Warm-Up Strategies

Heavier Loads

Some coaches advocate a warm-up set at a weight greater than 225 for one rep to get greater neural excitation. This may work for athletes anticipating more than twenty reps, but may be too taxing for those anticipating less than twenty.

Lighter Loads

I advocate a strategy based on my powerlifting experience — two warm-up sets: 135 for five and 185 for two, and then go for it.

Training Suggestions

Lactic acid tolerance is a big factor. Coaches have had success with various forms of endurance training. Some coaches will have athletes train with lighter loads like 185 and 205 pounds. Some coaches will have athletes practice max reps at 235, so 225 will feel lighter on test day. I personally like drop sets on day two.

Endurance Bench Workout

Up to a point, endurance is proportional to strength. You need to get the athlete as strong as possible. At the same time, endurance is a skill. You need to work on his endurance. Work on strength, endurance, and the specific skill of the test.

Understand the athlete is training to impress a scout, not you. You'll allow technical flaws not acceptable at any other time or with any other group. Our job is to help our athletes safely perform well and make the best impression possible.

Here's an example of an endurance bench routine for a 400-pound bencher who's current max at 225 is twenty reps.

Week One

Day One — Bench
135x5
225x3
275x1
315x1
340x5
300x10
225x max

Day Two — Incline
135x5
185x3
225x5

Bench Drop-Set
225xMax
185xmax
135xmax

Overhead Athletes and Overhead Lifts

Swimmers, baseball players, football quarterbacks and tennis and volleyball players would seem to have little in common as athletes. But when you work with enough of these overhead athletes as a strength coach, you notice a common predisposition to shoulder injuries, particularly rotator cuff tendonosis.

These sports require repetitive activities with the athletes' hands above their heads. The simple and logical fix is to avoid most overhead exercises. It's not that the athletes can't do them; the problem is the amount of time they already spend with their arms above their shoulders. Overuse is the enemy of the overhead athlete.

That said, not all overhead exercises are equally damaging. We'll do shoulder presses with dumbbells, but not with a barbell. We also avoid snatches and overhead squats, along with behind-the-neck exercises, which we don't do with anyone.

This is old news: The behind-the-neck position involves extreme abduction and external rotation and isn't safe for any type of athlete. It's especially dangerous for people whose sports involve serving, spiking or pitching.

Barbells in an overhead lift are not especially conducive to good shoulder health, either. Because they don't bend or rotate, the bar determines the mechanics of the shoulder joint, something you never want an unyielding hunk of iron to control. Ten years ago we didn't have many choices, and we used bars for overhead athletes out of necessity. Today some people just use bars out of habit, despite the fact there are now many alternatives.

A lot of cable machines now have dual handles for pull-downs and rows — a much better option than straight bars for overhead athletes, which are outdated for pulling exercises and should be even used sparingly for pressing. Dumbbell bench presses — flat or incline — get the job done.

For power, I like kettlebell overhead swings, since there's no catch phase to bang up the forearms and lots of eccentric challenge for the muscles of the upper back.

I also like the hang clean for the overhead athlete, assuming there's enough time to teach proper technique.

Another great tool for the overhead athlete is the medicine ball. We use it with all our players to varying degrees, but it's essential for the overhead athletes. Overhead throws with the med ball are one of the best power exercises, helping them develop the core power so vital to effective throwing. As a bonus, these offer terrific eccentric work for the rotator cuff.

Overhead athletes almost always need to focus on shoulder flexibility. The side-lying external-rotation stretch, also called the sleeper stretch, is a good choice. I also like wall slides, as noted earlier. In fact, I like wall slides for everyone.

Smart and experienced trainers like to remind gym rats there's no such thing as a best workout. That's true if we're talking about building bigger muscles or improving body composition. But when it comes to training athletes with the goal of increasing their speed, strength and power, the opposite is true. There really *is* a best way to do it.

The problem is what works for most athletes isn't a good choice for every athlete. That's when you have to make specific adjustments for individual players or types of players.

Sometimes this means adding targeted exercises to address imbalances and help prevent injuries.

But more often, training specificity is defined by what you *shouldn't* do in those special cases — avoiding exercises and movement patterns that create problems, or that make existing problems worse. This is the case with overhead work in athletes whose sports predispose them to rotator cuff overuse.

Strength Comparisons

Ideally, athletes should have the same or similar bench press and clean numbers. If you don't see this relationship, your athletes are spending too much time benching and not enough time on power movements.

I also like to see the total weight for a chin-up — bodyweight plus external load — be equal to or greater than an athlete's bench press one-rep max. In other words, a 280-pound bench presser who weighs 180 pounds should be able to do a chin-up with a hundred pounds external load.

Another area in which we evaluate strength is by comparing related exercises. It's amazing how many groove lifters or specialists we see. Strength isn't about how much done in a particular lift, but rather the ability to reflect that strength at numerous angles.

With this in mind, we developed the following relationships. Please note this is in many ways old-fashioned trial and error, developed over the last decade with our MBSC athletes.

Bench Press = 100%
using an example of a
300-pound one-rep max

Incline Bench Press
80% of bench press
or a 240-pound one-rep max

Dumbbell Overhead Press
40 to 50% of bench press
or a pair of 60- to 75-pound dumbbells

Overhead pressing is a lost art. It's startling to see the disparity in overhead pressing strength as it relates to bench-press strength. Most trainees are capable of much more in the overhead press, yet no one does the move anymore. This has been a prominent area of emphasis with our athletes.

We also use the following formula for any dumbbell variations:

Dumbbell Weight
80% of bar weight divided in half

So, continuing with the 300-pound bench press example:

• 80% (or a six- or seven-rep max) would be 240 pounds

• A dumbbell bench press six-rep max would be eighty percent of 240 pounds divided in half, or ninety-five pounds.

In other words, a 300-pound bench presser should be able to dumbbell bench press a pair of ninety-five-pound dumbbells six times.

For the incline bench press, we again use our eighty-percent rule. To determine a dumbbell incline six-rep max for the 300-pound bench presser, we take fifty percent of the one-rep max divided in half, or seventy-five pounds.

Another method is to take eighty percent of the flat dumbbell bench press weight.

Our theoretical 300-pound bencher should be able to dumbbell press ninety-five pounds for six reps. He should also be capable of a dumbbell incline of seventy-five pounds for six reps.

If we continue the trend and take eighty percent of seventy-five pounds, he should also be lifting sixty-pound dumbbells in the overhead press, as indicated above.

Overhead Pressing

The overhead press is where things typically fall off. Most athletes today need a lot of work on overhead movements. Watch athletes overhead press; many will make a concerted effort to turn any overhead exercise into an incline press. This allows the clavicular head of the pectorals to take over for the deltoids in the pressing action.

To offset this, we use seated dumbbell overhead presses to control hip motion better in our beginners. We progress from seated, to half-kneeling, to standing to force athletes to learn to use the shoulders instead of the chest.

If you want to develop shoulder strength, don't allow your athletes or clients to use a bench with a back. They can sit in place on one, but leaning back isn't an option. As soon as they lean back, they'll shift to a clavicular-pectoral version of an incline bench press.

For athletes, strength must exist on one-leg and must be demonstrated in more than just the bench press. The key is well-rounded strength, not an impressive performance on a pet lift. Whenever I have an athlete who arrives at our facility as a good bench presser, I immediately shift the focus to the hips and lower body.

If our athletes are going to do poorly at one of our test lifts, I hope it's the bench press. If they're going to be good at just one, let's hope it's the hang clean. I'll take hip power over prone strength any day.

The Strength Chart

The following chart represents what constitutes strong in some basic exercises for drug-free adult men.

> **Bench Press**
> 1.25 to 1.5 x bodyweight
> *250 to 300 pounds for a 200-pound athlete*
>
> **Clean**
> 1.25 to 1.5 x bodyweight
> *Same as above*
>
> **Front Squat**
> 1.5 to 1.75 x bodyweight
> *300 to 350 pounds for a 200-pound athlete*
>
> **One-Leg Squat**
> 0.5 x bodyweight for five reps
>
> **Chin-Up**
> 0.5 x bodyweight for a single rep

As we use mostly single-leg exercises and there are no industry standards to compare, I wanted to determine what might be considered strong in these exercises. We estimated single-leg squat strength, then we had to actually test our athletes. I found the results surprising.

Jay Pandolfo, then assistant captain for the New Jersey Devils, did ninety-five pounds for eleven reps on each leg. Our Boston University hockey captain did 110 pounds — a fifty-pound vest with thirty-pound dumbbells — for five reps on each leg. The average for our hockey team was eighty pounds for five reps.

Now when someone asks me to give them a parameter for single-leg strength, I can tell them eighty pounds for five reps is good for a one-leg squat. Excellent would be five reps with 110 pounds.

The same situation applies to upper-back strength and chin-ups. If someone asks me what's strong for a man, I say 135 pounds added to bodyweight for three reps.

When asked about female athletes, I'd say forty-five pounds for three reps.

Ask a strength coach what a good bench press is for a 200-pound male and chances are you'll get a reasonable answer. Maybe everyone won't be in agreement, but surely they'll all have an opinion.

Now, try asking a reputable strength coach what constitutes superior single-leg strength or first-class vertical pulling strength. Good luck finding the same level of agreement, if you get an answer at all.

What are the limits of single-leg and upper back strength? If you're going to train, you need a goal. If we're going to train for strength, we need to know what strong actually *is*.

The four-minute mile is a great example of breaking down athletic barriers. In 1957, Roger Bannister became the first to run a mile in under four minutes. On that day, he broke a twelve-year-old record. By the end of 1957 sixteen other runners had added their names to the list. It's amazing what someone will do once they've seen what's possible.

My goal is to raise the bar on both single-leg strength and upper-back strength by telling the strength and conditioning world exactly what is strong.

Developing Single-Leg Strength

Why We Train on One Leg

Running is a single-leg action, really a series of bounds. This is why vertical jumps correlate so highly to speed. Running is simply a series of horizontal bounds. Very little in life or sport is done with two feet on the ground. In fact, rowing is the only sport where both legs work simultaneously. In life, it rarely happens.

In the early 1990s when people like Vern Gambetta and Gary Gray began to point out simple anatomical lessons, all I could do was listen. Guys like Gray and Gambetta basically said our approach of conventional double-leg training was flawed, that our sagittal-plane-dominated world wasn't realistic.

Strength training has been and still is primarily sagittal plane and double-limb. However, we've used single-limb training for upper body for years and raved about its superiority: *We call it dumbbell training.* Dumbbell bench presses and incline presses are widely accepted, as are dumbbell rows. However, unilateral lower body training was frowned upon. Step-ups? Lunges?

My reaction then was, "What do you mean, do single-leg exercises? What about squats and deadlifts?" That single-leg squats or lunges done with only bodyweight might be beneficial to athletes or to those looking to gain more muscle mass was initially as foreign to me as it was or is to many readers.

Training really comes down to two things: anatomy and physics. Our knowledge of physics hasn't changed greatly over the last few decades, but our knowledge of what we now call functional anatomy has definitely advanced. The concepts presented in functional anatomy are what led me to functional training.

Single-limb training is a logical outgrowth of this new knowledge. It'll promote greater muscle growth and greater muscle strength because it works more muscles. Knowing the way the body works allows us to develop and use exercises that work not just prime movers, but also the stabilizers and neutralizers.

My athletes perform Olympic lifts at least twice a week and still generally perform front squats and deadlifts at least once a week. However, I see a future that may not include bilateral squats of any kind.

That doesn't negate the case for single-leg exercise either for performance or for muscle gain. The anatomical evidence for single-leg exercise is overwhelming. As a result, our athletes and personal training clients do lots of single-leg exercises.

When looking at the anterior chain we see the lateral subsystem. The lateral subsystem consists of the gluteus medius, the adductors and the quadratus lumborum. When we stand on one leg, as in a one-leg squat, we engage these three muscles we don't use much in a two-leg squat.

The key to the lateral subsystem is to engage these additional muscles in their normal role of stabilizers, not as movers. In a conventional squat, we strengthen the prime movers and neglect the stabilizers.

You may think, "We've trained this way for decades and it worked." Here's where I disagree: We've done it this way for years, but I'm not so sure it's been working. If what we were doing worked so well, why do we have so many ACL tears and so many bad backs? I truly believe single-leg training is the best way to prevent knee injuries and the best way to train around a back problem. Double-leg training may create double-leg strength, but it doesn't have the additional preventative value of single-leg training.

The other problem: Double-leg strength doesn't correlate to single-leg strength. I can't tell you how many athletes I've seen who can squat in excess of 500 pounds, yet can't do one single-leg squat because they lack the functional strength.

Single-leg strength is a quality frequently ignored in strength programs, but it's essential in the improvement of speed and the reduction of injuries. Single-leg strength and stability is the essence of lower-body strength, and is the most important quality in performance training.

Eliminating double-leg squatting may sound extreme to some, but it emphasizes the importance of single-leg exercise in any strength program. Unfortunately, most strength programs focus solely on conventional double-leg exercises such as squats, leg presses or the unequivocally nonfunctional leg exercises like extensions and curls.

Pelvic Stabilizers

The actions of the pelvic stabilizers are different in a single-leg stance than in a double-leg stance. Single-leg exercises force the gluteus medius, quadratus lumborum and the adductor group to operate as stabilizers and neutralizers, which are vital in sport skills.

The benefits of single-leg strength development are reinforced when we understand the importance of the adductor magnus as both synergist and stabilizer for the glute max in hip extension. Unilateral exercise forces the adductors to balance the abduction and external rotation component of the glute max.

Single-leg training is simply the logical process of using what we now understand about functional anatomy and applying it to training. The diagram to the upper right illustrates the muscular differences between double-leg training and single-leg

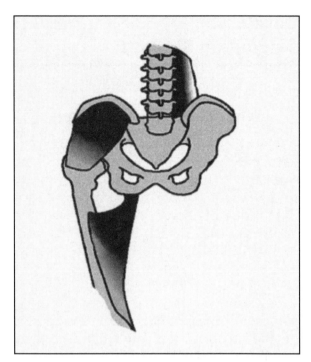

The pelvic stabilizers in single-leg action

training. The key stabilizers of the pelvis, so necessary in any running or jumping activity, receive little stress in conventional double-leg exercise.

Single-leg strength is beginning to be recognized as a key in injury reduction, and is becoming a staple of most reconditioning and knee-injury prevention programs.

Training one leg at a time is merely the application of functional anatomy to training. Almost everything in sports is done in a split stance, or by pushing off one leg from a parallel stance; it just makes sense to train the body that way.

With single-leg work, you can get more stress to your athlete's legs, build more usable strength, and potentially add more size by working around your client's back, which is often the weak link in bilateral exercises like squats.

When the goal is to build bigger, stronger legs, it's always a good idea to target those muscles without placing heavy loads on the spine.

Challenging
Single-Leg Strength

When I wrote *Functional Training for Sports,* I thought it was great we had athletes who could do a one-leg squat. I was an early proponent of unilateral training, and pushed both my male and female athletes to perform these exercises.

Eventually I noticed a sense of complacency among my athletes. They were just like me; they were happy they could do a one-leg squat with some level of external resistance. Some were actually getting pretty strong, routinely using twenty- or twenty-five-pound dumbbells.

Over time, the dumbbells became too heavy to properly lift into position, and the weight vests we used at the time only went up to a whopping twenty pounds. This meant the top weight we were comfortably able to add was about sixty pounds. To solve the loading problem, we purchased X-Vests. X-Vests can, in theory, be loaded up to eighty pounds; we made up forty- and fifty-pound vests.

The other problem we encountered was the same issue many coaches encounter in two-leg squats. As the load increased, the depth decreased.

To solve the depth problem, we began to use the same method we used to insure depth on our two-leg front squats. We placed a box behind the athlete and asked him to touch it. Now we could both dictate depth and increase the load.

The pistol version we used initially caused low back pain in some athletes, particularly those with long femurs. We solved that by using two boxes, one to stand on and one to use as a depth gauge.

Using a box to stand on allows a hip bend with the non-working leg dropping straight down. This eliminates the possible issues of hamstring flexibility in the non-working leg and a problem of deficient t-spine mobility. Now were able to concentrate on pure single-leg strength with fewer barriers to performance.

Classifications
of Single-Leg Exercise

One of the major changes of the last decade in the fields of strength and conditioning and personal training has been an increased emphasis on exercises considered both functional and multiplanar. Where many strength coaches and trainers previously relied on bilateral exercises like squats and leg presses, we now regularly use exercises like lunges and one-leg squats.

We'll next look at the menu of single-leg exercises to classify the relative differences and benefits of each exercise, and evaluate where these exercises might best fit into our programs.

As we use more and more single-leg exercises with our athletes, we've broken these exercises into categories and placed the exercises in progressions. One of the drawbacks of having a broad range of exercises available is determining which exercise is appropriate for which individual, and at what point in training should each be used.

We often see an advanced exercise like lunges capable of producing extreme soreness recommended as a cure-all for nearly every lower-body issue. The current thought in some circles seems to be when in doubt, lunge. Yet prescribing an advanced single-leg exercise for a beginner can be a crippling introduction to the world of unilateral training. Using lunges initially can make sports practice difficult for the next few days.

When looking at single-leg exercises, it's apparent they can be broken into knee-dominant exercises, variations of a squatting movement, and hip-dominant exercises, or those that prioritize the glutes and hamstrings and are variations of straight-leg deadlifts or bridging exercises.

Further investigation of the demands of single-leg exercises makes it necessary to break single-leg knee-dominant exercises into static exercises like one-leg squats, and dynamic exercises such as lunges and slideboard lunges.

In static single-leg exercises, there is no movement of the feet. One or both feet stay in contact with the ground. The body moves up and down in the sagittal plane or potentially side to side in the frontal plane, as in a lateral squat.

Static knee-dominant exercise can further be broken into either static unsupported or static supported exercises.

Static Supported Exercises

Single-leg supported exercises describe a one-leg exercise done with some support from the remaining leg. The non-working leg could either be in contact with the floor as in a split squat or on a bench. These are not dynamic exercises as they lack translation. The center of mass stays in the confines of the base of support and the feet do not move.

A split squat is what we call a single-leg, static, supported exercise. It's static: We're not moving. It's not a lunge. There is no step. It's supported: We have the back foot in contact with the ground, a box, bench, or something else. Other examples would include the one-leg bench squat, the lateral squat and the rotational squat.

The rear-foot-elevated split squat, while harder, is still a static, supported exercise. All we've done is shifted the load more onto the front leg. This is a harder exercise than the split squat, and probably a better exercise for the more advanced athlete. This is a really important single-leg strength exercise, but it's still static.

The pelvic implications of supported exercises are very different from the pelvic implications found in single-leg squatting, or other unsupported exercises. It's very different in terms of what it's asking the pelvis to do.

Single-leg supported exercises are a great introduction to single-leg training and should always precede the dynamic variations.

An additional benefit of single-leg supported exercise is these exercises are excellent for flexibility.

Static Unsupported Exercises

Static unsupported single-leg exercises consist of single-leg movements done on one leg only. The non-working extremity is not allowed to touch the ground or any other object such as a bench. The only true static unsupported exercises are variations of one-leg squats. These may be referred to as one-leg squats, balance squats or step-downs in various texts.

The single-leg squat is an excellent example of knee stability. We won't find an example better than that. As we look at a single-leg squat, we should think knee stability; this is the ability to exist in what we would call a single-leg, unsupported environment.

Many of the single-leg unsupported exercises are frequently used as dynamic warm-up exercises, and are excellent for more experienced trainees in that function.

Carryover Limitations

Until recently, I did not distinguish between static unsupported and static supported exercise. Strength and conditioning coach Karen Wood convinced me otherwise. Wood's rational is the limited functional carryover from the single-leg supported category to the single-leg unsupported category. In other words, performance of exercises like splits squats or rear-foot-elevated split squats did not carryover to performance in a true one-leg squat.

In static supported exercises, the hip rotators, adductors and glute medius do not take as active a role in stabilizing the femur. In true static unsupported exercises, the hip rotators, adductors and glute medius must actively work to prevent internal rotation of the femur.

Static unsupported exercises are essentially tri-planar, as the movement may be sagittal, but the stabilizers must also prevent movement in the frontal and transverse planes.

A static unsupported exercise becomes a tri-planar movement automatically as the stabilizers work as anti-rotators. Wood's thought process has caused me to program exercises in a manner we now define as progressive range of motion.

Progressive Range of Motion

Earlier in my career I would have scoffed at the idea of using partial movements. However, as I became involved in the rehabilitation of athletes with patella-femoral problems, I came to realize range of motion in the lower body needs to take a back seat to femoral control. Often in static supported exercises like a split squat or a one-leg bench squat, the athlete can move through a full range of motion, perhaps with significant loads, but still be unable to control the motion of the femur in an unsupported environment. In this case, lower-body strength is wasted because it does not fulfill its obligation to control the motion of the femur.

To illustrate the concept, in our facility, a single-leg squat will be done only to a pain-free range that demonstrates control of the femur relative to adduction and internal rotation.

In other words, it is not enough to squat low. The trainee must squat low while maintaining control of the femur from the hip musculature.

In progressive range of motion training, the bodyweight load remains constant, while the range of motion is progressively increased. Once the trainee demonstrates full, controlled range of motion, the programming reverts back to basic progressive resistance concepts.

In the same program or in the same workout, we may simultaneously be using a single-leg unsupported exercise with progressive range of motion as in partial one-leg squats, followed by a single-leg supported exercise done through a full range of motion.

Progressions

Split squats should precede lunges; lateral squats should precede lateral lunges; and rotational squats should precede rotational or transverse lunges. Failure to do this will result in exceptional soreness, possible disruption of the training program, and often a loss of confidence in the coach or trainer by the athlete or client.

The reason for the exceptional soreness lies in the sagittal emphasis of most training programs. Many times range of motion is consistently gained in the same plane of motion; motion out of the sagittal plane involves muscle fibers and action not previously encountered.

Athletes often report unusual levels of soreness in an area that appears to be the adductors or the medial hamstrings and it sometimes seems even worse with lunges. Rolfer and author Thomas Myers describes the adductor magnus as the fourth hamstring, and in fact the adductor magnus is the third most powerful hip extensor.

Adductor magnus assists in hip extension by providing a counterbalance to the external rotator capability of the glute max, the most powerful hip extensor. The combination of extreme knee and hip flexion in a single-leg exercise stresses the anti-rotator and extensor capabilities of the adductor magnus in a way completely unfamiliar. This causes unusual soreness that can be injurious or even confused with an actual groin strain.

Many athletes don't use the adductor magnus as a hip extensor until they begin to squat low or begin performing walking lunges. When they do these exercises, they activate the adductor magnus. The response is usually a painful one.

The adductors, primarily the adductor magnus, plays a critical role in sprinting, acting as both a powerful hip extensor and a counterbalance to the external rotating capability of the glute max.

Dynamic Unsupported Single-Leg Exercise

The remaining single-leg exercises would be classified as dynamic exercises. In dynamic single-leg exercises, the body is translated in either the sagittal plane (lunge, slideboard lunge, Valslide lunge, TRX lunge or walking lunge), frontal plane (lateral lunge), or transverse plane (rotational lunge).

Dynamic single-leg exercises are among the most significant soreness producers in the coach's toolbox, and should be implemented with great care.

A static supported version of the exercise should precede the dynamic version for a three-week period. Lunges should not be used until the trainee has done at least three weeks of split squats.

Accelerative and Decelerative Patterns

It is further necessary to categorize dynamic single-leg exercises into accelerative and decelerative patterns.

Accelerative patterns would be walking lunges and slideboard lunges. Accelerative exercises are pulling actions that mimic the mechanics of an athlete accelerating toward an object. These have high transfer capability to running.

Decelerative patterns would include conventional lunges, lateral lunges or any multi-planar, transverse or rotational version. The decelerative patterns have more application to braking and direction-change skills.

Decelerative exercises are excellent for injury prevention, whereas accelerative exercises will greatly enhance movement capability. Both types are necessary, but they should not be viewed as either strongly related or interchangeable since they are markedly different.

The accelerative dynamic single-leg exercises have been inappropriately named and misclassified. Walking lunges, Valslide lunges and slideboard lunges are actually hip-dominant exercises that look knee-dominant.

Although the action in a walking lunge or slideboard lunge appears to be the identical movement to a conventional push-back lunge, the muscle actions are entirely different. Conventional lunges are knee-dominant and quadriceps-oriented and don't produce unusual soreness. Any of the walking, slideboard and Valslide variations will produce exceptional soreness, particularly in the long adductors as noted above.

Effectively programming single-leg exercises takes on an entirely new dimension in light of this. In our programming, I have relied far too heavily on the static versions and have not used enough of the dynamic. In fact, the accelerative options may be the best one-size-fits-all choice.

Single-Leg Progressions

Dynamic Warm-Up

Incorporate static supported exercises in the warm-up, focus on double-leg exercises like bodyweight squats, and single-leg unsupported versions with more advanced athletes. A dynamic single-leg warm-up may be the most intense leg workout your client has ever done. It's advisable in week one to use only one or two basic double-leg exercises during the actual strength session.

If a moving dynamic warm-up is used, only back lunge walks should be programmed for the first three weeks. This will avoid the extreme adductor soreness often caused by forward lunge walks.

Weeks 1-3

Split squat, 1x3-4-5, *add one rep per week*
Lateral squat, 1x3-4-5
Rotational squat, 1x 3-4-5

Weeks 4-6

Single-leg strength

Bring in dynamic versions of the static unsupported exercises, one exercise per workout beginning with lunges and progressing to lateral lunges and eventually to rotational or transverse lunges. This progression of sagittal plane, to frontal plane, and eventually to the transverse plane was first proposed by physical therapist John Pallof.

Posterior Chain Training

After we eliminated back squats from our training programs, the results were a big reduction in back pain. We do a limited amount of double-leg deadlifting, a maximum of once per week, and never utilize a two-leg Romanian or straight-leg deadlift. Once I can better calculate single-leg loads in the squat, we may stop all our squatting and just use the single-leg versions.

I've already done this with our modified straight-leg deadlift. We use only the single-leg version and base loads off the hang clean one-rep max, a lift we'll never stop doing. We progress from a reaching one-leg straight-leg deadlift to a single-dumbbell modified one-leg straight-leg deadlift, abbreviated as 1L SLDL.

When the dumbbells get too heavy to hold in one hand, we switch to a two-dumbbell version or to a straight bar. The one-dumbbell version is more functional, but somewhere around eighty pounds the dumbbell gets too heavy to hold in one hand. When you suddenly switch from one eighty-pound dumbbell to two forty-fives, the load on the posterior chain increases by ten pounds, but it feels significantly lighter.

The problems we initially ran into when switching from conventional straight-leg deadlifts to the single-leg versions involved technique and load selection. We made two critical mistakes.

- The leg was too straight

- The load was too light

The solution to the first mistake came by way of Paul Chek. Chek contends an extended-knee straight leg over-recruits the hamstrings. Many athletes are weak in the glutes and synergistically dominant in the hamstrings, and this leads to hamstring problems. I modified our technique as specified by Chek and *voilà*, glute soreness. Chek recommends a consistent twenty-degree knee bend, and I concur.

The second problem related to load. How heavy is heavy? Because we don't do conventional deadlifts, I needed another parameter on which to base the formula. Since we test the hang clean, I decided to use a percentage of hang clean one-rep max as a starting point because the hang clean should give a reasonable estimate of the strength and power of the hip and back extensors.

We began with twenty percent of the athlete's hang clean max, which proved to be light, and we progressed rapidly. Most athletes will be able to handle eighty to a hundred pounds in one hand in a one-leg SLDL if pushed.

We had to progress to a straight bar or a two-dumbbell version because one dumbbell became too difficult. Athletes will easily be able to work up to fifty percent of their hang clean max with a bar or two dumbbells, a pair of seventies for a theoretical 275-max hang clean.

Determining Weight for Single-Leg Squats

True single-leg exercise must take into account both the athlete's bodyweight and the external load. In single-leg exercise, bodyweight functions as the majority of the load. Because of this, many coaches find it difficult to determine loads for one-leg squats. We have found it useful to follow the same process we use for jump squats using different percentages. In order to determine an athlete's load, we calculate total system weight.

Total system weight equals bodyweight plus front squat max

Example: A 200-pound athlete capable of a 400-pound front squat would have a total system weight of 600 pounds. We generally begin at forty percent of total system weight, then subtract bodyweight and divide by two to get a dumbbell weight.

In others words, forty percent of 600 is 240. (240-200)/2= 20 or 240 less bodyweight of 200, divided by two equaling 20.

This athlete would use twenty-pound dumbbells for sets of five reps.

The reason this matters is again illustrated by the example of the 300-pound athlete capable of front squatting 300 pounds. This athlete has the same total system weight, but would struggle with single-leg squats. In fact, the formula produces a negative number.

$$BW + FS = (TSW \times .4) - BW =$$
$$300 + 300 = 600 \times .4 = 240 - 300 = -60$$

Any athlete with a negative number will struggle with single-leg squats even without load. We still use five-pound dumbbells because they provide an effective counterbalance and actually make the movement easier. This is paradox; single-leg squats are easier with five pounds in each hand, but harder with ten.

Large loads for athletes with great strength-to-bodyweight ratios — generally above two times their bodyweight in the front squat — are best achieved by combining weight vests and dumbbells.

Progressions

Weeks 1-3
Reaching One-leg
Straight-leg Deadlift

The reaching action recruits the thoracic extensors while the action of reaching with the hands reinforces the lengthening of the back leg.

Weeks 4-6
Single-dumbbell One-leg
Straight-leg Deadlift

As the load increases, the load is now moved closer to the point of rotation. This results in less back stress and works great up to approximately eighty pounds.

Weeks 7-9
Double-dumbbell One-leg
Straight-leg Deadlift

We're now using loads of eighty pounds and up.

Single-Leg Exercises

The single-leg strength exercises we use are classified as levels one, two and three. All athletes, regardless of training stage, should begin with a level one exercise for the first three weeks of training. Almost all level two exercises can be done with external load by more advanced athletes, but athletes should progress only after they have mastered an exercise. After athletes have mastered a level one single-leg strength exercise, we progress them to level two.

- Half-foam roller, round side up

- Half-foam roller, round side down

- Airex pad

- Half-foam roller, placed on an exercise bench — unstable on top of unstable

Most of the single-leg exercises fit into the bodyweight progression. The athlete uses bodyweight only, with no external load for the first three weeks, but increases reps each week from eight to ten to twelve per leg. This is our basic progressive resistance concept.

More advanced athletes can begin with external load, such as a bar, dumbbells or a weight vest, but this should be discouraged initially if the athletes do not have experience with single-leg training, or are larger or weaker.

Heavier, taller or younger athletes will frequently struggle with single-leg exercise in the initial stages. Resist the temptation to rush into more difficult single-leg exercises if your population includes athletes with poor leverage or poor strength-to-bodyweight ratios. Almost all young athletes will fall into that category. As athletes become more advanced, any single-leg exercise can be added to the program as long as the athlete is able to do at least five quality reps.

Posterior Chain Hip-Dominant Single-Leg Training

The interesting thing about hip-dominant single-leg training is it is not only single-limb, but also single-joint. For years we have thought single-joint exercise a waste of time. Over time, I've realized it's not about how many joints work as it is about how many *muscles* work. The "no single-joint exercise" mantra may be an oversimplification. I may dislike a lateral raise or a leg extension because it isolates a single muscle in a non-functional manner, but I love one-leg straight-leg deadlifts.

The one-leg straight-leg deadlift is a single-joint exercise. The number of muscles working is what makes it better than a leg extension or a leg curl. It's not about the number of joints moving, it's about the combined action of moving a joint in one plane, while stabilizing in two other planes.

In the one-leg straight-leg deadlift, the action is a sagittal plane hip-hinge. However, the spinal erectors, lower traps and rhomboids must work to stabilize the spine and the scapulae. The hip rotators and pelvic stabilizers work to keep the pelvis moving in the sagittal plane. What appears to be a relatively simple single-joint exercise is actually an extremely complex exercise in muscle synergy that incorporates a huge amount of muscle. In addition, single-leg straight-leg deadlifts provide great stress to the glutes and hamstrings, while providing fifty percent less back stress than the two-leg counterpart.

The same can be said for the slideboard leg curl, where once again we have a single-joint action. Biomechanically some would claim it is the same action as a prone machine leg curl. Upon further review the slideboard leg curl becomes a far superior exercise because the glutes and hamstrings must work together to hold the hip in extension while the hamstring works alone to flex the knee. The slideboard leg curl in effect forces the hamstring to work from both ends in its two-joint function as a synergist of hip extension and a prime mover in knee flexion.

It's clearly not as simple as single-joint is bad, multi-joint is good. If you train athletes to improve performance or reduce the risk of injury potential, or bodybuilders looking to stress some little-used muscles, give one-leg squats, one-leg straight-leg deadlifts and slideboard leg curls a trial in your program.

Ponder this to increase your awareness of the myriad of options available to the strength and conditioning coach or personal trainer for knee-dominant single-leg exercise and the potential uses and progressions available.

Single-Leg Stability Training

The development of single-leg stability is potentially the cure-all for many of the chronic lower-extremity problems seen in athletes today. Numerous athletes suffer from knee problems such as chondromalacia patellae, patella tendinosis, or other patella-femoral syndromes.

Often these problems are attributed to problems with the knee joint itself or with the patella. Frequently trainers and therapists will describe these problems as patella tracking issues and recommend limited-range strengthening for the quadriceps. Although this is an outdated concept, many trainers and therapists still cling to these ideas.

Most athletes suffering from chronic knee pain generally share a common difficulty in stabilizing the lower extremity while performing a single-leg squat. This inability to stabilize is actually a hip dysfunction related to an inability to properly fire the glute medius, meaning it's a neuromuscular control issue, or a weakness in the glute medius.

A 2003 study done by Ireland, Willson, Ballantyne and Davis, described on page 66, concluded, "In the absence of sufficient proximal strength, the femur may adduct or internally rotate, further increasing lateral patellar contact pressure. Repetitive activities with this malalignment may eventually lead to retropatellar articular cartilage damage generally associated with this syndrome."

Ireland, et al, concluded healthy subjects had normal strength, while the subjects with patella-femoral pain had significant weakness. Although all subjects in Ireland's study where women, I believe the same results would be seen in men with patella-femoral pain.

Eccentric Single-Leg Squat

The eccentric single-leg squat begins to bridge the gap from isolated exercise to multi-joint exercise. Eccentric single-leg squats are excellent for any patella-femoral pain client. Clients suffering from patella-femoral pain often experience difficulty during the transition from the eccentric to the concentric contraction. Initially, the eccentric single-leg squat is done through a limited range of motion with no concentric contraction. The client lowers for the prescribed time and then stands up using both legs.

This is the pure eccentric-only version. Eccentric single-leg squats should begin with a short, pain-free range of motion and a long eccentric contraction of five or six seconds.

This exercise literally teaches the glute medius and glute max how to re-establish control of the femur. Remember, knees don't usually go bad. Instead, hips fail to properly and adequately control the knees.

With the eccentric-only single-leg squat, we're using a single-leg exercise to relearn femoral control.

Facilitating
the Glute Medius

In some athletes, the muscles that control the hip are either too weak to perform their functions or are not neurologically activated. As a result, instead of the gluteus medius, the support structures of the knee are forced to provide stability. This may mean pain in the iliotibial band, in the patellar tendon, or under the kneecap.

The gluteus medius is an often-neglected muscle of the hip; the primary function is to stabilize the lower extremity in single-leg activities such as running, jumping or squatting. Knee problems were previously blamed on poor quadriceps strength, and doctors and therapists prescribed nonfunctional exercise like leg extensions to solve the problem. Recently therapists and athletic trainers have begun to recognize the role of the gluteus medius in these knee conditions.

If an athlete seems to have the leg strength to perform a one-leg squat, but struggles with stability, we use a technique Gray Cook refers to as reactive neuromuscular training, or RNT. These athletes will easily perform the one-leg squat, but will be unable to keep the knee from moving into an adducted position. Although we would describe this as the knee falling in, the reality is this is a hip issue, specifically a glute medius issue. In many cases simply facilitating the glute medius will solve the problem.

We found ourselves trying to verbally instruct the athlete to not let the knee fall in. Very often this is a waste of time as the athlete is unable to make the connection between the instruction and the action. Shad Forsythe, performance specialist at Athletes' Performance in Los Angeles, came up with the following solution, also discussed on page 68.

Take a twenty-inch piece of Theratube or similar material and place it around both legs just below the knees. The tube should be light and easy to stretch. Have the athlete perform the squat with the legs connected. The action of the Theratube due to the pull into adduction gives a small neural stimulus to the abductors, particularly the gluteus medius.

We use this technique with both single- and double-leg squat patterns.

This is representative of Cook's reactive neuromuscular training concept. A low-level stress is applied to the muscle, in this case the glute medius, to cause the muscle to contract and contribute its proper level of stability. I really like this concept and we use it in a number of areas.

Once we've facilitated the glute medius, we use single-joint isolation exercises to teach athletes how to use the gluteus medius and to promote strengthening.

Two simple exercises, the bent-leg hip abduction and the straight-leg hip abduction, are used for this purpose. These exercises were proposed by physical therapist Shirley Sahrmann in *Diagnosis and Treatment of Movement Impairment Syndromes*.

Bent-Leg Hip Abduction

To perform a bent-leg hip abduction, have the client side-lying with the knees bent ninety degrees and the hips flexed to forty-five. The soles of the feet should be in line with the spine. This position is like the hook-lying position, lying on the back with the feet flat on the floor and both the hips and knees flexed, only on the side. The top shoulder and hip should be positioned slightly ahead of, or in front of, the bottom hip and shoulder.

Have the client abduct the leg, keeping the feet together with no rotation at the lumbar spine. The hips and shoulders should remain in line one over the other, and all the motion should come from the hip. Generally, sets of ten reps are done in week one, and two reps per week should be added.

Most athletes with hip weakness will erroneously make this a trunk rotation exercise. Athletes must abduct the thigh with no rotation at the lumbar spine.

In order to facilitate this, the athlete can be placed against the wall, or the trainer can stand behind the client with the lateral shin placed against the glute max. Whether the trainer uses his own leg or the wall, the instruction must be to abduct without pressing into the wall or leg. I prefer to use my leg initially as both the client and I can feel when the client presses.

The key is to make the motion one of abduction and external rotation, not lumbar rotation. In order to do that, the cue must be to lift the knee as high as possible without pressing against the leg or wall behind.

Straight-Leg Hip Abduction

Straight-leg hip abduction is another exercise to facilitate and strengthen the glute medius. This isolates the muscle so it will function better in its role as a hip stabilizer.

Mark Verstegen likes to call this process isolation for innervation. This idea reflects the debate of single-joint exercise versus multi-joint exercise. Many in the field of functional training think only multi-joint exercise is appropriate, but I believe isolation is fine for joints with high degrees of freedom like the hip or shoulder, or for joints that need high degrees of stability like the hip, shoulder or spine.

Note the foam roller inserted above the iliac crest

To instruct straight-leg hip abduction, have the athlete side-lying with both legs extended and the body in a straight line. Place a half foam roller under the athlete, just above the iliac crest. This will prevent the athlete from using the quadratus lumborum muscle to fake abduction via lateral flexion.

Wrap a five-foot piece of Theraband over the heel, to be grasped behind the leg. This serves as a stimulus for extension of the leg, and prevents the use of the hip flexors.

Have the athlete fire the glute max on the top leg to slightly extend at the hip, and keep the femur in slight internal rotation. From this position, the athlete will lift the leg to the side.

Another benefit to the straight-leg hip abduction exercise is it also recruits the lateral fibers of the external oblique muscle.

These exercises are valuable in helping clients learn to isolate and activate the gluteus medius, but attention to detail is critical. People will instinctively find ways to cheat on these subtle exercises.

Straight-Leg Mini-Band Walks

Straight-leg mini-band walks may be one of the most underrated exercises in the functional training world. This is a classic innervation exercise. Many of the functional purists criticize this exercise because we never walk with our legs straight, but try the exercise before you dismiss it. Isolation exercises for joints with significant mobility or for joints that need additional stability are not only acceptable, they're desirable, and the hip joint meets the criteria. When done correctly, the glute medius is directly affected as in no other exercise.

To correctly perform straight-leg mini-band walks, have the athlete:

• Begin with the abdominal muscles drawn in; the cue is tall and thin.

• The knees are slightly bent to about five degrees.

• Steps should be about six inches.

If possible, have the client watch in a mirror to avoid any motion except abduction at the hips. The appearance of the client should be one of gliding across the floor.

The shoulders should stay over the hips, avoiding a see-saw action from the ground.

Straight-leg mini-band walks should be viewed as a strength exercise. Work the client up to the Perform Better gray bands for significantly greater function in the hip abductors.

Superband X-Walks

Superbands from Perform Better can provide an even greater stress to the hip abductors, while also activating the retractors and depressors of the scapulae.

This exercise borrows a concept from physical therapist Alex McKechnie. McKechnie uses Theraband to activate the diagonal slings of the body. The thought is the body functions in diagonal connections. The cross-point of this connection is the lower back, where tissue known as the thoracolumbar fascia acts as a connector from the lower body to the opposite side of the upper body.

To perform the X-Walks, have the client stand on the Superband and grasp the right side of the band with the left hand and the left side with the right hand, creating an X.

Instruct the client to pull the shoulder blades down and back, and to proceed as in the mini-band walk. The X creates an adduction force that must be fought against while also activating the scapulae retractors and depressors.

Single-Leg Strength

Level One
Split Squat

The split squat is a great exercise for developing single-leg strength. This exercise is usually step one in our single-leg progression. With older, more experienced athletes, we jump right to a bodyweight version of the rear-foot-elevated split squat, a level two exercise.

Dumbbells or a bar can be added in the front-squat or back-squat positions. In fact, front split squats have become an excellent alternative strength exercise for any of our athletes with a history of back pain.

Tell your clients to think about contracting the glute of the back leg to properly stabilize.

Level Two
Rear-Foot-Elevated
Split Squat (RFESS)

The one-leg bench squat goes by several names. Bulgarian Angel Spassov referred to the exercise as a Spassov Squat in the '80s, and questionably attributed many Eastern European successes to its performance. We call it a rear-foot-elevated split squat. Terminology isn't important; execution is key, and this is one of our foundational exercises.

To coach the RFE split squat, have your athlete in a position similar to that of a traditional split squat, except with the back foot on a bench.

At this point there is one stable point of support on the floor and one somewhat less stable point on the bench. This is a slight decrease in stability from the traditional split squat and an increase in difficulty because the back leg can provide less assistance.

The exercise is more difficult for two reasons.

• More of the bodyweight is on the front foot

• Stability is decreased by the back foot position

The athlete descends until the front thigh is parallel to the floor and the back knee is nearly touching the floor. Like the split squat, this exercise is done with no foot movement and can improve the dynamic flexibility of the hip flexor muscles if performed correctly.

The athlete must continue to think about firing the glutes and keeping the abdominals tight or the additional motion will come from lumbar compensation rather than hip motion.

Another excellent way to teach the RFESS or split squat is what strength and conditioning coach Brad Kaczmarski refers to as the bottom-up approach.

If an athlete struggles with body position, start the exercise in a perfect bottom position with the knee on the Airex mat and come up. Each rep involves a reset at the bottom. This takes the Gray Cook bottom-up squat concept and applies it to single-leg training

This exercise can be done as a bodyweight exercise, following the 8-10-12 bodyweight progression, or as a strength exercise with dumbbells or a bar for as few as five reps, or perhaps three sets of five reps per leg.

Beginners will develop balance and hip flexibility, along with strength, size, and the all-important ability to endure a high level of discomfort while training. But the really dramatic results come when more advanced lifters load up the exercise. You can apply huge weights to your athletes' leg muscles with limited spinal compression.

In fact, the loading capability of the RFE split squats is unmatched by any other exercise that primarily targets the leg extensors, including the squat. When we started using heavy RFESS as the primary lower-body exercise for our athletes, we found they couldn't work both legs without taking a break between sides.

This might be our new squat down the road. We're moving completely away from the idea of double-leg squatting and there may come a time soon when all we're doing is rear-foot-elevated split squats on one day, and a static, unsupported single-leg squat on the other.

In all honesty, I'm hesitant to take the plunge of dropping double-leg squats, but when I see over and over the primary problem is the back, all the time... the back, the back, the back. And when I look at a guy doing 225 in a form of single-leg, foot-elevated squat, I have to wonder, do we ever need to load him with 450 pounds to get the effect we just got from 225?

Mark Verstegen lectures about logic training, and that's where I am with this. When we think logically, the only reason we continue double-leg squats is others saying, "That's the way we always did it." I don't think that's enough.

These unsupported exercises are going to allow significant loads, but nowhere near what we might see in the static, supported environment. The most we've seen unsupported is about 125, about half what we've seen in a rear-foot-elevated split squat. This becomes a really good strength exercise, and this is a big change for us in recent years. When we can get these great single-leg loads without having to put a massive amount of weight through the spine, it's a really big benefit.

One of the arguments against dropping double-leg squatting is the idea of the anabolic effects of really heavy loads. The RFE split squat allows us to get that effect, or at least a greater effect than if we just did the one-leg squats.

Technique Points

• An exercise bench works as the rear-foot platform for most, but if you find the stretch to the quads and hip flexors of your athlete's elevated leg is too extreme or uncomfortable, switch to a lower box or step. We find this necessary for some of our shorter lifters.

• The start of the exercise is a lot like a back squat: Have the client position the bar on the shoulders in a squat rack, lift it off the supports, and take a step back. From there, have your client lift one foot and place it on the bench behind. The top of the foot rests on the bench; this may be uncomfortable if he's used to doing this exercise with the toe on the bench. It may be easier to do it that way with lighter loads, but with heavier loads it's not — the range of motion is longer, and your athlete's balance will be worse. Break the habit early.

• We place an Airex pad or mat on the floor under the rear knee, and tell the athlete to touch the pad with the knee each rep. This creates consistent depth, and also serves to cushion the knee. This is especially helpful when we're testing our athletes' strength on this exercise.

• As you would in a back squat or barbell lunge, you must have your athlete keep the core tight and chest up. Core control is especially critical in the RFESS, as the elevated rear foot can create a back arch.

Testing the RFESS

Recently I performed a little experiment on our hockey players, a very compliant group of athletes. It wasn't research since we had no control group, but the results were so startling I think they would stand up under true scientific scrutiny.

For most of our postseason training sessions, we did RFE split squats instead of traditional front or back squats. My goal initially was to test a hypothesis about back stress and injury, but the conclusion went way beyond that.

After approximately six weeks, we did a repetition-max test. Each athlete took fifty percent of his one-rep max on the back squat and did as many RFESS reps as possible with each leg. Since we don't do back squats in our program, we estimated each athlete's max by adding fifteen percent to his one-rep max in the front squat. We then used fifty percent of that number.

The estimated one-rep maxes for the back squat ranged from 290 to 460 pounds, so our test weights ranged from 145 to 230. The strongest athlete lifted 230 pounds fourteen times with each leg. The weakest did fourteen reps on each leg with 145.

Another very interesting thing happened as I crunched the numbers. In order to project loads for upcoming workouts, I had to try to come up with a max for the RFESS. I did this by taking a rep-max chart and projecting out maxes. However, the results were bizarre. Almost every athlete's projected RFESS max was within ten percent of his best front squat. Yes, you are reading this correctly: The projected maxes corresponded almost exactly with the one-rep-max front squat.

I drew two immediate conclusions.

First, if we had spent six weeks working on our back or front squats with equal focus and intensity, there's no way any of these athletes could have lifted his estimated one-rep max fourteen times.

The strongest guy had a very respectable one-rep max of 405 in the front squat. That's the number we used to extrapolate a max back squat of 460 pounds. Is there any drug-free training program on earth that could increase his strength to the point he could lift either weight — his true one-rep max in the front squat or estimated max in the back squat — fourteen times? And to make it comparable, he'd need to do two sets of fourteen reps, since he did fourteen RFESS reps with 230 pounds *with each leg.*

If he got to the point where he could back squat 460 for fourteen reps, it would imply a one-rep max of around 675 pounds. Nothing's impossible, but this scenario comes pretty close.

That brings us to point number two, which is far more important: The experiment showed the athletes' legs could handle far more weight than their backs were capable of transmitting. This suggests, yet again, the back is the weak link in squatting. Bypass the back, and the legs can handle much heavier weights.

The results of the experiment make intuitive sense. What gets injured most often in squatting? The back. We now train legs with heavier loads, with the goal of increasing strength and size by bypassing the back.

Why isn't this conclusion completely obvious and uncontroversial? For starters, old-school gym culture puts the back squat on a pedestal. You can't convince traditionalists there's a more effective way to train the lower body for strength and size.

Second, the RFESS had a specific niche in older training programs: It was an exercise formerly done for fat loss, or for muscular conditioning, usually while holding dumbbells at arm's length. I can't recall any popular book or magazine recommending the exercise with a barbell, using heavy weights for low reps.

Third, the exercise is awkward enough to discourage lifters from pushing themselves to better performance. Lifters who've spent years mastering the back squat, and months or years with the front squat don't want to spend a few weeks getting comfortable with elevated split squats.

Finally, it's difficult for the guy who's worked like a slave to build bilateral strength in the squat to work with half his max in a single-leg exercise. I can relate; I wouldn't have considered it back in my powerlifting days. Since my only goal now is to help our athletes get bigger and stronger for their sports, it's a lot easier to be open-minded about better ways to accomplish that goal.

Level Two
Slideboard Back Lunge

The slideboard back lunge is rapidly becoming one of my favorite single-leg exercises, an excellent exercise combining single-leg strength, dynamic flexibility and moderate instability. In fact, my affinity for this exercise led me to convince Ultraslide to develop and market a five-foot version not appropriate for conditioning, but specifically made for exercises like slideboard lunges and leg curls.

One of the unique benefits of the slideboard back lunge is it looks like a knee-dominant exercise, but it's really a hip-dominant exercise. I've taken to using the comparison of horses and zebras. Although they look remarkably alike, they are not from the same family.

Craig Freidman of Athletes' Performance has argued the movement pattern of the front leg is more of a pulling action as the sliding foot moves forward. This pulling action may stress the hip extensors to a greater degree than the knee extensors.

Begin by using a bodyweight progression with this exercise because of the additional stretch and instability component.

The addition of a single kettlebell in the hand opposite the working leg makes this an even better glute exercise. The kettlebell produces an internal rotation force that increases glute max activity.

Much like the one-leg straight-leg deadlift, I like to load these asymmetrically until the load becomes too heavy for the hands. At that point we can switch to two kettlebells or two dumbbells. Our athletes have worked up to thirty-two kilo kettlebells and eighty-pound dumbbells.

Slideboard lunges have become my favorite exercise if forced to choose one lower body strength movement.

Level Three
One-Leg Box Squat
or Balance Squat

The one-leg box squat is the king of single-leg exercises. Some coaches refer to these as balance squats because the support of the back leg is now eliminated. It is the most difficult, and is also the most beneficial of all the single-leg exercises.

The one-leg box squat requires the use of a single leg without any contribution to balance or stability from the opposite leg. The pelvic muscles must function as stabilizers without the benefit of the

non-working foot touching the ground or a support bench. The stance leg must produce force without any assistance from the swing leg.

The importance of this training cannot be overstated, as pelvic muscle stabilization is needed in all sprinting actions.

Do not become discouraged if your athletes are initially unable to perform this exercise. Most athletes feel unsteady or clumsy the first few times. One of the major benefits of single-leg squats is the balance and proprioception developed.

This may be the only case of an exercise being easier with weight than without. The counterbalance will allow a client to keep the bodyweight back toward the heel. Strangely, five pounds in each hand helps, but ten pounds will increase the difficulty.

Another method to increase resistance for stronger athletes is to combine a weight vest with dumbbells. Stronger athletes find they are limited by their ability to lift the dumbbells to shoulder height as the weight increases. To counter this, we add a weight vest instead of increasing the weight of the dumbbells.

If the formula calls for seventy pounds, a twenty-pound vest can be combined with a pair of twenty-five-pound dumbbells. Strong athletes can work up to over a hundred pounds of external load, but in order do this you must purchase weight vests that allow loads over twenty pounds.

Level Three
Walking Lunge

The walking lunge is another great single-leg exercise and is mistakenly considered by many to be an easy alternative to the squat. In actuality, the lunge is a very productive addition to the program.

The key benefit of the lunge and the reason it is an advanced exercise is the leg muscles must cause deceleration as the body moves forward. We consider it a level three exercise because the body must be prepared for the deceleration component.

Lunges are an excellent dynamic stretching movement for the hip area, and should be included in strength training and warm-up routines for this reason alone. Athletes who have had groin or hip flexor problems will find the lunge a very beneficial exercise.

Lunges are not used by more coaches due to space issues than for a negative reason. The need for a bar and room to walk make walking lunges impractical. The advent of the portable mini-slideboard allows coaches and athletes to gain the benefits of walking lunges in a limited space through slideboard lunges.

The creation of the Valslide by celebrity trainer Valerie Waters has made the slideboard lunge a staple of our programs. The Valslide allows this exercise to be done on almost any surface safely and efficiently. If you don't have room for walking lunges, substitute with slideboard or Valside lunges.

Levels One through Three
Single-Leg Pause Squats

The single-leg pause squat is an exercise that works wonders for athletes with patella tendinosis or any patella-femoral syndrome. The exercise is listed as level one through three because it has so many potential applications.

The exercise may be a level one exercise due to its strong effect on femoral control. The single-leg pause squat can be used as a variation of the one-leg squat with a pause on the box or bench, or as an eccentric-only exercise. In either case, the single-leg pause squat is an excellent way to develop femoral control.

The eccentric version is a great way to begin pain-free training for athletes suffering from patella tendinosis. In the eccentric version, range of motion is limited to a range that is pain-free and can be controlled. Athletes with patella-femoral issues may initially only be able to control a quarter-squat or less.

If the athlete free falls to the bench or box, raise the height of the box. To raise the height of the box, Airex pads can be stacked or stackable steps can be used.

In order to facilitate better control of the femur by the glute medius, a mini-band or Theratube can be placed around the knees as detailed earlier. The non-squatting leg acts as an anchor and allows the glute medius of the squatting leg to exert an abduction force.

Program Design

Program Design Basics
Prevent Injuries in Training
Reduce Performance Injuries
Improve Performance
Program Structure

Developing Power and Speed

Strength Programming
Explosive Movements
Rep Range
Tempo
Time Under Tension
Essentials of a Sound Program
Ratio of Exercises

Training and the Central Nervous System

Circuit Training
Order of Exercises
Circuit Training Results
Peripheral Heart Action

Hypertrophy Training for Athletes
Body Types
High Volume Training (HIT)
The Mythology of Hypertrophy

Concurrent or Conjugated Periodization

Choosing a Training System
Periodization
Westside System

Efficient and Effective Workouts

Daily Leg Training

Four-Day Training Programs

Three-Day Workout Programs

Two-Day Workout Programs

Low Budget Programming

Sample Programs from MBSC

Program Design Basics

Program design and exercise selection are simple concepts we make more complex than necessary. You don't need to be trendy or cute in your exercise selection. In my thirty years of training and coaching, the basics have not changed much. What has changed is we now have a better understanding of why exercises have stood the test of time. Concepts like closed-kinetic-chain exercise and functional training only serve to validate what some of the early geniuses of strength and conditioning like Bill Starr, Fred Hatfield and Ken Leistner already knew.

Because of the success of *Functional Training for Sports* many people expect to find our athletes doing all sorts of outlandish exercises. Most coaches who visit are surprised to see our athletes performing front squats, hang cleans and press variations. The reality is our athletes don't stray far from the basics, and when they do it is for a good reason.

When I talk with trainers about programming, the conversation often goes something like this, "I use a little of your stuff, a little of Mark Verstegen's stuff and mix in a little of …"

In trying to describe how this works or potentially doesn't work, a food analogy may be the best route. Some people can really cook, others need cookbooks and recipes; some people write cookbooks, others read cookbooks. In the restaurant world, there are cooks and there are chefs. Cooks follow the recipes, chefs create the recipes. The key is to figure out if you are a cook or a chef.

Basic Guidelines

If you are creating your first program, you are probably a cook. You should find a recipe and follow it exactly. Think about it this way. If you were making something for the first time, would you take two recipes from two different cookbooks and combine them? Would you add ingredients from one of the recipes, while subtracting ingredients from the other? Everyone knows this is foolish in the kitchen.

Unfortunately, when it comes to program design this is exactly what many coaches and personal trainers do. I occasionally hear from athletes who trained with me who became coaches themselves. Instead of using a program that was successful in their training, they alter it. Then they email me the program and ask me to look it over. Invariably the program is a little of mine and a little of theirs, with maybe a touch of third party, a combination of recipes if you will. Also invariably, the program is poor. These are not experienced chefs, yet they have chosen to alter the recipe to suit their tastes. The better choice is to choose a recipe designed by a chef, and do a great job of making the meal.

In other words, *coach the heck out of the program.*

If you have been writing programs for few years, perhaps you are a sous-chef. The sous-chef is the second in command in the kitchen. Many third- and fourth-year coaches are sous-chefs. They have developed the ability to alter the recipe without spoiling the meal. They understand ingredients can be altered, but there should be a plan to be followed. The sous-chef also understands the ratio of ingredients matters, and he knows he can't yet cook to his own taste.

After five years of successful program design, you might now qualify as a chef. At this point you can contemplate bold changes to the recipe because you have extensive experience cooking. Vern Gambetta used to say, "It's okay to break the rules; just make sure you understand them first."

After five years you should no longer be watching a popular new DVD, only to abandon your whole program. Like chefs who don't abandon their chosen cooking style after watching an episode of *Hell's Kitchen*, you would only be making small changes to what should be a system.

Figure out if you are a cook or a chef. Don't be afraid to copy if you are a beginner. In fact, I encourage you to copy rather than mix. It's a mistake to blindly copy programs. It is a mistake to copy bad programs. However, it's beneficial to copy good programs. If you are not confident in your ability to create a program, feel free to copy.

The idea is eventually we all become chefs, but we all start out as cooks.

The real key to program design is not to adopt someone else's philosophy, but to develop your own. Coaches need to do what's best, not what's trendy, and should not simply copy someone else's system. In order for a coach to succeed at this, they need to do three very important things.

Think: *What will work best for my athletes?*
Question: *Ask yourself why this exercise is in the program.*
Analyze: *Look for programs that get the type of results you want.*

To create a great program, it is important to have some underlying goals or objectives. Your objectives should reflect your fundamental beliefs.

Objective One
Prevent Injuries in Training

Injury reduction is so basic it should not need to be mentioned. However, the proliferation of programs that flirt with or cross the line between safe and unsafe clarifies the need for this to be stated clearly.

In order to prevent injuries in the actual training process, we need to minimize risk. This does not mean eliminate risk, only minimize it. Everything you want to include in the program must be analyzed in terms of risk-to-benefit ratio. Is the benefit worth the risk inherent in the exercise? This ratio of risk to benefit changes with age and with levels of experience. Things like squats, deadlifts and Olympics lifts, although excellent exercise choices, are not for everyone.

There are two things we need to accept to become better coaches.

- Injuries in training are our fault.

- No one should be injured while training.

Speaking at a seminar nearly fifteen years ago, Vern Gambetta demanded coaches accept responsibility for injuries in programs they design. That statement was a turning point for me — until that day I was just another meathead strength coach who thought real lifters should have sore shoulders and sore backs, a by-product of training hard. Upon leaving that seminar, I took my first step toward becoming a real coach. I made a conscious decision to make my athletes better on the field, and keep them healthy in training.

Does this mean we train with machines and take no risks? No, it means we constantly balance risk-to-benefit ratios. What I do with a young healthy twenty-year-old is different than what I do with my thirty-five-year-old NHL clients. What I do with my thirty-five-year-old NHL clients is different than what I do with my fifty-five-year-old personal training clients. One size does not fit all, and neither does one exercise or one training program.

Risk ratio is the reason we do front squats versus back squats, and why we never use box squats. It is the same reason we do our Olympic lifting from a hang position above the knees rather than from the floor.

As coaches and personal trainers, we must constantly make choices to balance the risk-to-benefit ratio.

Objective Two
Reduce Performance Injuries

The second objective of a quality strength program is to reduce the incidence of injury in performance. Notice I wrote reduce instead of prevent; no coach will prevent injury — injuries will happen. However, it is critical to realize our primary goals are to reduce injury, not to improve performance.

In both the NFL and the NHL, the strength and conditioning program's success is measured by the ability to keep players in competition. In the world of sports, coaches take injury very seriously and strength and conditioning coaches who encourage their athletes to lay it on the line in training end up in a different line... the unemployment line.

The biggest take-away point is improved performance is not the primary objective. First, we need to keep training as safe as possible. Then we need to work to reduce injury potential during competition.

Objective Three
Improve Performance

Finally, we get improved performance.

There needs to be balance. A vanilla, machine-based program with no risk will not reduce the incidence of performance-related injury, and it won't improve performance. The key is developing the ability to balance risk-to-benefit ratio.

The ideal program is designed with those three goals in mind. It works on all aspects of training, but in a progressive manner to minimize exposure to undue stress. Of primary importance, the program improves performance, but never at the expense of health.

Program Design Points

Consistency

A bad workout is better than a missed workout. It is still better to go through the motions than to miss a training day.

Structure

Coaches need to figure out how to divide up the training time they are given. Figure out how much time you have and go for maximum results.

Density

Density is really a measure of work per unit of time. How much work can we fit into the time allotted? Good program structure leads to density.

The best way to achieve density is to pair exercises. This is a concept everyone should be using. Doing multiple sets of an exercise with two- to five-minute rests between sets should be done only by competitive lifters. Those who train athletes from other sports or who train non-competitive clients should be pairing exercises.

The next best way to achieve density is to use rest time for something other than rest. All of our core work and half of our stretching is done between sets while our athletes are resting from other exercises.

Program Structure

Structure is essential. The pre-workout process must include:

- Tissue density — foam roll

- Tissue length — stretching

- Tissue readiness — activation

Now think time: How many minutes can we devote to the above? This should be ten to twenty percent of training time for young healthy athletes, six to twelve minutes out of an hour.

With your older clients, expect to increase the preparation time as tissue density, length and readiness issues increase with age.

In the beginning of the workout we are preparing the muscles. In the next step we are preparing the athlete. A good dynamic warm-up can be done in five or six minutes and will be particularly successful once the tissue is prepared.

Developing Power and Speed

Once the muscles are prepared, the next step is power and speed development. After a good warm-up, we do plyometric exercises using bodyweight power and light implement work such as medicine ball throws.

This is also the time to add short sprints and sprint drills. Many of the sprint drills will have been done as part of the dynamic warm-up, but the actual sprints occur later. From a training density standpoint, I prefer to pair jumps and throws. One set of a plyometric drill is followed by a set of medicine ball throws; three sets are done in alternating fashion.

This allows adequate rest between sets of plyos without wasted rest time.

The nice thing about plyometric exercises and medicine ball exercises is they also provide an increased level of preparation for the nervous system.

The last thing done before entering the weightroom are sprints. We use a low volume of sprinting before our strength work, usually only five or six sprints of five to twenty yards.

For a young healthy athlete, power development in the weightroom revolves around the Olympic lifts. Older athletes may perform additional plyometric exercises like jump squats or Shuttle MVP jumps. Based on the age and health of the trainee, resisted exercises are selected to develop lower-body power.

We perform hang cleans, close-grip hang snatches, dumbbell snatches, or in the case of younger or older athletes, kettlebell swings to develop total-body power.

These will generally be done in a tri-set combined with a core exercise and an active stretch or mobility exercise. Instead of resting, the athlete will do core work and mobility work during the rest time.

The tri-set for an explosive lift will look like this:

- Explosive lift

- Core exercise

- Mobility work

Tri-sets are used for power exercises so the focus remains on the power exercise, and so the nervous system is not overstressed.

Strength Programming

The strength program looks similar to the power program, except we often move from tri-sets to quad-sets. In strength work, exercises are paired with other non-competing strength exercises, and the rest time is again filled with core and mobility work.

The most important thing to understand in program design is this: Time should never be wasted. To create a great program, first create a great preparation sequence. Then choose exercises appropriate for your population. Finally, use time as a precious commodity not to be wasted.

In the simplest terms, use the lifts that teach or force your athletes to do what you want them to do. Look at what you feel are the common errors of your clients, and design a program to include exercises that correct those errors.

For example, consider this list:

- Bodyweight lower-body exercises

- Front squats

- Box front squats — not the sit-down variation

- Pause or slow-eccentric bench

These exercises are important because they all represent an exercise variation to correct a critical flaw.

Bodyweight lower-body exercises get people on their feet. That's where life is.

Front squats virtually eliminate the back stress and technique flaws of squatting.

Box squats force depth, create hip mobility and actually reduce the load on the spine in terms of compression and torque.

Pause bench presses or eccentric-emphasis bench presses eliminate bouncing and arching.

Good exercise selection is purposeful and is designed to eliminate mistakes and correct errors.

Obviously, there are other criteria for exercise selection. I like Coach Mike Burgener's *Yes to the Fourth Power* idea:

Is it done standing?

Is it multi-joint?

Is it done with free weights?

Is it characteristic of explosive sports?

You can't always adhere to Coach Burgener's philosophy, but it's a great place to start.

Often coaches and trainers violate the most basic rules of program design. The information that follows represents a consensus of most successful strength coaches. In program design, certain rules must be followed to achieve success.

Explosive Movements First

If you are using Olympic lifts, they should always be done first in the program. Exercises with high technical and neural demand must be done at the beginning of a strength training session. I judge programs initially based on this one point. If an athlete asks me to look at a program and I see the program calls for him to perform an Olympic lift after he benches or squats, I automatically disregard the rest of the program. This may be an overreaction on my part, but these are the basics.

Exercises that stress the nervous system — like the Olympic lifts — must be done when both the muscular and nervous systems are fresh. This not only insures the effectiveness of the lifts, but makes them safer. The Olympic lifts require a high degree of skill and coordination, and athletes must be as fresh as possible when performing these exercises.

Multi-Joint Exercises Second

This concept has been stated over and over and will be stated one more time for emphasis. Most coaches get this part right; very rarely will you see a program that prioritizes single-joint exercise over multi-joint exercise.

Forget Single-Joint Exercise

The common single-joint exercises are a waste of time. There are some exceptions, as we've covered in earlier sections like hip abduction and adduction and scapulo-thoracic work. However, exercises like leg extensions, leg curls and triceps press-downs have little value to athletes. The time wasted on these exercises could have been used for exercises that have the same goal, but with far greater benefit.

Single-joint exercises for hinge joints like the knee and the elbow are a waste of time. Don't let anyone sell you on the injury-prevention angle. A good single-leg progression and some bridging will prevent or reduce injury incidence far better than single-joint machines.

Limit Machine Use

The only machines necessary in an athletic strength and conditioning program are adjustable cable columns or functional trainers. Adjustable cable columns allow rotary training — chopping and lifting actions — as well as standing row movements.

Every other exercise can be done better with a weight than with a machine.

The silliest trend in machines is those that mimic conventional free-weight exercises. The most important thing to have for a great program is space, and machines rob you of space.

Keep the Reps Low

No one gets strong doing reps. I almost never let my trainees do more than eight reps. If size is the goal, it's a different story, but if you want your athletes strong, stay under eight most of the year. And we never do more than three sets of an exercise, even for beginners.

One thing for sure, most trainees would do better training harder and not longer. In my early days I attempted to bomb and blitz my way to larger muscles as the magazines instructed, and failed miserably.

Later, Ken Leistner's thoughts on training made sense and helped me become a better-than-average lifter. Often I would come to the gym, warm up, do one heavy set of squats and leave. In the process, I got very strong. The process was simple. Have a goal for the day. Attain the goal. Go home.

One mistake I made over my career is spending too much time on foundational, hypertrophy-type exercise. Athletes need to lift heavy weights and have great variety in programming. However, if the objective is strength, they need to lift heavy. My proposed solution is to do hypertrophy-type work, but in a 5-10-20-rep format to get some low-rep emphasis. This is a variation of Charles Poliquin's 6-12-24 program. This means even in the high-rep phases, the athlete is still doing a heavy set of five reps.

We generally do:

5 reps at 82 percent

10 reps at 70 percent

20 reps at 58 percent

These sets are done in descending order. This means the heavy set is done first. You'll notice I break my own rule in this phase. The twenty-rep set is for endurance and targets a different type of muscle fiber. The important part of this sequence is it hits all ends of the spectrum. Strength is maintained with the five-rep set, and endurance and hypertrophy addressed with the ten and twenty. Do this for only one multi-joint exercise per day, or you will overtrain your athletes.

We select the weights by subtracting twelve percent from the five-rep set for the ten-repper, and again for the twenty.

Bench Press Example

200 x5 (- 24) = 175x10 (-21 lbs) = 155x20
The weights are rounded to the lower number.

Use Heavier Weights

The idea of light weights and lots of reps for athletes who don't want to build size is one of the biggest lies in the training and coaching world. Use less weight and more reps and you won't get big? Bodybuilders have been doing the exact opposite for years with great success; volume builds hypertrophy.
Remember volume, not weight, builds size.

Know the Workout Duration

Be realistic. I can't tell you the number of programs I have read that don't add up. Look at the time each set will take, and look at the rest time allotted. Do the math. I've seen programs that if done as indicated would have taken three hours.

Twenty sets is a good guideline for an hour workout. When you design a program, take the time to do the math, then to try the program to make sure your estimates are accurate.

Allow one minute for each set and at least one minute between sets; even this is fast. At this pace you could get in twenty sets in forty minutes.

Understand and Use Tempo

Tempo is a measure of the time a repetition takes. Tempo is usually described with three numbers.

• The first indicating the eccentric portion of the lift;

• The second indicating the time to pause at the midpoint, zero indicating a touch-and-go rep;

• The last number is the concentric phase.

In other words, if I did a normal rep, I would exhibit a 1-0-1 tempo. I have a few opinions on tempo.

• Normal tempo is 1-0-1. I have watched and timed many lifters and even a normal controlled rep was clearly 1-0-1.

• Most athletes have difficulty holding a tight position during the pause.

• I don't favor slow concentric movements.

I find myself using tempo less and less, and instead, what we do is vary the contraction type. Our only real use of tempo is in an eccentric emphasis phase or in an isometric phase. Often we combine the two in one phase where we do one exercise for each major movement with an eccentric emphasis or an isometric emphasis.

Examples

- Eccentric bench —
    Five-second lowers

- Eccentric chins —
    Five second lowers

- 5-5-5 RFESS —
    Five seconds at the top, five at the middle, and five at the bottom

- Eccentric or negative-emphasis glute hams

Jay Schroeder has re-popularized isometric exercise with holds, and the excellent work of Canadian strength coach Christian Thibedeau made eccentric training much easier to implement. Both of these systems rely heavily on tempo.

I tried eccentric training in the past with little success and the primary reason was I believed what I read. Research tells us a lifter should be able to handle more weight eccentrically than concentrically. Some estimates have run up to a hundred-and-twenty percent of concentric max. If you believe this, you are doomed to failure.

Most athletes cannot do an actual controlled eccentric with even a hundred percent of their max. If your athlete can bench 300 pounds, have him try lowering 360 pounds under control. What you would actually see is a yielding isometric where the athlete merely *attempted* to control the descent.

An athlete may eventually be able to lower more weight than he can raise, but the athletes I coach are not even close. I don't know where the studies were done that imply athletes can lower more weight than they can raise, but it doesn't appear to be true.

Most athletes are not used to lowering the bar with control and instead lift via elasticity. As a result, they are not able to lower the bar with control.

Thibedeau came up with some excellent guidelines for eccentric training. To develop eccentric strength, which will enhance concentric strength, he recommends the following:

75% 8 seconds lowering
     2 reps per set

80% 6 seconds lowering
     1 rep per set

85% 4 seconds lowering
     1 rep per set

One way to look at eccentric training is the number of seconds of controlled eccentric contraction should be roughly equal to the number of concentric reps the athlete is able to do. In other words, if your athlete bench presses 225 for five reps, he should be able to lower 225 for five seconds.

Charles Poliquin recommends thirty to seventy seconds of time under tension for hypertrophy. The concept of tempo ties closely into the concept of time under tension.

Time Under Tension

Time under tension is the total amount of time a set takes from start to finish. Ten reps at a 1-0-1 tempo would yield twenty seconds of time under tension.

Time under tension may have been one of the big overreactions of the last ten years. I have found time under tension, except in an eccentric sense, made very little difference in our workouts.

The theory was most hypertrophy workouts didn't include enough time under tension to truly stimulate hypertrophy. The thought was that for hypertrophy, sets needed to last at least thirty seconds, so a ten-rep set would need to be done at a 2-0-1 tempo at the bare minimum to produce significant hypertrophy. An eight-rep set would need to be done at 3-0-1 if we adhered to this concept.

However, my thoughts on hypertrophy have changed and I no longer think time under tension is such a big issue. I think hypertrophy has as much to do with genetics and diet as training stimulus.

Essentials of a Sound Program

A sound strength program must contain all of the qualities that follow. Omission of any one component sets the athlete up for imbalances, and may lead to injury or increased risk of injury.

Australian trainer Ian King developed some of these concepts in the late '90s, and they've since become universally used in modern training programs.

Core Strength

- You can call it pillar or anything you want, but understand it and make sure it gets done.

Power Training

- Power exercises, meaning Olympic lifts if you are comfortable coaching them, but equipment like the Vertimax, and exercises like jump squats or medicine ball throws all develop total body power.

Knee Dominant

- Knee-dominant exercise is a group of basically single- and double-leg squats; these can also be classified as lower-body pushing exercises.

Hip Dominant

- Hip-dominant exercises include straight-leg deadlifts and single-leg variations. Hip-dominant also encompasses bridging movements.

- The difference between hip-dominant and knee-dominant is best illustrated by the difference between the front squat and straight-leg deadlift. These exercises could be called lower-body pulling exercises.

Horizontal Press

• Horizontal pressing movements — bench press and pressing variations

Vertical Press

• Vertical pressing movements — overhead presses

Horizontal Pull

• Horizontal pulling movements — rowing motions

Vertical Pull

• Vertical pulling movements — chin-ups

Ratio of Exercises

Ignoring the essentials is one of the great failings of modern strength and conditioning coaches.

To evaluate whether your current program is hitting all of these critical areas, take your first phase of training and categorize each exercise. See if you have covered all of the categories at least once during the week and preferably twice.

Look at the ratio of horizontal presses to vertical or horizontal pulls, and the ratio of knee-dominant exercises to hip-dominant exercises. If these are not in a one-to-one relationship, you're using an unbalanced program that can potentially set your athletes up for injury.

An imbalance of horizontal presses to horizontal and vertical pulls will almost always lead to rotator cuff problems. An imbalance of knee-dominant exercises to hip-dominant exercises will lead to hamstring problems. Review this evaluation and compare it to your injury stats.

At the conclusion of every season, I look at the number and type of injuries and ask myself if I did everything possible to reduce the incidence of injury. This is how I came to many of the above conclusions.

I still remember a year in the early '90s when we had twenty football players with some level of rotator cuff tendinosis. When I looked at our program, I saw a typical strength program: lots of pushing, very little pulling. Most of the linemen could easily bench press their bodyweight, but few could do even one chin-up. It wasn't hard to find the problem.

After forcing our athletes to perform chin-ups and assisted chin-ups, our upper-back strength increased and their rotator cuff problems disappeared.

Program design is simple if you follow the rules. Coaches get into trouble when they program to their own likes or biases. Remember the purpose of the program is to reduce injuries and improve performance. We are not trying to create powerlifters, Olympic lifters, bodybuilders or strongmen. We are trying to create athletes. Strength training is simply a means to an end.

Training and the Central Nervous System

Any good strength coach knows it's more difficult for athletes with higher training ages to make consistent gains. How many years an athlete has been in the weightroom is reflected in his rate of strength gains. However, it's a mistake to accept this slowdown in progress as a fact of life. We all know beginners progress more rapidly than advanced athletes. The question is why.

An athlete can work all year to increase his bench press by a mere five pounds. We've all been there; if you haven't, you haven't really coached. A year of training to go from 400 to 405, a lousy one-percent increase.

The higher the training age, the less frequently the athlete is able to lift heavy. Training age is simply the number of years of serious training.

One problem with strength training is in the early stages athletes can bench three times a week and get strong. This is why high school kids have so much trouble accepting the idea that less is more.

Each athlete will have a period of free-strength development. Novice trainees will progress in an almost linear fashion with little effort. Any college strength coach will tell you the greatest gains come in the freshman year during this free-strength period. Gains past this point are always a struggle.

This latent period of strength gain appears to be highest in fast-twitch athletes. Fast-twitch novices will make progress above and beyond their peers often without expending equal effort. Two athletes can follow the same program, but the athlete with more fast-twitch fiber will certainly make greater gains.

The difference is the untrained, fast-twitch athlete can make tremendous gains during this time, while the slow-twitch athlete will make more moderate gains. Don't assume what occurs with genetically gifted athletes will happen with everyone.

Unique Characteristics of Beginners

Rarely have beginners been on an organized program. Most beginners, if they have trained at all, use a haphazard program that tends to develop the bench press and little else. Often beginners will bench press up to three times a week.

Beginners have usually never been on an organized in-season program. Just the implementation of in-season training stops the roller coaster of strength gain to strength loss.

Most beginners have never taken advantage of simple nutritional structure like pre- or post-workout nutrition. When we add the good nutrition element, it seems like magic happens.

In the college-age environment, we get approximately two years of free strength. Free strength is the wonderful progress provided by good program design and good nutrition. We're just organizing the training and forcing the trainees to adhere to a schedule in which they can't haphazardly choose what they do. Progress may be due as much to general organizational factors as to the actual programming.

What appears to happen is the athlete rises to the level his fast-twitch fiber dictates, and then stagnates. When the athlete stagnates, we begin to pressure him about nutrition and rest and supplements to attempt to squeeze out more progress.

The problems usually begin in year three as progress grinds to a halt or moves at a crawl. Now the athlete who has always improved in all test areas begins to experience periods of stagnation in certain lifts, usually the bench press as this lift often has the highest training age.

We have three problems here:

- First, in these relative beginners the bench press is probably the only lift with a training age greater than two; therefore, it'll be the first to stall.

- Second, the bench press targets much less muscle mass than an exercise like the squat.

- Third, the body may have genetic limits for certain lifts, much like bodyfat set-points. The bottom line: Not everyone is capable of a double-bodyweight bench press.

Sports performance training has an inherent problem. In preparing for a season, we need concurrent improvement in all quantities. We can't make strength a priority and not work conditioning; our athletes will be out of shape. We can't make conditioning a priority and forget about strength; the players will get injured and pushed around. It's a little bit of a catch-22.

Here are some of strength and conditioning coach Jason Ferrugia's thoughts.

- Move to a three-day lifting program instead of four — Initially I thought I could never do this, but I have done it with my Boston University athletes for the past three summers. I would only consider this for highly trained athletes who train year-round. In my training business and with my professional clients, we still stay with a four-day program.

- Group CNS-intensive work on two days. My previous goal was to spread work over four days. What Jason suggests is more of a classic, old-school upper-lower split. I compromised with some changes I think will work. The end result is my day two and day four workouts will be brief, and will only involve pressing, with all other work done on days one and three.

- Use one lower-body day per week. In our system, we were really doing what amounted to four lower-body workouts a week. The program called for knee-dominant exercises on days one and three, and hip-dominant exercises on days two and four. The new program will keep all lower-body work on the same day.

This is the most significant change in our entire program design structure, and as with everything, it's still a work in progress. What this change means in our case is instead of hitting each pattern twice, we hit each pattern once.

Here's the program design background. Before, our program centered around splits as follows:

Monday and Wednesday

Explosive lift — Snatch
Vertical pulls
Knee-dominant — Double-leg
Horizontal pulls
Knee-dominant — Single-leg

Tuesday and Thursday

Explosive lift — Clean
Horizontal press
Hip-dominant — Straight-leg
Vertical press
Hip-dominant — Bent-leg

In this system, each of the major patterns is hit twice per week. After considering Ferrugia's recommendations, I realized we might be better off hitting each of the lower-body patterns once a week instead of twice. My original thought was legs can handle more volume; Jason's response was in effect the opposite. He thought we should hit each upper-body pattern twice per week, but needed to decrease the volume of lower-body work As I thought about it, I began to agree.

What I'd failed to factor in was all the CNS-intensive lower-body training the athletes perform.

- Olympic lifts

- Squats

- Single-leg squats

- Deadlift variations

These are all exercises in the weightroom that tax the CNS to some degree. Now let's make a list of the other work considered CNS-intensive.

- Sprints

- Plyometric drills

- Sled pulls and pushes

- Interval conditioning

The upper body wasn't getting near the CNS stress the lower body got.

Twenty years ago in my competitive lifting years, the only CNS-intensive work we performed were squats, deadlifts, and possibly some running for conditioning.

Now look at the list: Olympic lifts, plyos, sled work, single-leg work. We've continued to pile on the CNS-intensive lower-body work, while doing the same old upper-body stuff we'd always done.

As we return to a four-day program, this is what the workouts would look like.

Monday and Wednesday

Explosive lift — *Jump squat Monday;*
Hang clean Wednesday
Vertical pulls

Knee-dominant — *Double-leg Monday;*
Single-leg Wednesday
Horizontal pulls

Hip-dominant — *Straight-leg Monday;*
Bent-leg Wednesday

Tuesday and Thursday

Explosive lift — None
Horizontal press
Core stability exercise
Vertical press
Rotary stability exercise
Triceps exercise
Shoulder prehab exercise

We train four consecutive days in the summer — all lower body is done on Monday and Wednesday and only on Mondays would we actually compress the spine. Wednesday is a heavy hang clean day, followed by single-leg knee-dominant work.

We have come full circle in our under-reaction/overreaction world. Our workouts now look like — dare I say? — old-school legs and back and chest-shoulder-arm splits. I shudder when I think about it.

Circuit Training

Many coaches tout the value of the work capacity developed in circuit training, but we don't want work capacity at the expense of technique, particularly in a beginner. Most athletes need a huge amount of supervision, and supervision is difficult in circuit training. We have at least ten athletes, and often over twenty-five, working in a circuit at one time.

This is very difficult to coach. In fact, it is next to impossible to get a reasonable amount of coaching done in a group working a circuit. The coach or coaches must manage time, traffic flow, effort and often injury adjustments. This leaves very little time for technical coaching.

In addition, circuits have a two major built-in drawbacks:

- Inability to do power exercises

- Olympic lifts are difficult to include in circuits

The fatigue generated in circuits makes Olympic lifting a poor choice for inclusion. We don't want an athlete doing a set of power cleans as the tenth exercise in a circuit. As a result, we can't include Olympic lifts.

Order of Exercises

In a circuit, there really is no exercise order. There is a sequence, but no order. Some athletes will overhead press before bench pressing. One athlete will do front squats as the first exercise, another will do it as the last. If you believe order of exercise performance matters, you have another strong reason to dislike circuit training.

The reason we do circuits is simple, yet requires some explanation. I began doing circuit training with my athletes two years ago, primarily for team-building purposes.

We were coming off a season that was not up to our expectations. Our greatest shortcoming was not that we weren't fast enough or strong enough, but we were not a team; in many ways this was a group of individuals who lacked a common goal. My thoughts began to shift toward teamwork and team-building ideas and I got stuck on the idea we needed to work harder and we needed to work together.

An old thought came to mind based loosely on an idea originated by Mike Arthur at the University of Nebraska in the '80s. Nebraska experimented with circuit protocols they dubbed the Survivor Circuit. In the early '90s, I experimented with a basic adaptation of the Survivor Circuit consisting of ten basic strength exercises arranged in a sequence of lower body, upper pull, upper push, core and back to lower body.

At the time Arthur developed the program, research showed a circuit of major muscle group exercises performed for sets of ten repetitions produced a huge increase in growth hormone production. However, what I remembered most was these circuits were hard and the athletes vomited. What I wanted to see was our athletes working as a unit against a clock, pushing each other. I paired guys who worked hard with those who were underachieving, and off we went.

The first circuit we used is described next.

Modified Survivor Circuit
The Ten-Rep Circuit

Weights used were approximately sixty percent of one-rep max

Station 1
Trap Bar Deadlift, 10 reps

Station 2
TRX Inverted Row, 10 reps

Station 3
Alternate Dumbbell Press, 10 reps

Station 4
Ab Wheel Rollout, 20 reps

Station 5
Front Squat, 10 reps

Station 6
Chin-up, 10 reps

Station 7
Close-grip Bench Press, 10 reps

Station 8
Single-leg Straight-leg Deadlift, 10 reps

Station 9
Bench Press, 10 reps

Station 10
Front Plank, 30 seconds

The sequence was not perfect, but we were able to cover all of the major areas of the body. I had been obsessed with trying to design the perfect program, a perfect balance of sets and reps. What our athletes hadn't been getting were the effects of peer pressure. Athletes pushing each other through a circuit was causing an overall increase in effort.

It's easy to get caught up in minutia. How CNS-intensive is the training, how much rest between sets? What is the sequence of exercises? What happens to the guy who squats first versus last?

When we overanalyze, what we often miss is the human element. When I think of many of the coaches I know who are having great success with strength increases, one thing they all have in common is the emphasis on effort and environment.

As we progressed through our first few weeks of circuits, some very strange things happened. In spite of doing a workout that theoretically would not provide great strength increases, we were getting exceptional strength increases. I was dumbfounded. We were doing a program that should not produce strength gains, but the athletes were getting stronger.

I called Alwyn Cosgrove and told him of the discovery. Alwyn summed it up simply as he always does, "Psychology trumps physiology every time." It is far too easy to get caught up in the science, and forget young athletes will respond under pressure.

Another phenomenon occurred that was even stranger: The athletes loved the circuits. They felt like a team; everyone was equal, and no one could hide or skip a set.

The intention was to do these circuits for a few weeks and return to our traditional programming, but our captains intervened and asked that everything be done as a group in circuit-style.

My first thought was it was impossible.

My second: How are we going to do this?

I began to develop power circuits to get our med ball and plyo work done, and muscle endurance circuits for our endurance days. The program quickly morphed from a typical Boyle program into something much different.

Later, we experimented with a combination of modified HIT training, circuits and more peer pressure. In order to get more strength emphasis in the front squat, bench press and hang clean, we did a test almost every day before our circuits. If we were Westside athletes, this would have been our max-effort work.

For most of the summer we did a max effort every day we trained. Tests might be a one-, five- or ten-rep max on any lift, but what the tests all had in common was an attempt to get as many perfect reps as possible with all the teammates watching.

Peripheral Heart Action

The use of circuit training the past few summers led me to try to explain the science behind the circuits and why they may work from a physiological perspective. One concept is called Peripheral Heart Action (PHA) training. The idea of PHA training was originally developed by Dr. Arthur Steinhaus in the 1940s. Steinhaus was a man way ahead of his time; his thoughts could have easily been written last week, instead of fifty years ago.

The person who brought Steinhaus' work to the forefront was a former Mr. America named Bob Gadja. In the '60s Gadja developed a world-class physique by ignoring the pump-oriented training popular at the time and instead used Peripheral Heart Action.

The idea of PHA is to use circuits that cause continuous circulation of blood from the upper body to the lower body. Gadja avoided the pump style of training that focused on a particular muscle group and focused on a total-body approach to deliberately move the blood from the lower body to the upper body via peripheral heart action circuits. He called it the anti-pump. Gadja was viewed as a non-conformist, but his physique was not.

Fred Hatfield discussed Peripheral Heart Action in *Powerlifting: A Scientific Approach* in 1981, and as mentioned previously, Mike Arthur resurrected a form of circuit training in the '80s at the University of Nebraska. Still, overall circuit training has been viewed with skepticism by the strength community.

In the HIT world — Nautilus, Hammer, one set to failure — athletes often obtained excellent results with circuit-like one-set programs. The circuits moved from big multi-joint exercises to small bodypart exercises. What distinguished HIT training was a different definition of the word intensity.

To a strength athlete, intensity means weight on the bar. What intensity a set would be meant at what percentage of the one-rep max the work was done.

Intensity is entirely different from the HIT perspective: Intensity means working hard. A set of twenty reps might be considered low intensity in the conventional strength world and high intensity in the HIT world.

We won a National Championship training in very un-Boyle-like fashion, and intensity played a major part. To be clear: I do this with my Boston University Hockey team and with no one else. I do not do this with my NFL clients, my NHL clients or my sports-performance clients. If you don't have a group like mine, I strongly caution against this type of work and instead advise the strength programming as described in this book.

If you have a group of athletes with solid technique and want to change the intensity, give circuits a try.

Hypertrophy Training for Athletes

I train a lot of young athletes. These high school and college kids almost always need to gain solid weight in order to compete at a higher level. In the world of sports, hardly anyone is big enough.

And yet I never train athletes with the goal of producing muscle hypertrophy. That is, I never use bodybuilding methodology to make athletes bigger. We want propulsive muscle mass, muscle that can contribute to the higher goal of more explosive movement capability. We want bigger legs, a bigger back, and thicker spinal erectors.

In other words, I want bigger athletes, but only if the new size is functional, and only if it comes with minimal gains in bodyfat.

Why would I avoid bodybuilding techniques if these would make our athletes bigger? Aren't bodybuilders pretty much the gold standard for their ability to gain lean mass with minimal bodyfat? The answers are interesting and surprisingly counterintuitive. Hypertrophy training for athletes isn't as simple as it seems.

I'll never forget watching the Senior National Weightlifting Championships in Seekonk, Massachusetts, in the early '80s. At the time I was a powerlifter as well as a strength coach, and as an all-around musclehead, I'd been to more bodybuilding shows and powerlifting meets than I can recall. But this was the first time I'd seen Olympic weightlifting up close, and I was hooked.

What stuck in my mind were the physiques. They were developed exactly the way I wanted to develop my athletes — massive through the upper back, lower back and legs. And, aside from the super-heavyweights, they'd developed this mass with very low bodyfat.

To my eyes, it was evidence that form follows function.

Body Types

Over time I learned an even more valuable lesson: The process of building a functionally bigger and stronger athlete depends on the athlete. We can't train them all the same and expect the same results.

Let's start with the mesomorph, the guy who gains muscle the easiest. It seems the mesomorph can get bigger and stronger just by looking at a weight. Put him on a bodybuilding program and he gains. Put him on a Westside program and he gains. Give him a steady dose of Olympic lifts and he gains.

His training response in many ways is a false positive. A trainer who succeeds in putting muscle on a mesomorph is convinced his methods are uniquely effective, even though the reality is the athlete is genetically predisposed to hypertrophy. That can cause problems for the other athletes the coach trains, because they won't respond the same.

Another false positive comes when a novice lifter starts training. We could call this the honeymoon period of training, when little-used muscles like the pecs, lats, biceps, quads and glutes spring to life, straining the seams on T-shirts and forcing him to give up his Levi 501s for relaxed-fit jeans that offer more room to grow.

When previously untrained, those muscles grow on just about any program you give them... until the body adapts to the program and stops growing. That's when the coach has to look carefully at the issue of stimulus and response.

If your athletes aren't getting the response you want from your training programs, the problem could be:

- too little stimulus

- too much stimulus

- too little recovery

If a coach is working from a template that succeeded with mesomorphs, he may not be able to detect which of these problems is in play when dealing with other skinny or stocky athletes.

Particularly perplexing are the ectomorphs — thin, bony guys, the true hardgainers. The ectomorph seems to be doing everything right. That is, he's doing what worked for his more genetically gifted peers, but fails to gain size or strength. He sees his friends or teammates succeeding with volume-based programs, so he turns into a copycat, assuming he needs the same... and more. The result is years of frustration because the ectomorph doesn't tolerate or respond to stimulus like the mesomorph.

I can certainly relate. I was something of a hardgainer myself, and found I did best with HIT-like programs from guys like Ken Leistner and Stuart McRobert. When I'm training a tall, skinny basketball player, we'll achieve hypertrophy with a high-intensity, low-volume workout program combined with a hypercaloric diet.

At the opposite extreme is the pure endomorph, like the collegiate linemen with thirty-percent bodyfat. No matter how we train him, any muscle he gains is going to be accompanied by some fat. The fat he gains isn't functional, but it doesn't encumber him the way it would on a running back, shortstop or point guard. We'll give him a moderate-volume training program, and try to reduce his bodyfat level with a high-protein, limited-carb diet.

High Volume Training (HIT)

This brings us to a much larger question: Is conventional hypertrophy training based on high-volume bombing and blitzing of individual muscle groups a mythical effect produced by drugs? Or is it an actual response to volume?

The way we train athletes today isn't all that different from the way bodybuilders trained through the 1970s when I started lifting. Back then, the physique-training guidelines still focused on mastering basic exercises like the squat and deadlift. Even the bodybuilders who came up in the dawn of the steroid era were extremely strong in the major lifts.

By the time the super-high-volume training protocols were ubiquitous, it was hard to know if they worked for drug-free lifters. The bodybuilders who promoted them in magazines were all using steroids. If a drug-free bodybuilder had success with such high volume, he was probably a mesomorph who would've had success with lots of different programs.

Hardgainers like me just got smaller and weaker when we tried bombing and blitzing individual muscle groups. Stuart McRobert described the problem succinctly: *If you aren't getting bigger or stronger, your program doesn't work.* You can't stray too far from progressive resistance and expect to get results with drug-free training, whether you're talking about hypertrophy or athletic performance.

Classic linear periodization includes a hypertrophy stage in which athletes do higher-volume, lower-intensity workouts "to increase lean body mass and develop an endurance (muscular and metabolic) base for more intense training in later phases and periods." That's a direct quote from *Essentials of Strength Training and Conditioning,* the textbook of the National Strength and Conditioning Association.

Even when I have my athletes use higher-volume workouts, the focus is never on hypertrophy. There's no correlation between muscle size and performance, but there seems to be a direct correlation between muscle strength and fundamental athletic skills like the vertical jump and short-distance sprints. If my training programs produce athletes who jump higher and run faster, I'm doing my job and earning my pay.

Putting size on our athletes is an ongoing concern, but we pursue it with basic exercises — squats, deadlifts, presses, rows, chins — and the proper diet for the individual athlete.

If we choose to focus on particular muscles like isolated shoulder training, it's to maintain balance and prevent injury. Beyond that, you will never see our athletes doing anything that reminds you of conventional bodybuilding, unless the exercises mentioned above are your idea of conventional bodybuilding.

There's another reason why I push back against bodybuilding-style training for athletes: In my experience, it takes their focus off our goal of training, which is performance. If my athletes have extra time to spend in the weightroom, I want them working on their weaknesses, not pumping up their biceps to improve appearance.

Athletes, male and female, who worry more about appearance than performance have come to a crossroads. It's time to make a choice. If they're interested in modeling, they should by all means pursue it. But if they want to play sports, they need to train like athletes.

A lot of our athletes are going to develop a muscular look, but it's not because we're trying to achieve it. They're natural mesomorphs and their training produces rapid rewards. Some of these guys can train poorly and eat wrong and still look like they're doing everything right. These are the outliers who constantly confuse the rest of us.

On the other hand, some of our hardest-working athletes look like they hardly train. As long as their performance reflects the time and effort they've put in, I'm happy.

The bottom line is this: I don't want our athletes to train to look better. I want them to look better because they train.

The Mythology of Hypertrophy

In personal training, we encounter two types of clients. We have the clients, usually men, who desire hypertrophy, and we have the clients, usually women, who view hypertrophy as a disease. In order to effectively and honestly develop training programs for both types of clients, it is important to revisit what we think we know about the development of hypertrophy.

As a result of performing some eccentric emphasis strength work, I began to question what I had always taken for granted about hypertrophy. I began to look at some of the accepted ideas about training in general, and about hypertrophy in particular, that many of us in the fields of strength and conditioning and personal training accept as facts.

Let's take a look at some of these myths about hypertrophy.

Myth:
A good, controlled rep takes four seconds to complete

This is the number one problem in the myth of hypertrophy training. If a well-performed repetition takes four seconds to complete, trainees should do eight to twelve reps for hypertrophy, correct? Many of today's leading strength and conditioning coaches are big proponents of tempo emphasis in program design. Let's examine this concept a bit further.

A recent article stated eight to twelve reps would take thirty-two to forty-eight seconds, and therefore would fall in the hypertrophy range of thirty to seventy seconds time under tension. In my experience, this is one of the most basic misconceptions in training for hypertrophy.

At our facility, we performed a little informal research with a metronome. We made a metronome CD — one beep tone per second — and had it play while our athletes trained. The purpose of this tempo CD was to force our athletes to slow down the eccentric portion of the lift by consciously trying to lower the bar for five seconds. The by-product of this experiment was I was able to watch many people lift with a loud metronome beat in the background.

What I observed surprised me. Good controlled lifting in my gym was at best 1-0-1 tempo. I observed this over and over, and realized our conventionally performed eight- to twelve-rep sets were taking from sixteen to twenty-four seconds to complete. In order to produce hypertrophy, it would be necessary to consciously slow down the reps to break the thirty-second barrier.

Test this yourself. Have your client lift as he normally would and time the set. I'll bet ten reps will take ten to twenty seconds. Normal or natural tempo is much closer to 1-0-1 than 2-0-2. This alone throws off our entire concept of training or not training for hypertrophy. My long-held erroneous belief in the assumption of how long a rep should take, and consequently how long a set takes, is probably why some of my athletes have had some difficulty gaining size. Believing what I read and not challenging assumptions may have caused some athletes and clients to progress at a slower rate.

How do we train for hypertrophy if that is the goal? I don't like deliberate slow concentric motion. This means in order to produce hypertrophy, we would need to slow the eccentric portion of a ten-rep set down to two seconds.

This 2-0-1 tempo will just reach the thirty-second mark, thought to be the bottom end of the range for hypertrophy. This type of approach — slow eccentric, fast concentric — should also produce more functional hypertrophy than deliberately attempting to perform the concentric portion of the rep more slowly, and it will certainly allow the use of a higher load.

Myth:
Use free weights for hypertrophy

Do muscles have the capability to recognize types of resistance? Can a muscle tell the difference between a weight, a band or a spring? I don't think so. One of my favorite lines of miscommunication is, "This will give you long, lean muscles like a dancer." This is akin to telling people you can turn an apple into an orange right before their eyes. You can no more help a short, stocky client create long, lean muscles than you can make him taller.

Exercise will remove subcutaneous bodyfat and reduce intramuscular fat stores, but changing the source of resistance in a resistance-based exercise will not produce a muscle that looks different. Muscles can't discern the difference between resistance generated by bodyweight, a piece of iron or a piece of rubber.

We may need to produce a resistance that will cause fatigue to occur at the thirty-second point or later to induce hypertrophy.

If weight training had to be done with a free weight to produce hypertrophy, lat pull-downs would be a better exercise than chin-ups for upper-back development. Thousands of bodybuilding articles tell us the opposite, but the resistance in a chin-up is "only" bodyweight.

If you want hypertrophy, program light weights and more reps. The common prescription for female trainees — light weights, lots of reps — leans more toward a bodybuilding, mass-producing prescription than away from it.

For less hypertrophy, stay in the five- to six-rep range with higher loads to generate less time under tension, and do fewer sets. The result: less time under tension, less volume and less hypertrophy.

The fact is, training is about time under tension and the point of fatigue. We can produce hypertrophy with weights or without.

Myth:
Lift light weights, do more reps

Light weight is an oxymoron. Why would anyone lift light weights? I often talk to trainees, particularly women, and hear some variation of *I have eight-pound dumbbells, and I do the same routine three times a week.* When I ask why one would train with such light weights, the response is usually, "I don't want to get too big."

This is based on a major misperception. Ask a natural bodybuilder how much time and effort goes into gaining ten pounds of quality muscle. Most male natural bodybuilders will tell you it takes about a year. For a woman, it could be two years. Our eight-pound-dumbbell-waving client need not be concerned about too much hypertrophy.

Hypertrophy may be more about diet and genetics than anything else.

The Truth about Hypertrophy

Hypertrophy may be the goal for some clients and considered an unwanted by-product of training by others. In either case, it should not be a great concern. The reality is, hypertrophy for most non-anabolic-using clients is very hard to come by. And one unfortunate problem with hypertrophy training is our concept of how to train for hypertrophy has also been heavily influenced by steroid users.

Hypertrophy may in fact be a function of diet and bodytype and really have very little to do with training style. However, that does not negate the facts previously stated; we need to at least understand tempo and have a realistic view of how long a set takes.

In either case, I would still avoid the conventional three to four exercises per body part favored by bodybuilders. Instead, program one or two exercises for each movement pattern, and if hypertrophy is the desired result, emphasize slower eccentric contractions.

Another common misconception is single-joint exercise is better for hypertrophy. Instead, with a client interested in hypertrophy, stay with basic multi-joint exercises like bench presses, front squats and chin-ups. It is amazing to watch people waste time with lateral raises and other single-joint exercises when they have not performed a single overhead pressing movement.

The bottom line is the exercises most beneficial are often the most difficult to do. The body doesn't always like a good taste of hard work. Sometimes, at least at first, it hurts.

The public is uninformed, and often as trainers we're just playing along. We talk to clients about tone and about changing muscle structure to long dancer's muscles. People in our industry need to see this is as salesmanship and not science. Why not tell our clients the truth?

Concurrent or Conjugated Periodization

As we struggle with the concepts of periodization, much of the confusion comes from the fascination of many in our industry with the Westside Barbell philosophy. Westside advocates conjugate periodization, a term many trainers don't understand.

The large differentiating factor to remember is training athletes is not like training powerlifters; this is the basic problem. Powerlifters are athletes, but athletes are not powerlifters. Trying to integrate the concepts used by elite powerlifters into the training of athletes is difficult.

Physical therapist Bill Hartman clarifies:

"Concurrent is training multiple qualities simultaneously. Conjugated means linked. Conjugate periodization is variant of concurrent programming and still trains multiple qualities, but with an emphasis on one aspect while maintaining the others with limited volume in each training block.

"The point a lot of folks miss is each preceding training block of emphasis is designed to enhance the following block, which makes it conjugated or linked.

"For example, if a high-level athlete requires greater power output, a block emphasizing increased volume of maximal strength while maintaining power, followed by a reduction in volume of maximal strength work and an increased emphasis and volume of power should raise power to a higher level than if both are worked equally in consecutive training blocks."

Think about Hartman's definitions and you'll see the confusion. In a sports-training setting, we are always concurrent and sometimes conjugate. Out of necessity, we constantly train multiple qualities, but unlike powerlifters, we train more than strength qualities.

The powerlifter's end goal is always strength. He may add dynamic days to develop explosiveness, but at the end of the day, the goal is simply to lift more weight.

As you understand the concepts better, you'll see training athletes is always concurrent and sometimes conjugate. Our programs were conjugate or concurrent periodization for twenty years; I just didn't realize it.

In the off-season we train for power at least three different ways. Olympic lifts use heavy loads to train for power, while plyometrics use primarily bodyweight. Medicine balls use small external loads in comparison to the significant loads used in Olympic lifting.

While I am training an athlete for power, I am concurrently training him for strength. At certain times, notably preseason, we decrease the strength and power emphasis and have a greater energy system emphasis.

Along the same lines, I listened to Al Vermeil on the Strength Coach podcast on my way to work one day. Al is a wise man, and he said, "Keep a thread of everything in your program." As soon as he said it, I stopped my car and wrote it in my ever-present notebook.

Take your pick, concurrent or conjugate. The bottom line in sports training is we never train just for strength or just for power or just for speed. We need to train concurrently for all of the above in the off-season, and keep at least a thread of all of it in the program year-round.

Choosing a Training System

Most coaches do not choose a system of training; it chooses them. Coaches tend to either follow the crowd, or follow their own training preference. We'll look at the evolution of training systems to provide insights into the pros and cons of each. The key is to take pieces where applicable to form a workable system for each client's needs.

Set and Rep Schemes

For beginners, too much has been said about sets and reps. Programming is not nearly as important as execution. Many high school and college coaches have excellent sets and rep schemes implemented with poor attention to technique. This is a mistake. KISS: Keep It Simple, Stupid.

We should be strength and conditioning coaches, not computer geeks. I love Excel spreadsheets as much as anyone, but the continuing trend of good programming done poorly is disturbing.

You are only as good as the technical proficiency of your athletes.

Progressive Resistance Exercise

The easiest method of progression for beginners is to add five pounds per week to the bar as long as the athlete can perform the exercises with perfect technique. For more experienced lifters, add two-and-a-half pounds per week to the heaviest set.

This system is called Progressive Resistance Exercise (PRE) advocated by Stuart McRobert's hardgainer crowd. Many big-time strength coaches reject this type of program as too simple, but the PRE program formed the basis of almost all of the training for our college freshmen athletes. Periodization was minimal and we employed PRE almost exclusively.

The advantages of a progressive exercise program are evident.

- The system works extremely well with beginners, and may be all many athletes need.

- PRE can be combined with other methods for a simple periodized program.

Have your client perform two or three sets per exercise after the warm-up sets. The sequence is as follows: warm-up set first, heavy set second, heavy set plus or minus five to ten pounds third. With the third set, decide whether the athlete should go up, go down or stay at the same weight.

By following a program of progressive resistance exercise, your athletes could improve 260 pounds per year with this method. No athlete will make five-pound increases for an entire year, but most athletes will be happy with much smaller gains in any lift. In theory, an athlete able to front squat an unloaded forty-five-pound bar for ten reps would be squatting ninety-five pounds for ten reps by week ten. By week twenty, he would be squatting 145 for ten reps. Some of our female athletes have become incredibly strong by using this system.

By the end of the first training year, this system must be replaced by a periodized system, but because of the rapid gains in strength in year one, we found a more structured percentage-based system actually resulted in holding back some of our beginning athletes.

Twenty-Rep Tests

One method we often use after the first three weeks of training to determine whether we are using appropriate loads is what we call a twenty-rep test. In week three of the program, we take the set two weight — the heaviest set — and tell the athlete to do twenty reps in as few sets as possible.

Weight Adjustments for 20-Rep Scheme — Percentage-Based
Weights on left — Reps across top

Wt	10	11	12	13	14	15	16	17	18
10	10	11	11	11	11	12	12	12	12
20	21	21	22	22	23	22	24	24	25
30	31	32	32	33	34	33	35	36	37
40	41	42	43	44	45	45	47	48	49
50	51	53	54	55	56	56	59	60	61
60	62	63	65	66	68	68	71	72	74
70	72	74	75	77	79	79	82	84	86
80	82	84	86	88	90	91	94	96	98
90	92	95	97	99	101	102	106	108	110
100	103	105	108	110	113	114	118	120	123
105	108	110	113	116	118	119	123	126	129
110	113	116	118	121	124	125	129	132	135
115	118	121	124	127	129	131	135	138	141
120	123	126	129	132	135	137	141	144	147
125	128	131	134	138	141	142	147	150	153
130	133	137	140	143	146	148	153	156	159
135	138	142	145	149	152	154	159	162	165
140	144	147	151	154	158	160	165	168	172
145	149	152	156	160	163	165	170	174	178
150	154	158	161	165	169	171	176	180	184
155	159	163	167	171	174	177	182	186	190
160	164	168	172	176	180	183	188	192	196
165	169	173	177	182	186	188	194	198	202
170	174	179	183	187	191	194	200	204	208
175	179	184	188	193	197	200	206	210	214
180	185	189	194	198	203	206	212	216	221
185	190	194	199	204	208	211	217	222	227
190	195	200	204	209	214	217	223	228	233
195	200	205	210	215	219	223	229	234	239
200	205	210	215	220	225	229	235	240	245
205	210	215	220	226	231	234	241	246	251
210	215	221	226	231	236	240	247	252	257
215	220	226	231	237	242	246	253	258	263
220	226	231	237	242	248	252	259	264	270
225	231	236	242	248	253	257	264	270	276
230	236	242	247	253	259	263	270	276	282
235	241	247	253	259	264	269	276	282	288
240	246	252	258	264	270	275	282	288	294
245	251	257	263	270	276	280	288	294	300
250	256	263	269	275	281	286	294	300	306
255	261	268	274	281	287	292	300	306	312
260	267	273	280	286	293	298	306	312	319
265	272	278	285	292	298	303	311	318	325
270	277	284	290	297	304	309	317	324	331
275	282	289	296	303	309	315	323	330	337
280	287	294	301	308	315	321	329	336	343
285	292	299	306	314	321	326	335	342	349
290	297	305	312	319	326	332	341	348	355
300	308	315	323	330	338	343	353	360	368

This weight should correspond to a ten-rep-max load, but we want to know the actual numbers. Ideally the athlete should take this set to technical failure, the point at which he can't complete reps with proper technique.

Loads for the next week would then be recalculated based on the number of reps done. The chart on the previous page illustrates how this is done.

Use 200 pounds in the far left column as the example weight. If your athlete does 200 pounds for fourteen reps instead of the expected ten, the weight for the next week would be adjusted to 225 for ten reps instead of 205 pounds. This system allows us to insure no athlete is drastically underachieving in a situation where we are not prepared for actual max testing. This is a repetition-max test used to adjust weight.

Linear Periodization

Periodization is a European concept practiced in the US for most of the '80s and '90s, and at the time it was introduced, it represented a significant improvement over methods previously used.

Linear periodization takes our PRE scheme and adds linear repetition variation over a series of weeks. It builds a system of gradually decreasing volume usually measured by total number of reps done on the major lifts, and increases intensity measured by the weight on the bar over the length of the training cycle.

Linear periodization was made popular in the strength and conditioning community through Mike Stone's *NSCA Journal* article, *The Theoretical Model of Strength Training*. Mike Stone and John Garhammer were instrumental in the '80s in bringing advanced concepts to strength and conditioning through their work with the NSCA. This system was once considered advanced, but may even be too simple for the experienced athlete. Phases in linear periodization were generally four weeks long, consisting of three heavy weeks followed by an unload week. A basic periodization diagram appears below.

One of the drawbacks of any form of periodization with beginners is the percentages used are basically guesswork. The athletes usually have not been tested, and even if tested, the athlete generally progresses so rapidly in the early weeks that percentage projections quickly become inaccurate.

For this reason we use PRE for all of our beginner programs, and use a twenty-rep test at the end of week three. We can then see if the prescribed loads have been too light and make adjustments.

Bodybuilding Method

The bodybuilding method has rapidly fallen out of favor over the last decade as education in the field of strength and conditioning has progressed. Generally coaches using a bodybuilding method to train their athletes are ex-bodybuilders simply using what they learned in their own

	Phase 1	Intensity	Volume	Phase 2	Intensity	Volume	Phase 3	Intensity	Volume
Reps	3x10	60-77%	30	3-5x5	80-87%	15-25	4-6x3	90-97%	12-18
Tempo	Not generally dictated in American systems								

training. This is an extremely inefficient method for athletes since bodybuilding, like powerlifting and Olympic lifting, is a sport more than an actual training system.

Bodybuilding is characterized by high-volume workouts generally broken down by body part, has very little athletic application and is often time-consuming due to a multi-angular approach. This style of training frequently results in misplaced emphasis, as the aim of a competitive bodybuilder is improved appearance, not improved performance.

Bodybuilding can also be extremely counterproductive in those looking to lose weight, because high-volume workouts will result in muscle hypertrophy. However, high volume may be helpful to athletes who need to gain additional mass.

Undulating Periodization

Undulating periodization was popularized in the '80s by Canadian strength coach, Charles Poliquin. Poliquin wrote the article *Five Steps to Improving Your Football Strength Program* published in the *NSCA Journal*, and it quickly established him as an expert in the area of periodization of training.

The program described by Poliquin took the Stone model one step further. In the Stone model of linear periodization, volume decreased in a linear fashion, while intensity increased. In the method Charles advocated, volume and intensity undulates over the course of the training cycle. The phases are either an accumulation phase — an accumulation of volume or time under tension — or an intensification phase, an increase in load.

• The intensification phase generally consists of more sets, fewer exercises, and reps in the single to triple range.

• The accumulation phase has more emphasis on variety and tempo.

• As a rule of thumb, athletes perform no more than six exercises per day, done in three pairs.

• Workouts are designed to be done in one hour or less to limit cortisol build-up.

• This undulating periodization is characterized by three-week phases with no unload weeks.

Poliquin was also the first strength coach in the US to popularize the concept of exercise tempo. He brought this concept from Australian writer Ian King, as he wrote extensively about the theories of tempo and time under tension, particularly as these related to the accumulation phase. Charles stated a ten-rep set could be done in twenty seconds using a one-second eccentric contraction and a one-second concentric contraction. This would mean the set generated twenty seconds of time under tension for the muscle, time under tension being a measure of how long the set lasts.

This would be described as ten reps at a 1-0-1 tempo. One second down, one second up with no pause. Poliquin postulated that any set could be made to produce hypertrophic response. In other words, five reps done at a 2-0-2 tempo would produce the same hypertrophy result as ten reps done at 1-0-1.

These articles were the first time ideas like undulating periodization, tempo and time under tension were introduced to American strength and conditioning coaches.

Even if time under tension is not the key, varying the contraction type and including isometric work and eccentric work may have been an underlying message that was missed.

Four-Phase Undulating Periodization

When contemplating the concept of paired exercises, the conclusion is obvious: Paired exercise sequences make better use of time.

In the Poliquin method, practicality becomes an issue due to equipment availability. Care must be taken to make sure athletes are pairing the correct exercises.

	Phase 1	Intensity	Volume	Phase 2	Intensity	Volume
Reps	3x8	60-77%	24	4-6x3	90-97%	12-18
Tempo	Varied, Eccentric/ Pause / Concentric — Example: 3/1/1					
	Phase 3	Intensity	Volume	Phase 4	Intensity	Volume
Reps	3-5x5	80-87%	15-25	4-6x3	90-97%	12-18
Tempo	Varied, Eccentric/ Pause / Concentric — Example: 3/1/1					

The Westside System

In the current strength and conditioning world, the favored system of the masses is a Louie Simmons' Westside Barbell approach, which is centered around powerlifting-style training. Although Simmons has made some wonderful contributions to the field, I cannot advocate most of the methods.

• Although Simmons presents his training as evidence- and results-based, it may in fact be neither. There is no independent research I have seen validating the training concepts advocated by Westside.

• Most of the results demonstrated are colored by the use of performance-enhancing drugs.

• The Westside system is designed to produce powerlifters, not athletes. Powerlifting is a sport consisting of three lifts: the squat, bench press and deadlift.

The essence of the Westside system revolves around improving these three lifts. The not-so-logical conclusion is improvement in the three powerlifts leads to improved sports performance. Although in a simplistic sense the improvement of force production will lead to some changes, our knowledge of functional anatomy leads us to conclude that training for sport must be more specific and improve strength qualities unique to the single-leg nature of most sports.

On the other hand, Simmons, like Stone and Poliquin, must be recognized for pushing the envelope and redefining the sport of powerlifting. Simmons' ideas about speed of movement and variable resistance were the first advances in training for strength in a long time.

My objection to the variable resistance methods lies in practical concerns in our group setting. Simmons' two most significant contributions are in the use of bands and chains for variable resistance.

Heavy chains are attached to the bar, and as the bar is lowered, the chain gathers on the floor; the weight is reduced by the amount of chain accumulating on the floor. As the bar is raised, the weight increases as the chain comes off the floor. This is an ingenious concept of applying variable resistance in a free-weight environment. The load more closely matches the strength curve and allows the lifter to accelerate the bar. However, as discussed on page 206, for groups this used to be expensive and impractical until companies began to commercially produce lifting chains.

Another Simmons innovation is the use of heavy elastic bands to provide resistance similar to the chain idea. Bands are anchored to the power rack and placed around the ends of the bar. As the load is lowered, the bands decrease in elastic energy and the load becomes lighter. As the lifter raises the bar, the load increases due to the tension placed on the bands, again a free weight being used in a variable-resistance environment. This is a stroke of genius, but does require a coach to purchase bands and to monitor the condition of the bands. A broken band in this situation could be disastrous.

Simmons' methods are brilliant, but besides being empirical in nature, they can be costly, time-consuming and, in the case of bands, potentially dangerous. This does not discount Simmons' ingenuity, but in a group setting such as ours, makes these methods somewhat questionable from a practicality standpoint.

The idea of using one sport like powerlifting or Olympic lifting to train for any other sport is a well-intentioned idea, but not a sound concept.

Coaches may take some concepts from the Westside Barbell school of thought to help an athlete improve in the bench press, and may use ideas from the training of Olympic lifters to help an athlete improve in the hang clean, but to succeed, we must eventually help the athlete produce and reduce force on one leg.

Olympic Lifting

Much like the Westside system, some coaches have adopted a philosophy based on the sport of Olympic weightlifting. Athletes are again trained for another sport to hopefully improve ability in their sport. Olympic lifting is a sport, and attempting to train athletes like Olympic weightlifters is often like putting a square peg in a round hole. What makes a good Olympic weightlifter from a lever-system standpoint may not make a great lineman or power forward.

A program of Olympic weightlifting or powerlifting will not provide the proper musculo-skeletal stresses necessary to truly improve sport performance. Athletes need to work in single-leg environments to most efficiently and effectively improve sport performance. Lifts like the squat, bench press and hang clean are part of the solution, but must be complemented with specific exercises to develop the single-leg extension patterns of the hip and knee.

High Intensity Training (HIT)

High intensity training or HIT, as it has come to be called, was the brainchild of the Nautilus inventor, Arthur Jones, and is an extremely interesting phenomenon in the world of strength and conditioning. Although the system appears to have a limited basis in exercise physiology, high intensity training has a long history and a very loyal and dedicated following.

There are a few varieties of HIT; proponents range from professional strength and conditioning coaches who believe strongly in the original Nautilus philosophy of one set to momentary muscular failure done on a circuit of machines, to guys like Ken Leistner and Stuart McRobert, who advocate a similar philosophy based around basic free-weight movements. What all of the proponents of HIT share is the belief that less is more. The proponents of HIT believe in very hard, very brief work.

One big problem with this type of system is a zeal bordering on fanaticism. HIT is a small but interesting splinter group in the world of strength that should be investigated before it is discounted.

There is clearly a mental benefit to asking athletes to work to complete failure. The HIT system will work well in team sports settings where intrinsic motivation is an issue. My major point of disagreement with the proponents of HIT lies in their stance on power development. In HIT, no power work is performed. Most proponents believe moving a load with speed is inherently dangerous. As a result, neither plyometrics or Olympic lifts are used.

The work of exercise physiologists in the area of the stretch-shortening cycle and the force velocity curve make this stance difficult to defend. Proponents of HIT believe we lift for strength and separately practice sport skills, and there is no neurological midground. Some proponents of HIT are beginning to use plyometrics to develop the stretch-shortening cycle, although many of the early proponents saw no need for such exercises.

Combination Approach

The reality is no single system provides all the answers. A sound training program will take strength ideas from powerlifting, power ideas from Olympic lifting, speed ideas from track, and injury-prevention concepts from physical therapy. The integration of all these disciplines will lead to the ultimate program.

In any case the most important point in program design is to choose a system you understand, and choose exercises you are comfortable teaching.

Efficient and Effective Workouts

Having training knowledge is one thing. Being able to take that knowledge and use it to design a program is another thing entirely. The key to being able to design great programs is being able to filter information. You can't make a change every time a new idea comes across your desk. You need to look at new information and filter out the hype.

The more time you spend with your athletes, the better your results will be. For this reason, I am a proponent of four-day-per-week training programs. Some coaches prefer three sessions per week, but program design is easiest and most efficient in a four-day program.

Daily Leg Training

Until three years ago, daily leg training was a staple of our program, and in our three-day programs we still do lower body work every day. The emphasis used to switch from knee-dominant exercises on days one and three to hip-dominant exercises on days two and four. Our observation had been this was not a problem. The key we believed was in alternating the dominant joint from day to day.

Although the glutes and hamstrings are obviously used in squatting exercises on days one and three, there did not seem to be a detrimental effect in focusing on the glutes and hamstrings on days two and four. We successfully used this system for close to ten years and had done so without any real difficulty. In our summer training programs we train on a Monday through Thursday schedule, but still did not seem to have issues with overtraining or injury even when training four consecutive days.

As noted in the section on the CNS-intensive training on page 248, Jason Ferrugia gave me food for thought and experimentation with regard to the four-day schedules, and as a result, we made some drastic changes.

The second portion of the strength and power program consists of a pair of major multi-joint exercises, again complemented by a stretch for one of the two muscles or muscle groups worked.

On days one and three, squat variations or deadlift variations are paired are with a vertical pulling movement. A stretch for the hips is generally done between sets of lower body and whatever variety of pulling movement is scheduled.

On days two and four, the bench press, incline bench press or some variation (formerly paired with a straight-leg hip-extension exercise like a single-leg straight-leg deadlift) are done. These are now tri-setted with a core exercise and stretch for the upper back region.

The third portion of the strength and power workout is a tri-set, or in some cases a quad-set. Three or four exercises are done, sometimes in conjunction with a stretch. Without using a tri-set or quad-set, it is difficult to address all that must be done in the program.

This is a compromise, but keeps the workout to approximately one hour. Research indicates strength workouts longer than an hour can result in significant cortisol build-up. Adding a third pair of exercises would add ten to fifteen minutes to the workout, whereas making the second pair into a tri-set or quad-set results in very little additional time.

The third portion of the program will vary depending on the specific phase of the program, but generally will include an overhead or vertical press, a rotary exercise, and some type of rehabilitative or specialty work for the hips or shoulders.

On days one and three, some type of rotary stretch for the low back is included. On days two and four, a stretch for the hamstrings is performed. These stretches are always active-isolated stretches.

The following section includes worksheets for each variation of the program to facilitate your program design.

Four-Day Workout Programs

Training four times a week is the gold standard in training programs. The following chart takes the components discussed previously and demonstrates how these qualities fit into a four-day workout.

This table is the key to programming. Once you understand the concept, the table is like a fill-in-the-blank template for workouts.

As you can see, torso or core work is done every day, and med ball training is done twice a week. Two days focus on the core strength and stability exercises described in the core strength chapter, and two days are power days with the medicine ball.

In the next portion of the workout, the focus is again on power development through Olympic lifting.

Olympic lifts are done on lower body days to concentrate the CNS load. Snatches are done on Mondays in conjunction with a heavier leg day. Hang cleans are done on the second lower body day — Wednesdays for us, Thursdays for most M-T-Th-F routines — in conjunction with more single-leg lower body work.

On days two and four we do upper body strength training.

This is the basic template for a healthy athlete, but not for every athlete. For athletes with injury problems who are unable to Olympic lift, we may substitute jump squats, jumps on the Vertimax, or jumps on the Shuttle MVP. The important thing is to get some explosive, resisted hip extension, not to force everyone to Olympic lift.

Olympic movements should not be paired with other exercises. Exercises with a high neural and technical demand should not be coupled. The explosive, total body nature of these exercises is not conducive to combinations.

Four-Day Workout Program

Day One	Day Two	Day Three	Day Four
Movement Skills and Conditioning — One hour			
Warm-up Linear	Warm-up Multi-directional	Warm-up Linear	Warm-up Multi-directional
Linear Speed Plyometric	Lateral Speed Plyometric	Linear Speed Plyometric	Lateral Speed Plyometric
Linear Conditioning	Lateral Conditioning	Linear Conditioning	Lateral Conditioning
Torso Power — Med Ball	Torso Strength/Stability	Torso Power — Med Ball	Torso Strength/Stability
Power and Strength Development — One hour			
Explosive — Olympic	Upper Body	Explosive — Olympic	Upper Body
Stretch — Quad and Psoas			
Pair One	**Pair One**	**Pair One**	**Pair One**
Knee-dominant, Double-leg	Horizontal Press, Supine	Knee-dominant, Double-leg	Horizontal Press, Incline
Stretch — Lat	*Stretch — Chest*	*Stretch — Lat*	*Stretch — Chest*
Vertical Pull	Hip-dominant Straight-leg	Vertical Pull	Hip-dominant Straight-leg
Tri-set One	**Tri-set One**	**Tri-set One**	**Tri-set One**
Knee-dominant, Single-leg	Vertical Press or Rehab/Specialty	Knee-dominant, Single-leg	Vertical Press or Rehab/Specialty
Horizontal Pull	Hip-dominant Bent-leg	Horizontal Pull	Hip-dominant Bent-leg
Stretch —Rotational	*Stretch — Hamstrings*	*Stretch — Rotational*	*Stretch — Hamstrings*
Rotary or Rehab/Specialty	Rotary or Rehab/Specialty	Rotary or Rehab/Specialty	Rotary or Rehab/Specialty

Four-Day Program Design Worksheet

Fill in the blanks with exercises from the proper category.
To design a four-day program, use two sheets.

Day One	Exercise	Day Two	Exercise
Explosive/ Olympic		Upper Body	
Stretch — Quad/Psoas			
Pair One		**Pair One**	
Knee-dominant, Double-leg		Horizontal Press, Supine	
Stretch — Lat		*Stretch — Chest*	
Vertical Pull		Hip-dominant Straight-leg	
Tri-set One		**Tri-set One**	
Knee-dominant, Single-leg		Vertical Press or Rehab/ Specialty	
Horizontal Pull		Hip-dominant Bent-leg	
Stretch — Rotational		*Stretch — Hamstrings*	
Rotary or Rehab/ Specialty		Rotary or Rehab/ Specialty	

Three-Day Workout Programs

Three-day workouts may follow a few different patterns depending on the situation. If the workout is a Monday, Wednesday and Friday pattern, each workout is total-body. This is the plan illustrated in the sample program and worksheet on the following pages.

In a school setting, three-day programs can also be done Monday, Tuesday and Thursday, or Tuesday, Thursday and Friday to increase time utilization in the weightroom. The difference here is we would have two consecutive days and one non-consecutive day.

The two consecutive days would be performed like the four-day split — use the four-day worksheet — with the non-consecutive day being a total-body workout.

In other words for a Monday, Tuesday and Thursday program use day one and day two from the four-day program and on Thursday do a total-body workout.

Three-day programs include numerous compromises. It is no longer possible to work each specific area two times during the week. Vertical pressing and hip-dominant exercises might only be done once a week, while double-leg knee-dominant exercises and horizontal pressing may be done twice per week.

If you fill in the blanks with the exercises of your choosing for a three-day program, you have twenty-five percent fewer blanks to fill in than in a four-day program. As a result, compromises must be made, and the overall effectiveness of the workout is potentially decreased by the same twenty-five percent.

Three-day workouts aren't inherently bad, but you have to realize it is more difficult to put the pieces together in a three-day program.

Three-Day Workout Program

Day One	Day Two	Day Three
Movement Skill and Conditioning — One Hour		
For warm-up, speed development, plyometrics conditioning and core work. The days are alternated linear-lateral-linear in the first week and lateral-linear-lateral in the second week. This allows three linear workouts and three multi-directional workouts every two weeks.		
Explosive/Olympic	Explosive/Olympic	Explosive/Olympic
Stretch — Quad/Psoas		
Pair One	**Pair One**	**Pair One**
Knee-dominant, Double-leg	Horizontal Press, Supine	Knee-dominant, Double-leg
Stretch — Lat	*Stretch — Chest*	*Stretch — Lat*
Vertical Pull	Knee-dominant, Single-leg	Vertical Pull
Tri-set One	**Tri-set One**	**Tri-set One**
Knee-dominant, Single-leg	Vertical Press	Horizontal Press
Horizontal Press, Incline	Horizontal Pull	Horizontal Pull
Stretch — Hamstrings	*Stretch — Rotational*	*Stretch — Hamstrings*
Hip-dominant Straight-leg	Hip-dominant Bent-leg	Rotary or Rehab

Three-Day Program Design Worksheet

Fill in the blanks with exercises from the proper category.

Explosive/ Olympic		Explosive/ Olympic		Explosive/ Olympic	
Stretch — Quad/Psoas					
Pair One		**Pair One**		**Pair One**	
Knee-dominant, Double-leg		Horizontal Press, Supine		Knee-dominant, Double-leg	
Stretch Lat		*Stretch Chest*		*Stretch Lat*	
Vertical Pull		Knee-dominant, Single-leg		Vertical Pull	
Tri-set One		**Tri-set One**		**Tri-set One**	
Knee-dominant, Single-leg		Vertical Press		Horizontal Press	
Horizontal Press, Incline		Horizontal Pull		Horizontal Pull	
Stretch Hamstrings		*Stretch Rotational*		*Stretch Hamstrings*	
Hip-dominant Straight-leg		Hip-dominant Bent-leg		Rotary or Rehab	

Two-Day Workout Programs

Two-day workout schedules really force us to modify some of the initial recommendations. All of the necessary exercise categories are clearly more difficult to address in a two-day program.

In reality each category is addressed once per week. Each day features a knee-dominant exercise, a hip-dominant exercise, a pushing exercise and a pulling exercise.

A good solution for two-day programming is to use combination explosive movements like the clean, front squat and push-press, or the snatch, back squat and push-press.

Still another possibility is to use exercises like the high incline press (a combination of vertical and horizontal press), dumbbell curl and press (a vertical press plus elbow flexion), dips, V-handle pull-ups with the nose to the bar (a combination of chin-up and row functions), or chin-ups to the sternum, a combination of chin-up and row. These exercises fall in the in-between category, and as a result are more useful in two-day programs.

Two-day programs should be reserved for in-season lifting or for endurance athletes who do not have the time or physical energy and recovery to strength train three or four times per week.

Two-Day Workout Program

Warm-Up *Combine linear and lateral concepts*	
Linear Plyometrics	Lateral Plyometrics
Core *Use a combination of conventional core and med ball*	
Day One	**Day Two**
Explosive/ Olympic / Combo	Explosive/ Olympic/ Combo
Stretch Psoas	
Pair One	**Pair One**
Knee-dominant Double-leg	Knee-dominant Single-leg
Stretch Chest or Quad	Stretch Chest or Quad
Horizontal Supine Press	Incline Press
Tri-set One	**Tri-set One**
Vertical Pull	Horizontal Pull
Stretch — Lat or Hamstring	
Hip-dominant Bent-leg	Hip-dominant Straight-leg
Rotational or Rehab	Rotational or Rehab

Low-Budget Programming

Recently I was approached by one of my former athletes, a two-time Olympian, now coaching women's high school hockey. As a former Olympic team member, the coach is well aware of the need for training, but faced the same hurdles so many high school coaches face: how to get these young women to train with no equipment and no facility.

We had three main issues:

- To be effective this program had to be done at the rink immediately after practice. If not, attendance would be a problem.

- The program would have to be done in a narrow area in front of the bleachers with twenty women at a time.

- The program had to be implemented with no budget.

I thought back to my early *NSCA Journal* days and the excellent articles written by Istvan Javorek about the innovative training he had done at his community college in Kansas. Then I thought about Dan John's outstanding work with complexes, and the solution became obvious: bodyweight and dumbbells in combinations.

Armed with a limited selection of dumbbells and the knowledge we had bleachers, a progressive program began to take shape.

Initially the program would be done primarily with bodyweight. The dumbbells would only be used for two exercises, a dumbbell row and a combination of half-squat, hammer curl and overhead press.

This would make the workout:

- Simple

- Time effective

- Muscularly effective

We chose one exercise for each area:

Power
Squat jumps, 3x5

Upper Push
Push-up, 2x max, up to 10

Knee Dominant
Bodyweight split squat, 2x10

Hip Dominant
Forward-reaching single-leg
straight-leg deadlift

Upper Pull
Dumbbell row

In addition, we added the half-squat, hammer curl and overhead press segment to give an introduction to total-body combinations and hopefully form the basis for future explosive combos.

Progressions were easy. For split squats we added dumbbells in week two and moved to a rear-foot-elevated split squat in week four. For push-up progressions, we elevated the feet on the bleachers.

For the dumbbell row, the plan was to try to procure dumbbells of increasingly larger sizes as strength increased. Upper-body pulling exercises are the most difficult to replicate without equipment.

We changed the reaching single-leg straight-leg deadlift to a single-dumbbell version when we felt the athletes were ready — technique was the greatest issue — and eventually to two dumbbells.

The idea was to gradually increase the complex to a squat, cheat curl and push press combination if the girls continued to gain technical proficiency.

To begin we had two goals:

- To be consistent and train three days a week

- To become technically sound

If we became consistent and technically sound, the wonders of progressive resistance exercise would do its magic. Split squats would become rear-foot-elevated split squats, initially with bodyweight and eventually, like the initial split squat, done with dumbbells. Eventually, we might get to real single-leg squats.

Total time for the first workout was about twelve minutes. We introduced the workout and let the players perform it.

Squat jumps were done first, followed by paired push-ups and split squats. Reaching single-leg straight-leg deadlifts were paired with dumbbell rows, while the squat-curl-press was the finisher.

Workout one was a little ugly as we struggled to teach seventeen total beginners out of a group of twenty. Workout two went much more smoothly as they started to understand the process. Workout three began to look like a team lift.

We received odd looks from the collection of parents, siblings and figure skaters in the rink, but slowly those switched to looks of respect as they saw the team work.

Dumbbell rows and overhead presses were a work in progress, but the overall progress was nothing short of amazing. Over a period of a few weeks, a group of young women, most of whom had never lifted a weight began to grasp the basic concept of progressive resistance exercise.

The key to this program is that it is balanced, simple and cheap. This is exactly what a high school coach needs. Stop making excuses if your equipment is limited. Take some time to ask yourself how to get the job done.

Then start rounding up some old dumbbells and get your program started.

Static Stretching and Mobility Circuits

Our Boston University Hockey Team mobility program begins with a foam roll, followed by a ten-station static stretch circuit and a ten-station mobility circuit prior to each workout. We also use *Workout Muse 50-10* tapes. The tapes are made for fitness bootcamp training, but are perfect for this application. The recordings let us focus on coaching. The actual exercises are listed below.

Stretch	Switch Every Minute
1	Right Hamstring, Left Hamstring
2	Right Hip Flexor, Left Hip Flexor
3	Table Hip Rotator Right, Table Hip Rotator Left
4	Table Groin Right, Table Groin Left
5	Box Hip Flexor Right, Box Hip Flexor Left
6	Stretchmate Lat (Side to side, switch at 30 seconds)
7	TrueStretch Pec
8	Wall Hip Rotator Right, Wall Hip Rotator Left
9	Wall Rectus Right, Wall Rectus Left
10	Tennis Ball T-Spine
Mobility	
1	Lateral Squat
2	Split Squat
3	Rotational Squat
4	Single-Leg Straight-leg Deadlift
5	Valslide Hip Flexion
6	Stability Ball Internal Rotational
7	Half-kneeling Ankle Mobility
8	Seated T-Spine
9	Wall Slides
10	Push-up

Plate Circuit

The Plate Circuit is a thirty-on, thirty-off circuit done with a partner. For athletic adult men, use a thirty-five-pound plate; adjust accordingly for younger or female athletes. Partner one performs the exercise listed and passes the plate to partner two. For these circuits we use *Workout Muse 30-5-30* tracks. The exercises are arranged in a Peripheral Heart Action sequence of lower body, upper push, upper pull, core. In this circuit we want to work for a full thirty seconds focusing on getting as many reps as possible with good technique.

35-Pound Plate Circuit
Low Plate Squat
Weighted Push-up
One-Arm Row
Plate Crunch
Wheelbarrow
Overhead Lunge Walk
Staggered Push-up
One-Arm Row
Plank Circuit, R-F-L, ten-second holds
Single-leg Straight-leg Deadlift
Neider Press
Lateral Squat
Snatch
Car
Diagonal Plate Raise

Ten-Rep Circuit

The ten-rep circuit is a physically demanding workout based on Mike Arthur's Nebraska Football Survivor Circuit. Exercises are done with a partner in a "you go, I go" format. We try to pair athletes of contrasting ability, like a hard worker paired with an underachiever. We stay on a one-minute clock using *Workout Muse 50-10* tracks. The exercises are arranged in Peripheral Heart Action sequence of upper push, core, lower, upper pull in order to stress but not overstress. Individual muscle groups may get up three or four minutes to recover, however the systemic stress remains strong. Focus here is on ten reps, only with heavier loads. This is not intended to be a muscle endurance workout.

Ten-Rep Circuit
Dumbbell Bench
Plank Row
Trap Bar Deadlift
Dumbbell Row
Dumbbell Press
Single-leg Straight-leg Deadlift
Dumbbell Incline
Bar Rollout
Rear-foot-elevated Split Squat
Chin-up

Day Three Workout Variations

There are three variations of the day three workout. The first is an Olympic workout followed by a series of dumbbell complexes loosely based on the work of Istvan Javorek. The dumbbell complex is done without putting the dumbbells down. The complexes take over a minute to perform and consist of basic bilateral exercises. Rows are done second in the complex as they tend to be the most difficult exercises to perform with proper technique. Athletes here are grouped three or four to a platform for work-rest purposes. Dumbbell weights are thirty percent of hang clean max, divided by two. This means an athlete with a three-hundred-pound hang clean would use forty-five-pound dumbbells.

Variation One

Day 3	Tempo	Rest	Week 1	Reps	Week 2	Reps	Week 3	Reps
Clean	Exp	3 min	192	x3	192	x3	192	x3
			204	x3	204	x3	204	x3
			204	x3	210	x3	216	x3
			204	x3	204	x3	210	x3
Dumbbell Complex 1 =	Exp	4 min	42		42		42	
Two-DB Snatch x5 +			42		42		42	
Double DB Row x10			42		42		42	
DB Front Squat x 10 +			42		42		42	
DB SLDL x10 +								
DB Curl/ Push Press x10								

Variation Two

This second option includes a hang clean, followed by a bodyweight circuit. The bodyweight circuits are based on Craig Ballantyne's turbulence training work.

Day 3	Tempo	Rest	Week 1	Reps	Week 2	Reps	Week 3	Reps
Clean	Exp	3 min	188	x3	188	x3	188	x3
			211.5	x3	217.375	x3	223.25	x3
			205.625	x3	211.5	x3	217.375	x3
Bodyweight Circuit								
Squat Jump	x10		x2		x3		x3	
Alt Lunge	x10 ea							
Inverted Row	x15							
Lunge Walk	x10 ea							
Chin-up	x10							
Push-up	x20							

Variation Three

Variation three is what we call our functional circuit. The functional circuit allows us to incorporate all of our diagonal pattern exercises on the Keiser equipment. It is done in the same fashion as our ten-rep circuit. Ten reps of each exercise are done with a partner on a 50-10 clock.

Station 1	Half-kneel Chop
Station 2	Half-kneel Lift
Station 3	Anterior Reach with Cable
Station 4	Keiser Squat
Station 5	Extreme Core Trainer
Station 6	Cross-arm Keiser Pull-down
Station 7	Kneeling Push-Pull
Station 8	Vibraflex Squat Hold
Station 9	Powerplate Push-up
Station 10	Powerplate Split Squat

MBSC Summer 2007

Phase One	
Foam Roll 5 Minutes	Glutes and Hip Rotators, Lower and Upper Back, Posterior Shoulder, Adductors
Stretch 5-10 Minutes	Lateral Ham 3D, Hip Rotator 3D, Table Adductor, Table Quad, Table Hip Flexor
Mobility Warm-up 15-20 Minutes	Seated T- Spine, Half-Kneeling Ankle Mobility, Leg Swings Band Pull-apart Series X-Band, Split Squat x5, Lateral Squat x5, Rotational Squat x5
Active Warm-up 20-25 Minutes	Single-leg SLDL w/reach, x10 each, Lateral Skip, Cross-behind Skip, Cross in-front Skip, Shuffle, Carioca, Lateral Crawl
Ladder 25-30 Minutes	Shuffle Wide + Stick F/B, Cross in Front, F/B, Cross Behind F/B In-In-Out-Out, F/R/L, Scissors R/L
Plyos Medicine Ball 30-35 Minutes	Day 2: Single-leg Box Hop, 3x 3 R/L Day 4: Lateral Bound + Stick, 3x5 each Med Ball: Standing Overhead, 2x10 Half-kneel Side Twist, 2x10
Drills 35-40 Minutes	Superband Shuffle, 1x5 yards each 1-2 Stick (2 hoops), 3x3 each Hand to Knee Drill, x5 each Crossover + Stick, 2x3 each side
Conditioning	Slideboard, Intervals x30 seconds Week 1 = 6x; Week 2 = 7x, Week 3 = 8x

Phase One	
Foam Roll **5 Minutes**	Glutes and Hip Rotators, Lower and Upper Back, Posterior Shoulder, Adductors
Stretch **5-10 Minutes**	Roller Groin, Roller Split, Roller Hip Flexor, Roller Heel to Butt, Spiderman, Hip Rotator
Activation **10-15 Minutes**	Hip Left Psoas Combo, 3-5x10 seconds Exterior Rotation, 3-5x10 seconds AD/ABductor Isos, 3-5x10 seconds Elbow Push-ups, 3x8,10,12
Active Warm-up **15-25 Minutes**	Knee to Chest, Leg Cradle, Heel to Butt, Heel to Butt with Lean, Single-leg SLDL with Reach, Overhead Back Lunge to Hamstring, Spiderman, High-knee Skip, High-knee Run, Heel-ups, SL Walk, SL Skip, Back Pedal, Backward Run
Power **25-30 Minutes**	Plyo *Day One:* Box Jump, 3x5 *Day Three:* Single-leg Box Jump, 3x5 Med Ball, Kneeling Chest (on turf with partner), 2x10
Speed **30-35 Minutes**	Lean/Fall/Run, x3 Right and Left *Resisted:* Sled March, Week One x5; Week Two x6; Week Three x7 Sled Crossover, Week One x4; Week Two x5; Week Three x6
Conditioning	*Days One and Three:* Tempo Week One x10; Week Two x12; Week Three x14

Four-Day Program, Day One

Day 1	Tempo	Rest	Week 1	Reps	Week 2	Reps	Week 3	Reps
Kettlebell Swing	Exp	4 min		x10		x10		x10
				x10		x10		x10
Stretch- Yoga Table x10 w/ 2 sec hold				x10		x10		x10
Landmine			2	x12	2	x14	2	x16
Chin-up	1:00		BW	x8	BW	x8	BW	x5
			BW	x8	15	x8	19	x Max
					11	x8		
Front Box Squat 12"box	1:00		95	x8	201	x8	201	x8
or RFE Single-leg Squat			95	x8	235	x8	260	x Max
					235	x8		
Stretch — Stability Ball IR x8								
Side Plank Circuit			2x	30 sec	2x	40 sec	2x	50 sec
One-arm Single-leg Row	1:00			x8		x8		x8
				x8		x8		x8
Single-leg SLDL	1:00		41	x8	46	x8	51	x8
				x8		x8		x8
Face Pull				x8		x8		x8
				x8		x8		x8
Half-kneeling Stability Ball Lift				x8		x8		x8
				x8		x8		x8

Four-Day Program, Day Two

Day 2	Tempo	Rest	Week 1	Reps	Week 2	Reps	Week 3	Reps
Bench Press	2/0/Exp	1:00	165	x8	165	x8	176	x Max
			165	x8	170	x8		
					165	x8		
Stretch — Band or TRX Lat, x8								
Core: Ball Rollout			2	x20	2	x30	2	x40
Kneeling Alt Curl and Press	2/0/Exp	1:00	41	x8	47	x8	53	x8
				x8		x8		x8
Stretch — Wall Slides (forward if necessary) x10, x12, x14								
Core: Straight-leg Sit-up Progression								
Supine Hip Flexion with Lumbar Roll			2x10		2x12			x Max
Shoulder Circuit	2/0/Exp	1:00	BW	x8	BW	x10	BW	x12
				x8		x10		x12
Tri-set with Pilates Ring Adduction				x10+10		x12+12		x14+14
				x10+10		x12+12		x14+14
Tall Kneeling Alt Push/Pull				x10		x10		x12
				x10		x10		x12

Four-Day Program, Day Three

Day 3	Tempo	Rest	Week 1	Reps	Week 2	Reps	Week 3	Reps
Clean or KB Swing	Exp	4:00	154	x5	154	x5	154	x5
			159	x5	164	x5	174	x5
In week three, increase set three if set two is easy			159	x5	164	x5	?	x5
Stretch — Yoga Table, x10 with 2-second holds								
Landmine				x12		x14		x16
Single-leg Squat	2/0/Exp	1:00	67	x8	67	x8	67	x8
(To touch on box)			67	x8	75	x8	84	x8
					67	x8		
Rotational Inverted Row		1:00		x15		x15		x15
				x15		x15		x15
						x15		x15
Stretch — Stability Ball IR x8								
Side Plank Circuit			2x30 seconds		2x40 seconds		2x50 seconds	
X Pull-down	2/0/2	1:00		x15		x15		x15
				x15		x15		x15
				x8		x12		x15
Slideboard Lunge	2/0/Exp	1:00		x8		x12		x15
Slideboard Leg Curl				x8		x10		x12
				x8		x10		x12
Half-Kneeling Stability Chop				x8		x8		x8
				x8		x8		x8

Four-Day Program, Day Four

Day 4	Tempo	Rest	Week 1	Reps	Week 2	Reps	Week 3	Reps
Alt DB Incline	3/0Exp	1:00	56	AMRAP	59	AMRAP	59	AMRAP
			56	AMRAP	59	AMRAP	62	AMRAP
Stretch — Band or TRX Lax x8								
Core: Ball Rollout				2x20		2x30		2x40
Push-up	2/0/Exp	1:00		x Max		x Max		x Max
				x Max		x Max		x Max
Stretch — Wall Slides x10, x12, x14 (forward if necessary)								
Core: Straight-leg Sit-up Progression								
Supine Hip Flexion with Lumbar Roll				x10		x12		x14
Shoulder Circuit	2/0/Exp	1:00	BW	x8		x10		x12
			BW	x8		x10		x12
Tri-set with				x8		x12		x15
Pilates Ring Adductor				x10+10		x12+12		x14
Kneeling Anti-Rotation Press				x8		x8		x8
				x8		x8		x8

2009 MBSC Program Goals

*My thanks to Sam Leahey
for compiling this material.*

• Reduce the potential for injury during activity (training & competition)

• Increase explosive power and strength

• Improve linear and lateral speed, agility and quickness

• Provide an environment that promotes self confidence as well as individual and athletic improvement

Program Design Principles

Learn basic bodyweight exercises first, including squat, push-up and chin-up.

Begin with bodyweight progressions.

Week 1: 3 sets of 8 reps

Week 2: 3 sets of 10 reps

Week 3: 3 sets of 12 reps

Week 4: Begin external loading, five pounds per week. If unable to add weight, use machines or elastic assistance.

Progress from simple to complex
Level 1 to 4 or 5

• Explosive movements first

• Multi-joint second

• Volume and intensity progression

• Bodyweight: 8 reps, 10 reps, 12 reps, then external load and/or instability, generally no less than 5 reps

• Externally loaded — linear PRE-based periodization for beginners, undulating program for more advanced athletes

Strength Program Components

Double-Leg Knee-Dominant

Single-Leg Knee-Dominant

Straight-Leg Hip-Dominant Extensions
Single- and Double-Leg

Bent-Leg Hip-Dominant Extensions
Single- and Double-Leg

Midsection Strength — Core

Horizontal Press

Vertical Press

Horizontal Pull

Vertical Pull

Explosive Power Development

Conditioning Program
*Done primarily after resistance
training but sometimes before*

Linear

Tempo Runs
Outside or treadmill, bike if injured
or
Shuttle Runs
25- to 50-yard intervals

Lateral

Slideboard Intervals, twice per week

Weekly Format			
Day 1	**Day 2**	**Day 3**	**Day 4**
Movement Skills — one hour			
Warm-up Linear	Warm-up Multi-Directional	Warm-up Linear	Warm-up Multi-Directional
Pair	**Pair**	**Pair**	**Pair**
Linear Plyometric Med Ball Chest Throw Linear Speed Development	Lateral Plyometric Med Ball Overhead and Rotation Throw Lateral Speed Development	Linear Plyometric Med Ball Chest Throw Linear Speed Development	Lateral Plyometric Med Ball Overhead and Rotation Throw Lateral Speed Development
Power and Strength Development — approximately one hour			
Tri-Set	**Tri-Set**	**Tri-Set**	**Tri-Set**
Explosive Lift Jump Squat/Snatch Core Anti-Rotation Mobility Exercise	Horizontal Press Active Isolated Stretch Upper Back Core Anti-Extension	Explosive Lift Hang Clean Core Anti-Rotation Mobility Exercise	Horizontal Press Active Isolated Stretch Upper Back Core Anti-Extension
Quad-Set	**Tri-Set**	**Quad-Set**	**Tri-Set**
Vertical Pull Active Isolated Stretch Knee-Dominant Double-Leg Straight-Leg Sit-up	Vertical Press Active Isolated Stretch Side Plank	Vertical Pull Active Isolated Stretch Knee-Dominant Single-Leg Straight-Leg Sit-up	Vertical Press Active Isolated Stretch Side Plank
Tri-Set	**Pair**	**Tri-Set**	**Pair**
Horizontal Pull Hip-Dominant Straight-Leg Active Isolated Stretch Hamstrings	Core — Chop Shoulder Prehab Exercise Hip Prehab Exercise	Horizontal Pull Hip-Dominant Bent-Leg Active Isolated Stretch Hamstrings	Core — Lift Shoulder Prehab Exercise Hip Prehab Exercise
Possibly Conditioning — one hour			

Training Program Flow

Pre-Workout Self-Myofascial Release

Static Stretching
Table or roller sequence
Hip Flexors, Lateral Hamstrings, Hip Rotators, Other

Activation
Glute Max, Glute Medius, Psoas, Scapula Retractors, Scapula Depressors

Warm-up (15 minutes)
Every session (linear, multi-directional, lateral)

Plyometrics 2-4 x per week
Balance between linear and lateral days

Medicine Ball Throws
Paired with plyos for rest to work ratio

Speed Development

Explosive Training
3-4 minutes rest between sets
Olympic lifts or jump squats
Teaching progression is hang clean progression,
one-arm dumbbell snatch, close-grip hang snatch
One or two pairs of exercises,
then one tri-set of three different exercises,
60 to 90 seconds rest between sets

Core Training
Every session, alternating
Core strength, anti-extension, anti-rotation, hip stability, lateral stability

Joint Mobilization on Lateral Days
Tennis ball peanut t-spine, seated twist with t-spine bend, ankle mobility wall drill, leg swings,
split squats, lateral squat, rotational squat, wall slides

Lower-Body Strength Program
2 x per week
Double-leg knee dominant, single-leg knee dominant
and hip dominant, straight leg and bent leg

Upper Body Strength and Balance Program
Pushing and pulling

Sled Pushes or Pulls

Post-Workout Static Stretching and Self-Myofascial Release

Develops single-leg strength, dynamic flexibility and increases proprioception.

Linear Day Warm-up
15 minutes

High knee walk
High knee skip
High knee run
Heel-ups
Straight-leg skip
Straight-leg deadlift walk
Backward run
Backpedal
Backward lunge walk, begin in week two
Forward lunge walk, begin in week four

Linear Day Warm-up
Emphasis on Flexibility
15 minutes

Heel-up with internal rotation
Walking heel-up
Walking heel-up with SLDL
Overhead lunge walk
Backward lunge walk with twist
SLDL walk forward
SLDL walk backward
Straight-leg crossover

Lateral Day Warm-up
8 minutes of agility ladder
5 minutes of lateral dynamic flexibility

Lateral Squat
Stationary Spiderman

Plyometric Training

Linear (three to five sets of five jumps)
Lateral (three sets of five landings on each leg)
These are paired with medicine ball throws.

Phase 1
Single Response, Stabilization
Box Jump, Box Hop, Lateral Box Hop
Six landings, three on each leg

Phase 2
Multiple Response, Stabilization
Hurdle Jump and Stick, Hurdle Hop and Stick,
Heiden and Stick, Zigzag Bound and Stick

Phase 3
Multiple Jumps, Introduction of Elastic Component
Hurdle Jump with Bounce, Hurdle Hop with Bounce, Zigzag Bound With Bounce

Phase 4
Multiple Jumps, Elastic Response
Hurdle Jumps and Hops (linear and lateral), Power Skip, Lateral Bound,
Crossover Bound, Cross-Behind Bound

Medicine Ball Progressions

Three sets are done while paired with the above plyometrics.
We often do these from kneeling, standing parallel, split stance, or with a step.

Overhead Throw with Step
Single-Leg Front Twist Throw
Staggered Overhead Throw
Standing Overhead Throw
Standing Side Twist Throw
Standing Side Twist Throw with Step

Linear Speed Development

Phase I
Weeks 1-3
Noncompetitive Speed
Lean, Fall, Run Drill *or* 90-Degree Lean, Fall, Run Drill, 6 x 10 yards

Phase II
Weeks 4-6
Short Competitive Speed
Ball-Drop Drill, dropped from shoulder height, 5-7 yards

Phase III
Weeks 7-9
Long Competitive Speed, increase intensity or volume, never both
Against partner with 10- to 20-yard tag zone
Chase sprints or break-away belt sprints from standing or lying positions

Lateral Speed Development

Agility Progression

Level 1
(first three weeks)
One-Two Stick
Level 2
One-Two Cut
Level 3
Assisted One-Two Cut
Level 4
45-Degree One-Two Cut

Speed Progression

Level 1
(first three weeks)
Lateral Hoop Run and Stick, Three Hoops
Level 2
Lateral Hoop Run and Stick, Five Hoops
Level 3
Lateral Hoop Run and Stick, Seven Hoops
Level 4
Lateral Hoop Run with Return, Two Hoops

Knee-Dominant Exercises

Double-Leg Strength
Progress from one level to next or unstable surface
Front Squats, Kettlebell Sumo Deadlift, Trap-Bar Deadlift
Front split squat for back pain clients

Single-Leg Strength
Progression from one level to next or unstable surface

Static Supported
Level 1: Split Squat
Level 2: One-Leg Bench Squat, Lateral Squat, Rotational Squat

Static Unsupported
Level 3: One-Leg Box Squat Variations
Progressive Range of Motion Exercise
Single-Leg Pause Squats for Patella-Femoral Conditions

Dynamic
Decelerative
Conventional Lunge, Lateral Lunge
Any Multi-Planar Version — Transverse or Rotational

Accelerative, Hip-Dominant
Level 1: Valslide Lunge, Slideboard Lunge
Level 2: Foot-Elevated Slideboard Lunge

Hip-Dominant Exercises

Level 1:
First three weeks
Cook Hip Lift, Slideboard Leg Curl *(eccentric only)*, Hyperextension, Hyperextension Hold

Level 2:
Foot-Elevated Hip Lift, Modified Straight-Leg Deadlift,
One-Leg Straight-Leg Deadlift (Progressions)

Level 3:
One-Leg Hyperextension, One-Leg Good Morning,
Slideboard and Stability-Ball Hip Extension Variations

Level 3:
Slideboard Leg Curl (eccentric and concentric phase), Stability-Ball Leg Curl

Level 4:
One-Leg Stability-Ball Leg Curl

Accelerative Dynamic Single-Leg Exercises

Level 1:
Walking Lunge, Valslide Lunge, Slideboard Lunge

Level 2:
Foot-Elevated Slideboard Lunge

Hybrid Exercises for Knee and Hip

Level 3:
One-Leg Squat and Touch

Core Strength

Sahrman's Straight-Leg Sit-up Progression, arms straight, then folded in front
Turkish Get-up Progression

Anti-Extension
Front Plank
Stability Ball Rollout (Phase 1)
Abby Dolly Rollout – Forearms Down (Phase 2)
The Wheel or Abby Dolly Rollout – Forearms Up with Hands Only (Phase 3)
Valslide/Slideboard Rollout (Phase 4)
Barbell Rollout (Phase 5)

Anti-Lateral Flexion
Side Plank Short Lever
Side Plank Long Lever
Side Plank with Feet Elevated
Side Flexion

Anti-Rotary
Level 1:
Half-Kneeling Stability Chop, Half-Kneeling Stability Lift (slow and controlled)

Level 2:
Half-Kneeling Sequential Chop, Half-Kneeling Sequential Lift (speed increases)

Level 3:
Standing Dynamic Chop and Lift (squat, rotate, press/pull); Lift progresses to one leg

Rotary
Anti-Rotation Holds
Landmine
Kieser Push/Pull
Convertaball Twists

Hip Stability
Bodyweight Squat with Theratube, Single-Leg Squat with Theratube, Bent-Leg Hip
Abduction, Straight-Leg Hip Abduction, Straight-Leg Mini-Band Walks, Superband X Walks

Not direct core exercises,
these use deep abdominal muscles as anti-rotators:
One-Leg Squat, One-Leg Straight-Leg Deadlift, Kettlebell Slideboard Lunge, One-Arm
Dumbbell Snatch, Feet-Elevated BOSU Push-ups, TRX Inverted Rows

Core Stability
Quadruped, Supine Bridging, Lateral Bridge Exercises

Quadruped Progression
Quadruped Hip Extension Over Bench (5 reps of 5-second holds)

Quadruped Hip Extension
Bent-Leg, Dowel-Parallel Progression with Knee on Airex Pad

Level 1:
Bent-Leg, Dowel-Parallel (5, 8, 10 reps of 5-second holds)

Level 2:
Add 2.5 pound ankle weights

Quadruped Hip Extension
Bent-Leg, Dowel-Perpendicular Progression with Knee on Airex Pad

Level 2:
Bent-Leg, Dowel-Perpendicular Progression (5, 8, 10 reps of 5-second holds)

Level 3:
Add 2.5-pound ankle weights

Level 4:
Alternating Arm and Leg (5, 8, 10 reps of 5-second holds)

Supine Progression
Level 1:
Cook Hip Lift (3 sets of 10, 12, 14 reps each leg)

Level 2:
Hands-Free Cook Hip Lift

Isometric Supine Bridge Progression
Level 1:
Isometric Supine Bridge (3 x 30-second holds)

Level 2:
Isometric Single-Leg Supine Bridge (3 x 15-second hold each leg)

Level 3:
Bridge with Alternate March (5, 8, 10 x 5-second hold each leg)

Upper-Body Strength Program

Vertical Pulling and Pushing, Horizontal Pulling and Pushing, Scapulo-thoracic Training

Vertical Pulling Movements

Chin-up, Neutral-Grip Pull-up, Pull-up,
Alternate-Grip Pull-up, Sternum Chin-up

Horizontal Pulling Movements
All done with one foot in contact with the ground, except the inverted and rotational rows

Level 1:
Dumbbell Row, Inverted Row, One-Arm One-Leg Row (static hip),
One-Leg Squat and Pull

Inverted row progression if needed: Knees bent feet on floor, knees straight feet on floor, knees straight feet on bench, add weight vest or knees straight feet on stability ball

Level 2:
One Arm One-Leg Dumbbell Row (opposite or same side hand), One-Arm One-Leg Row (Dynamic Cable), One-Arm Two-Leg Rotational Row, Squat and Pull

Pressing Exercises

Progression:
Feet-Elevated, Weight Vest, Unstable Surface (feet or hands), Unstable Surface with Feet Elevated, Unstable Surface with Feet Elevated and a Weight Vest

Barbell Bench Press, Dumbbell Bench Press, Alternate Dumbbell Bench Press, Incline Dumbbell Bench Press, Alternate Incline Dumbbell Bench Press, Push-up, Feet-Elevated Push-up, Core Board Rotational Push-up, Dumbbell Rotational Push-up, Stability-Ball Push-up

Prone Shoulder Circuit

Y, T, W, L
Progression: Two sets of eight reps in each position with no weight and no rest between positions, then add to reps per week up to sixteen reps in each position, then go back to eight reps with very light dumbbells.

In Closing

Final Thoughts

The questions I get in the Strength Coach forum and at conferences are as likely to be about my work life as they are about specific training problems. I'd like to close with a little advice to the young coaches and trainers about our working lives in the training business.

We've learned much the past decade that will have a huge impact on how you train your athletes and clients, and our industry will continue to change and grow. As I noted throughout the book, it's vital not to get caught in the trap of believing so intently in your training philosophy you're unable to recognize the value of new thinking.

Your favorite writers and coaches will be wrong from time to time, myself included. I'm becoming famous for changing my mind, and these days I think that's a good thing. In fact, things in this book will be adapted to new information, and perhaps even soon.

Keep reading, keep watching DVDs, and get to live seminars. In reality, it's best to reverse those in priority, because in a live seminar you're getting the presenter's thoughts as of that day. Production time for a DVD presentation is usually only two or three months. Books are great and thorough references, but they take most of a year or more to write, and often another year to publish. That's a long time in our changing field.

Another good alternative for continuing education are the electronic podcasts and webinars... current, live information without the travel. Conferences are better for a variety of reasons, and I encourage you to make an annual conference a priority, but today's electronic options such as strengthcoachpodcast.com and scwebinars.com help bridge the gap when budgets and schedules are tight.

Keep a mix of all formats in your continuing education, but don't let up on learning. That's the main thing.

The activity of building a training business and becoming productive is a process, a process of time and energy. The number one thing you can do for productivity is get up early. Successful people don't hit the snooze button. I heard a great tip once about waking up:

When the alarm goes off, get your feet on the ground.

I have lived by this for at least twenty years and now rarely need an alarm.

Years ago I read the advice to get out of bed instead of rolling over at first wake-up. The concept is related to sleep quality and I have found it to be true: Fifteen extra minutes of sleep usually leaves me more tired. If I wake up within thirty minutes of when I am supposed to, I get my feet on the ground.

People notice they get email from me at 4:45 a.m. because I get up, go to my computer, and check my email. I love to get my day started and accomplish things on my list before daylight. It makes me feel more productive, and sets the day on a good roll.

I read another efficiency hint once: If you can respond to an email in under a minute, do it immediately. I have adopted that policy as best I can and it has really helped. I can interact with about a hundred people a day and do most of it before my family gets out of bed. This also allows me to help my wife by throwing in a load of laundry, and I get to spend time with my children in the morning when they get up.

I also make a point to write everything down. I keep a notebook with me at all times for article ideas, program ideas, notes and to-do lists. It's much too easy to forget; I can't trust my memory for the little things.

Another trick I've found helpful in this business is not doing paperwork at work. This sounds silly — no paperwork at work — but I try to coach, observe and interact with my coaches and clients at work. I do paperwork at home in the morning.

To save time and increase work productivity, avoid going out to lunch. What a waste of time; the lunch hour is for "normal" people who don't like their jobs and need an hour away from it. Those who want to succeed never waste even a half-hour sitting and eating. Lunch takes me all of five minutes.

Another benefit of an in-facility lunch is it helps with weight control. I can't go into a sandwich shop and not walk out with a bag of chips, and often I've eaten the bag before I even get the sandwich. Instead of going out to eat, I keep protein shakes handy, and eat every three hours while I work.

Dinner is a different story. Dinner is family time. I bank my lunch hour so I can use it at dinner with my family.

In learning and time usage, I have a tip from the great Zig Ziglar. He calls this one Joining Automobile University, using the commute time to learn and to be more productive. I often spend two hours a day in the car, when I make all my phone calls for the day and record my podcast interviews. Audiobooks, podcasts and electronic recordings abound to greatly increase your business and training knowledge; when the workday is done, it's time for Automobile University.

As a coach or professional trainer, there comes a point when you realize your gym time is no longer all about you. Learn to do brief workouts. If you are a busy trainer, you don't have time to lift for two hours. Try to do four or five high intensity cardiovascular workouts a week. For me these are either twelve- to fourteen-minute threshold rides, usually a five-mile Airdyne ride done for time, or a series of distances for time. My favorites are timed miles or half-miles with a planned heart rate recovery. These workouts take a maximum of twenty minutes.

In addition, I love Craig Ballantyne's *Bodyweight 100* program. It currently takes me less than four minutes to get a full body lift. I try to lift twice a week, but probably average one workout every five days.

As I have said over and over, the secret is there is no secret. Read about how to save time and how to be more productive. Read *The One Minute Manager*. That's a great start.

Pick up little tricks. Success is really is about getting up and being organized. I find time to personal train ten to fifteen hours a week, work as a college strength and conditioning coach, and coach pro athletes eight hours a week, all the while keeping up with writing projects, email questions, the strengthcoach.com website and strengthcoachblog.com posts.

I love the idea of the *ready-fire-aim* approach. I would rather have accomplished one thing than thought about three.

Here's another great tip, and I wish I could remember who to credit for it: Be a ninety-percent person. If a success-oriented person strives to do a hundred percent, he'll rarely complete anything. That last ten percent kills you, and it stalls you. I don't worry about making every article or DVD perfect. I always want to deliver a quality product, but I don't obsess over it anymore. Don't over-plan or over-think, just strive to get a lot done. Make a list and start checking stuff off.

I hope you find this book to be a great ninety-percent effort. Just remember, for a true hundred-percent person, a ninety-percent effort still gets an A.

Terminology

Prone vs supine
Prone is lying face down; supine (spine down) is face up.

Superior vs inferior
Superior means closer to the head; inferior means closer to the feet.

Medial vs lateral
Medial refers to nearer to the center; lateral refers to farther from the center.

Posterior vs anterior
Posterior is toward the back; anterior is toward the front.

Distal vs proximal
Distal means farther from the torso; proximal means closer to the trunk.

Extension vs flexion
Extension straightens a joint; flexion bends the joint.

Supination vs pronation
Supination and pronation are used to describe action at the feet or forearm. In the feet, supination refers to excessive outward action; pronation refers to the ankle turning in. With the forearm, supination refers to turning the palm up; pronation refers to turning the palm down.

Medial vs lateral rotation
Medial rotation turns toward the center of the body as in internal rotation; lateral rotation turns away from the body externally.

Inversion vs eversion
Inversion turns the foot or hand in; eversion turns out.

Elevation vs depression
Elevation means upward; depression means downward. These terms are most often used to describe faulty scapula position, too high or too low.

Protraction vs retraction
Protraction moves a joint forward; retraction moves it backward.

Adduction vs abduction
Adduction brings the limb in toward the body; abduction moves it away.

Dorsiflexion vs plantar flexion
Dorsiflexion at the ankle is to bring the toes toward the shin; plantar flexion points the toes away.

Joint mobility vs flexibility
Joint mobility encompasses the ability of the joint to move through it's full range of motion; flexibility is about muscles, not joints, and is about lengthening.

Stability vs mobility
Stability is the muscle, tendon and ligament action needed to hold a joint in position; mobility requires the correct muscle action on one side of a joint and the necessary muscular flexibility on the other to produce full movement through a joint's range of motion.

Activation vs dormant
Activation means an action to trigger a muscle to fire well; dormant refers to an inactive muscle group, at varying levels from fully inactive to fully engaged.

Tendons, ligaments, fascia, myofascia
Tendons connect muscles to bones; ligaments connect bone to bone; fascia is connective tissue that covers soft tissue from head to toe, superficial to deep; myofascia is fascia covering muscle.

Lordotic vs kyphotic vs lordosis vs kyphosis
Lordotic is the curve of the spine bending to the front; kyphotic bends toward the rear; lordosis describes too much lumbar curve; kyphosis describes too much bend at the thoracic spine (to the rear).

Bilateral vs unilateral

Bilateral refers to both sides of the body working together; unilateral is one side working alone.

Concentric vs eccentric

Concentric shortens the muscle; eccentric lengthens, ie in biceps curls the concentric action brings the wrist toward the shoulder; eccentric returns the wrist to the side.

Isometric vs isotonic

Isometric changes the muscle tension without changing the length; isotonic changes the muscle tension while changing the length.

Origin vs insertion

Origin of a muscle is the stationary attachment site of muscle to bone; insertion is the mobile attachment end site.

Primer mover, synergist, antagonist

Prime mover is the main muscle that carries out an action; synergist assists the prime mover; antagonist performs the opposite action.

Planes of Movement
Sagittal, Frontal, Transverse

Sagittal refers to forward or backward; frontal (aka coronal) refers to side to side; transverse refers to rotational.

Sagittal plane motion would include forward and backward motions, like sit-ups, back extensions or biceps curls. The sagittal plane cuts through the center of the body, so the motion is front to back or back to front, including straight forward running. Squats involve flexion (forward motion) and extension (backwards on the way up), so would fit mostly into the sagittal plane.

Frontal plane motion would include leaning from left to right as in sidebends and lateral raises. Picture jumping jacks for a good image of movement along the frontal plane.

Transverse plane motion is the hardest to comprehend because the plane is horizontal as it divides the top from the bottom. It's hard to get our heads around it being a rotating action. The main thing to remember is rotation.

An example of a transverse plane exercise would be floor to overhead diagonals with a medicine ball, and a transverse activity might be swinging a golf club.

Continuing Education

Books

Anatomy Trains
Thomas Myers, Leon Chaitow, D. Juhan

Athletic Body in Balance
Gray Cook

Bigger Faster Stronger
Greg Shepard

Brawn
Stuart McRobert

Core Performance
Mark Verstegen

Diagnosis and Treatment of Movement
Impairment Syndromes
Shirley Sahrmann

Goals!
Brian Tracey

How to Win Friends and Influence People
Dale Carnegie

Low Back Disorders, Second Edition
Stuart McGill

Mechanical Low Back Pain
James A. Porterfield, Carl Derosa

Muscles
Testing and Function with Posture and Pain
Florence Peterson Kendall, et al

Physical Examination of the Spine and Extremities
Stanley Hoppenfeld

Seven Habits of Highly Effective People, The
Stephen R. Covey

Continuing Education

Books

Starting Strength, Second Edition
Mark Rippetoe, Lon Kilgore

Strongest Shall Survive, The
Bill Starr

Trail Guide to the Body, Third Edition
Andrew R. Biel

The Trigger Point Therapy Workbook, Second Edition
Clair Davies, Amber Davies

Ultimate Back Fitness and Performance
Stuart McGill

Ultra-prevention, The 6-week Plan That
Will Make You Healthy for Life
Mark Hyman, Mark Liponis

DVD Training

Functional Strength Coach 3.0 DVD Series
A Joint by Joint Approach to Training
Michael Boyle
Visit Perform Better for details

Online Webinars

Strength and conditioning webinars from a variety of presenters
Visit strengthandconditioningwebinars.com

Continuing Education Seminars

MBSC Mentorship
See bodybyboyle.com

Perform Better One-day Workshops
Perform Better Summits
Gray Cook's Functional Movement Screen Course
See performbetter.com for the above

For regular updates as our thinking evolves, new insights, photos, videos and explanations of anything in the book that may have been confusing, and for quick suggestions to your most complicated programming questions, join your peers at StrengthCoach.com.

Low Back Disorders 86
low back pain, *see back pain*
low-budget programming 276
lower-crossed-body model 87
lumbar
      extension 91
      flexion 32
      range of motion 98
      spine 98
lunges 47, 77, 218

M

manual therapists 76
massage, *see soft tissue*
Mattes, Aaron 56
maximum oxygen consumption 130
      see also VO2 Max
MBSC/Mike Boyle Strength & Conditioning 36
McBride, Jeffrey 85, 86
McDougall, Christopher 153
McGill, Stuart 85, 86, 88, 91, 100, 103,
      106, 190-191
McKechnie, Alex 49, 228
McRobert, Stuart 205, 254, 255, 260, 266
Mechanical Basis of Human Running Speed 171
Mechanical Low Back Pain 33, 97
medicine ball 184, 240
mesomorph 254
mini bands, *see bands*
mobility, general 37, 43, 45-49
      ankle 32
      circuit 278
movement specificity 134
multifidus muscles 103, 106
multi-planar lunges 48
Muscle Activation Technique (MAT) 50
muscle fibers 50, 129
muscular specificity 134
Myers, Thomas 56, 93, 218

N

National Academy of Sports Medicine
      (NASM) 56, 68
National Strength and Conditioning
      Association (NSCA) 255
NFL Combine 167
NSCA Journal 262

O

oblique strain 41
off-season training 183
older client 178

Olympic lifting, alternatives to 163
Olympic weightlifting 157, 240, 266
one-arm dumbbell snatch 101
one-leg exercises, *see single-leg*
open-chain 78
overhead athletes 209
overhead press 211
overuse injury 61, 151

P

pain, general, *see also specific pains* 74, 151
Pallof, John 64, 80, 220
Pandolfo, Jay 212
Parker, Johnny 59
patella-femoral pain, see knee pain
pause squat 233
pelvic
      floor 103
      position 200
      stabilizers 102, 214
pelvis 76
performance testing 132-133
Perform Better 14, 15, 79, 94, 228
periodization 259, 262-264
Peripheral Heart Action (PHA) 252
physical therapy 150
physiological testing 132-133
planes of movement 307
plank 88, 190
plate circuit 279
plyometrics 70, 72, 77, 240
Poirer, Chris 14
Poliquin, Charles 23, 60, 123, 242, 263
Porterfield, James 33, 97, 101
posterior chain 121, 200, 220
power development 157, 164, 178, 240
preseason conditioning 136
      see also conditioning
pressing exercises 204
program design 236, 245
progressing plyometrics 72
progression concept 80
progressive range of motion 67, 217
progressive resistance exercise 260
proprioception 72
psoas 32, 77, 78, 91, 113, 118
push-ups 206

Q

Q angle 71, 148
quad-dominant 121
quadratus lumborum 77, 213, 227
quadriceps 52
quadruped exercises 87, 103-104

R

range of motion 33
ratio
    of exercises 246
    of pulling to pressing 26
reactive neuromuscular training (RNT) 68, 225
reactive work 73
rear-foot-elevated split squat 176, 229
    see also split squat
reciprocal inhibition 91
rectus femoris 113
rehabilitation 59, 78
rep ranges 242
retro walking 70
Richardson, Hodges and Jull 85-86
Robbins, Paul 132
Rolf, Ida 56
rollouts 88-89
Romanian deadlift 122
Rose, Greg 14
Rospkof, Greg 50
Ross, Barry 202
rotational
    lunges 47
    medicine ball throws 184
    squats 47, 77, 218
    training 93
    of the lumbar spine 98
rotator cuff 26, 63, 64, 209
rowers 150
running 138, 146, 148, 150

S

sagittal plane 67, 220, 310
Sahrmann, Shirley 33, 38, 41, 59, 85, 86,
    88, 91, 93, 97, 113, 120, 226
sartorius 113
scapulae retraction strength 64
scapulae retractors 56
Schroeder, Jay 244
Schwinn Airdyne, *see Airdyne*
screening, *see Functional Movement Screen*
seated psoas contraction 118
segmental proportion 176
self-massage 51
shoulder pain 48, 63
Shuttle MVP 70, 178, 240
shuttle runs 135, 146
Signorile, Joe 178
Simmons, Louie 196, 206, 265
    see also Westside Barbell

single-joint exercises 242
single-leg
    deadlifts 62, 67, 123, 223
    exercise 216, 221
    squat 62, 67, 77, 102, 176, 212, 232
    stability 223
    unsupported exercises 67
sled training 186, 187, 188
slideboard 77, 79, 89, 136, 147, 181
    leg curl 70, 124, 223
    lunge 102, 219, 231
slow-twitch fiber 130
snatch 63, 101, 160
snatch grip 63
soft tissue 67, 76, 117, 153, 239
special strength 186
specific strength 187
speed
    at the cellular level 129
    development 240
    training 129, 167
spinal load 61, 200
split squat 47, 80, 218, 228
    see also rear-foot-elevated
sports hernia 74
sport-specific training 175
spot reduction 109
sprinting 78, 79, 167, 169-170, 240
squat 44-45, 61-62, 67, 77, 176,
    195-196, 198, 200-202, 212, 232
    depth and knee stress 197
    form 44
stability 37, 72
stability-ball leg curl 126
stability-ball rollouts 89
stairclimbers 148
Staley, Charles 21, 143
standing lift 39
Starr, Bill 236
start drills 173
static stretching 54, 77, 278
static supported exercises 216
static unsupported exercises 217
stationary bike, *see Airdyne*
steady-state cardio 140
Steinhaus, Dr. Arthur 252
StepMill 148
step-up lift 39
Stone, Mike 262, 263
Strack, Dr. Donnie 50, 61, 75

W

X

Y

Z